DOWNLOAD YOUR FREE SOFTWARE NOW!

This book is designed to be read alongside your Human Design life chart, which reveals your personality blueprint.

    To create your chart visit www.humandesignforusall.com. Follow the instructions, download the Windows-based software, and take the first step on your Human Design journey to find out who you really are.

A Revolutionary New System
Revealing the DNA of Your True Nature

HUMAN DESIGN

Discover the Person
You Were Born to Be

CHETAN PARKYN

WITH STEVE DENNIS

New World Library
Novato, California

New World Library
14 Pamaron Way
Novato, California 94949

Page 7: "Your True Self" © Margaret I. Jang 2005, www.onesourcelearn.com

Library of Congress Cataloging-in-Publication Data
Parkyn, Chetan, date.
Human design : discover the person you were born to be / Chetan Parkyn with Steve Dennis.
    p.   cm.
At head of title: a revolutionary new system revealing the DNA of your true nature
Includes index.
ISBN 978-1-57731-941-2 (pbk. : alk. paper)
1. Astrology. 2. Self-realization—Miscellanea. I. Dennis, Steve, 1971– II. Title. III. Title: Introducing a revolutionary system that unlocks your true potential.
BF1729.S38P37 2010
133.5—dc22   2010023468

First New World Library printing, September 2010
ISBN 978-1-57731-941-2
Printed in Canada on 100% postconsumer-waste recycled paper

g New World Library is a proud member of the Green Press Initiative.

10 9 8 7 6 5 4 3 2 1

I dedicate this book to Osho,
with gratefulness

"Nothing is good. Nothing is bad. When this dawns
in your consciousness, suddenly you are together,
all fragments have disappeared into one unity. You are crystallized,
you are centered. This is one of the greatest contributions
of Eastern consciousness to the world."

Osho

Your True Self

Within the sanctity of your inner being,
is your true self, a part that remains unseen.
A quietness, surrounded by joy and peace,
filled with calmness, hidden until you seek.

It's uncluttered by your future or your past,
only the "now," the "present," is what lasts.
Your true self is eternal and must grow
to new heights, your soul already knows.

For you to reach this sacred state of mind,
release ego and the poisons that it finds.
Then surrender; trust in what you truly feel,
but be aware to what is and isn't real.

Integrity will guide you on your quest,
let truth prevail to help you act your best.
If you can overcome the need to prove or win,
then you will find your true self deep within.

And when united with your inner self,
you will find there is no greater wealth.
Eternity is real and so very divine,
once your true self reveals itself to shine!

Margaret I. Jang

CONTENTS

FOREWORD

Every so often, there is a discovery that catalyzes an enormous shift in understanding, allowing for personal awakening. Very rarely, there comes along an individual capable of conveying something esoteric so that the rest of us can benefit from its truth. The Human Design system's complexities and Chetan Parkyn's clarity are demonstration of those two unique happenings coming together for the common good, a system long overdue finding perfect fusion with a teacher who has always been ahead of his time.

I have always been one who seeks, looking for clues that could unravel the mystery of life and allow me to become a better person. That's why I particularly remember the defining moments in life when one becomes acquainted with a self-awareness that opens the eyes and turns on the lightbulbs.

For me, one such moment was the auspicious day when I was introduced to the English gentleman Chetan Parkyn and given a Human Design reading. It was more than a decade ago, on the island of Maui, Hawaii, that this stranger with friendly eyes and a velvet voice started to "read" my "design for life" as if he had known me since the day I was born.

I'd had previous experiences with astrology and other forms of readings, but nothing could compare to the prescience of a system that was, through Chetan, reading my true nature and resonating with every instinct, emotion, thought, and sensation I had ever felt. One technical chart and one man from Shropshire, England, combined to inform me of the person I was designed to be and the life I was designed to lead. In that moment, Human Design emerged as a dynamic crystal ball into my world, past, present, and future. It unlocked an inner code I'd never encountered in other disciplines, a code I could apply to my way of being, my decision making, and my clarity about what and how I thought and felt.

This multifaceted system has also enabled me to better understand the "designs" of others, shining a light on certain behaviors and attitudes of those intimate in my world, including my children and friends.

Ten years later, I continue to check in with Chetan and keep that original Human Design chart as a constant companion and guide. It has become my road map through life. I get to be my own hero. I get to be in control of my runaway train when that happens, remembering that I'm always in the driver's seat. It has been cathartic and invigorating to know that it's okay to be who I am, and to know when to move into action and when to retreat. Believe me when I say that what you are about to discover is liberating stuff!

For many memorable years I played a significant part alongside my former husband, Anthony Robbins, witnessing the enormous difference people felt when they harnessed an inner power, motivating themselves to accomplish great things. I traveled the world as both a cocreator and a witness to a phenomenal rise in self-awareness, seeing at first hand how personal empowerment could transform lives. "Awakening the Giant Within" was ripe for its time. Likewise, Human Design is ripe for today's world and brings the same potential for self-empowerment. It is a journey of self-discovery that can, and should, be taken and applied to the family and community. I say this because its effect on my life continues to be profound. It served me and induced strength at my lowest ebb, and now, when I am healed and happy again, it allows me to experience the joy of freedom and lasting fulfillment. Quite simply, it has allowed me to know myself.

I encourage you, too, to jump into this inner knowledge about yourself and celebrate the gifts within, thanking the illumination granted by Chetan, whose genius and huge heart have made this system logical and applicable to our lives.

Becky Robbins

INTRODUCTION

"I wanted to dismiss Human Design as cobblers,
but you read me to the point where I couldn't deny it.
You should write a book about this one day."
DS, Yorkshire, UK

Just be yourself," they say. How many times have we heard that? It's often said to help ease a nervous first date, a daunting social invitation, or the first day on a new job. There is always someone armed with that well-intentioned advice: "Don't worry, just be yourself and everything will be fine!"

The problem is this: how many of us know what being ourselves actually means? Who is this "true self" — the private inner being that hides behind the mask it wears for most public interactions, that *real* person we are when stripped of our ego and acts of social graces aimed at winning respect, approval, or popularity?

Psychologists the world over would say that millions of people pass through life without ever realizing what constitutes their true self. It's as though we have forgotten our unique individuality in the collective rush to be all things to all people, to fit the picture-perfect portrayals in magazines, television dramas, and movies. It's as though the naturalness and authenticity with which we were all born — and which we unleashed with unaffected abandon as children — have been crushed, repressed, or even disallowed.

Instead, conformity and responsibility in adulthood have combined to distort or shrink our true natures. Millions of us parade as someone other than our true selves without even realizing it, adopting an "acting personality" shaped by the conditioning of our pasts and the judgments, expectations, and rules of others. Along the way, we've picked up and collected traits and acceptable responses that are deemed the "norm," so there's always a tendency to act as we *believe* we should act, or how we've been *trained* to act, all the time keeping our inner beings bound and gagged.

In that regard, I am reminded of a woman who sought me out to help rediscover a lost connection to the real person who, she said, had mysteriously disappeared during her marriage. Jayne told me:

> *All I want is to be myself again, act like myself again, feel like myself again. I don't want to be this person I've created and become. I know the real me is different, waiting to get out and be braver, less afraid of being hurt, less worried about the judgments of others, less afraid of taking on the world, desperate to laugh and dance again. She's in there. I know she is. But I've no idea where to look anymore. I need to be reminded of the me that has become lost.*

Like Jayne, most of us adopt a persona — a word that originates from the Greek for "mask." But what really matters is the authentic person behind the mask, that we are "seen" and recognized for who we truly are.

In writing this book I hope to bring you back home to the essence and safe harbor of your inner being, reuniting you with the person you were born to be and the life you were meant to live. That's why this is not a self-help book but a self-reminder, directing you to rediscover the essence and uniqueness of the *real* you.

What I'm introducing is a one-of-its-kind system and self-awareness tool called Human Design, a system where science meets spirituality, a system that intends you to be loved, accepted, and understood for who you are. Which is why it asks one question at the outset: "Are you living your Human Design?"

This system is built on the wisdom that the acceptance and embracing of your true nature are the essence of finding personal happiness, fulfillment, and freedom, which, in turn, can lead to finding and creating healthier relationships.

This book is the culmination of fifteen years in the field of Human Design. I have immersed myself in its truths, giving one-on-one readings and holding group seminars, and it has been a long-held wish of mine to share its prescient insights with a much wider audience because of the quiet revolutions it kick-starts.

I have lost count of the people who have walked through the front door of this system and emerged through the back exit renewed and invigorated. Once its truths become apparent, it induces an awakening that is both empowering and transformative. It provides concrete information for you to act on by altering the way you view yourself and approach interactions with others.

In the words of educator Stedman Graham: "When you have a sense of who you are and a vision of where you're going in life, you then have the basis of reaching out to the world, and going after your dreams for a better life."

Once you apply this system's knowledge to your life, the possibilities are endless. But knowledge is not the only qualification I bring to the table. Experience has also been my teacher, and I personally have Human Design to thank for bringing me back "home" and changing my life — a life that was seemingly going nowhere back in 1975.

I was sure the perfect storm was going to consume our hundred-foot motor yacht. There almost seemed a surreal lull between the heaving rolls of the forty-foot swell as we were driven across the Atlantic Ocean, a lull between life and death. I remember the chill, the pitch darkness, and the freezing spray of Atlantic water as this hurricane storm suddenly struck two days out of Bermuda. I was at the wheel, between Nassau and Malta, when the mother of all waves hit and the boat was knocked sideways. I gripped the wheel for dear life, convinced we were capsizing and that death was imminent.

Then, with agonizing slowness, the boat righted herself. It was a terrifying experience. This journey through the hurricane lasted for nine days and nights. I remember tying myself onto a bunk with ropes, wedged between two wooden drawers, and disappearing into a place beyond prayer. Two days after nearly capsizing, as the storm still raged, it was my birthday — always a time of review and reflection. I took a break in the gray light of day and hunkered down in one of the speedboats tied to the top deck to smoke a rare cigarette by way of meager celebration. As I did so, everything inside me went quiet, the storm around me seemed to mute, and I had a sudden realization of how miraculous our escape had been. I thought to myself, "Surely there's more to my life than this!"

I had dropped out of school in England, traveled the world for two years, and then completed an apprenticeship before earning a mechanical engineering degree at university. After taking one or two small jobs in Europe, I'd ended up repairing and delivering luxury motor yachts around the world. But after we'd arrived in Malta and I'd thanked the gods for my survival, I packed it all in and retreated to the Shetland Islands, to the north of Scotland, to take stock of my life. All I knew was that I needed to get away.

I started asking that "Who am I?" question, and don't mind admitting that such introspection led to a pretty dark time. The remoteness of my croft house on a hilltop in the middle of nowhere was almost a perfect analogy for the personal wilderness in which I'd lost my sense of self. During those eighteen months in the Shetlands, my dad, Roderick Parkyn, passed away. Another rope tethering my stability started to fray. Then, one night, sitting in the candlelit gloom of the croft, a week after scattering his ashes on his favorite seashore in Scotland, I felt his unmistakable spirit enter the room. Those who have known grief and have felt another's spirit will know what I'm talking about. It was a powerful experience and one that released me from my isolation. In a quiet but reassuring voice within I heard him telling me, "It's all right. You can go now."

A couple of days later, I was sitting on the front doorstep, flipping through *Exchange & Mart*, when with some synchronicity, this ad jumped out and called to me: "Free Trip to Nepal for Diesel Mechanic." Propelled by Dad's reassurance, I applied and successfully landed the job — as both mechanic *and* driver for the trip to Nepal. This was the start of an exhilarating journey of self-discovery.

I soon found myself driving a Magic Bus on the hippie trail to India, a place that ultimately became my home for five of the next eleven years. In 1979 I was introduced to the ashram of Osho, an enlightened master who at the time was known as Bhagwan Shree Rajneesh. Being in his company is another story for another time. For now, let me just say that he continues to touch my heart very deeply.

One guidance Osho offered was that if people had really personal questions about themselves, they should visit a "shadow reader" in Bombay (now Mumbai). Of course, I had to do it. This remarkable man met me, smiling, at the door of his apartment. He was clean-shaven, in his late thirties, wearing a billowing shirt and trousers, and there was a bright twinkle in his eye. In a parking area below his apartment, his son proceeded to measure the length of my shadow, cast onto the ground by the sun. Back upstairs, the shadow reader did some calculations, rolled his chair along a huge bookshelf, pulled out one of many identical-looking volumes, turned to a page, and started reading in Sanskrit, a classical language of India. Among many things, he predicted that my personal awakening would happen later in life. I would be introduced to a system, would master it and then teach it.

"System? What system? What is he talking about?" I thought.

His advice was that I should experiment with reading for people to learn the skills of interaction while imparting personal and important information relevant to their lives.

One week later, I met a psychic palmist who gave me a fast-track introduction on how to read hands and faces. And so it was that after some practice-makes-perfect I began to read palms. It came naturally to me and I loved it. My travels took me to America, Switzerland, Brazil, Holland, Germany, and Japan before I settled in Hawaii for the next nine years, reading the stories contained within people's hands.

Then, in 1993, I heard that a woman friend was organizing classes for a man called Ra Uru Hu, who was introducing a system to America called Human Design. I was sent a curious-looking chart that was supposed to represent my life's design, and it dawned on me that this was the very system the shadow reader had talked about.

Its origins were intriguing. Ra, a Canadian previously known as Alan Krakower, had been a born cynic who had worked as a newspaper advertising salesman and filmmaker but had gone through a series of major disappointments, which had led to his flying to Europe and catching a bus to Spain. A casual remark by a fellow passenger had directed him to the island of Ibiza. There, an event took place that changed his world.

On the evening of January 4, 1987, he was returning home on foot with his dog, Barley Baker, when he saw a light shining from inside his remote cottage. He knew perfectly well that the lamp had no oil in it, so he wondered what was going on.

As man and dog entered the property, Barley started to growl, then fell prone to the floor. Ra himself described feeling some kind of internal explosion. Within moments, he was standing in a pool of his own perspiration. He then heard a male "voice" insisting he get to work. He was receiving something profound from the Universe. Call it channeling. Call it inspiration. Call it what you will. But he started writing and sketching and continued for eight days and nights. From those writings, Human Design came into being.

As surreal as that story may sound, its inescapable truth can be witnessed in this book, for these are the teachings that Ra brought into the world, a gift from the Universe. It is a system that simply works.

For the next seven years I traveled regularly from Maui to attend classes with Ra, and in the same way that I had learned to read palms, I taught myself to read Human Design life charts. I started giving readings to friends and clients and began to see that the information was both meaningful and empowering. After four years, it was time to articulate all I had learned to a wider audience and I started teaching classes about the system.

One of the people who came to these classes had a profound impact on me, and it felt as if she was opening a whole new magical doorway. Carola was a spiritual astrologer and counselor, and she could see in her own way how clearly we were connected. Ultimately, she invited me to move to be with her in California and we married. She started using Human Design in her counseling practice and also noticed how it assisted clients to move through certain issues and find clarity about who they were as individuals.

I, too, was well aware of the empowering impact the system could have on people. For many people, it truly was the difference between being lost and then feeling found, granting them permission to be themselves once more.

Human Design isn't a guarantee for happiness, nor will it remove the challenges and pain of normal life. But I've seen how it can change lives. It changed mine. Now I intend it to change yours.

Most of us, at some point, have become frustrated with our lot and whispered self-searching questions such as "Who am I?" "What am I doing with my life?" "What is my purpose?"

It seems more and more people are engaged in an endless search these days — searching for the perfect career, perfect partner, and perfect life. The very word *searching* means looking for something that is lost, lacking, or missing, and we fall into the trap of believing that all the answers lie outside ourselves.

Yet the answers already lie on the inside. Those answers are detailed in a design of which the Universe is the architect, a design of the person you were programmed to be, your Human Design. It is a document that represents your blueprint for life — a blueprint of your personality. Once you've become acquainted with this information, you will know whether the life you're living fits with your design.

This is not some New Age concept; its accuracy is inescapable and timeless. It is not a philosophy or a belief; it is an actuality rooted in science that speaks its own power. Nor does it require the attraction or manifestation of wishes or desires. There is no asking, visualizing, or positive thinking required, because its truth already exists within us.

When I assert that truth, I'm not making some fashionable statement of rhetoric; I quite literally mean the truth is within — like a set of tools within a boxed set, waiting to be picked up and used to carve out a niche and purpose in life.

Another lady, named Margaret, discovered this truth when she realized her life was out of synch with her Human Design. As she later told me after a reading:

> *I realize that I was being someone else for too long. I see now that everything I was doing was contrary to my Human Design. But the moment my true nature was seen and appreciated, I felt alive again. I've used the tools you gave me, and it feels as if this system has provided the key which has unlocked my true self.*

This book, in conjunction with the free downloadable software, will reveal your unique design and give you that same key, providing a chart that illustrates all the ingredients that make you who you are:

- It pinpoints your intrinsic nature and what makes you tick.
- It details the sorts of people you "click" with and the kinds of environments that bring out your best.
- It reveals your true self's underlying nature, preferences, personality traits, strengths, weaknesses, abilities, dynamics, and built-in chemistry.
- It reminds you of the needs and feelings you're either celebrating or resisting.
- It explains how you can make decisions that foster happiness and fulfillment.

Once reacquainted with your "design for life," you will start to feel the ripples across all areas of your existence:

In relationships and friendships, it determines the dynamics between people, allowing you to see where there is synergy, conflict, or nothing in common.

In the family and at home, it explains differences between siblings and highlights the practical and emotional interactions between parent and child, husband and wife.

In the workplace, it illustrates to employers or clients the different natural abilities within each person — a vital tool for improving collective productivity.

In the classroom, it shows teachers the capabilities of each pupil and how to bring out the best in each child.

On the social scene, it makes you aware of the magnetisms at play and why you are drawn to certain people and repelled by others.

Relationships with yourself, your partner, friends, parents, siblings, colleagues, and bosses are all impacted by the power of this system. And through it we can learn to understand one another on a much deeper level, thus becoming more effective and empathetic parents, friends, lovers, and colleagues. It is the most logical, freshest, and clearest insight into the self that there could ever be.

Introduction

I can confidently say that you won't have seen anything like it before, so prepare for an intimate odyssey whose final destination is a true understanding of the person you were designed to be.

Prepare to meet yourself. Prepare to meet the *real* you.

Chetan Parkyn
San Marcos, CA
May 2010

1
Meet Yourself

The Life Chart

After my Human Design reading, I felt recognized on so many levels. I've met myself, and it feels right! I can now move forward into the rest of my life with confidence, joy, and enthusiasm.

MM, Colorado

Human Design is ripe for these changing times, encouraging us to meet ourselves head-on and be responsible for who we are. It is a system that takes the torch from the hand of astrology and carries it to the next level, providing both an accurate guide for life and a self-assessment device. Human Design is astrology's natural successor, something old making way for something new. No longer will it be enough for human curiosity to simply ask of others: "What is your sign?" You will want — and need — to know more.

For example, if you were born under the sign of Libra, you'll already know how different you are from fellow Librans, and yet you have to read the same forecasts. Without an in-depth astrological reading, you are collectively defined with a one-size-fits-all label. But Human Design, through this book, unveils and celebrates your unique individuality.

With that in mind, perhaps a better opening question for future social introductions could be "Forget your sign; what's your design?"

So, how does it work?

Human Design draws from four ancient wisdom traditions to become a system in its own right that provides a technical-looking design of the person you were born to be. It uses data to determine your exact placement in time and space relative to the solar system and star fields around you at the precise moment of birth. But whereas in astrology the sky is divided into twelve compartments (the signs of the zodiac), Human Design divides it into sixty-four. This correlates to two things: first, the sixty-four codons of the human genetic code; and second, the sixty-four hexagrams of the *I Ching*, a tool used by the Chinese to better understand human nature. Each one of these sixty-four compartments carries a unique meaning, allowing us to see, in depth, which characteristics make up our being.

We are all, in effect, human cells interacting within one giant energy vessel, the Universe, impacted by what is called a neutrino stream. Neutrinos are minute particles that travel near the speed of light, passing through everything. If we, as humans, live in an atmosphere of air, the Universe lives in an atmosphere of neutrinos. These are the very emissions of all the stars in the sky, and our bodies are being bombarded by trillions of them every second of the day. Because neutrinos have mass, they exchange information with everything they pass through, including us. So, at the moment of birth, we are imprinted with neutrino information, which leaves a genetic thumbprint, determining the nature we will carry throughout life.

Imagine the sky above us divided into sixty-four equal compartments. Within each of these compartments there are star fields "breathing out" neutrinos, trillions at a time, in all directions. These neutrinos pass through the planets, exchanging information as they go. When those same neutrinos pass through us at the exact time of our birth, they leave that planetary-flavored information embedded within us. It's as if they gently "bump" our human vehicle as we enter the world, leaving an indelible impression on our beings and shaping how we are going to interact in life.

In 1987, when Human Design was first developed, neutrinos were merely a theory. But proof arrived in the late 1990s when scientists in Japan and Canada established that neutrino particles change 'flavors' and, therefore, must have mass. This discovery, it was said, explained the "missing mass" of the Universe.

In these rapidly changing times, science is uncovering more and more about the mysteries of life. Human Design is where science and spirituality come together like never before to inform you about the essence of your life. It provides a way of reading your genetic neutrino imprint, of seeing your own design.

To create the chart that will reveal your blueprint for life:
1. Install the software using the download link hosted on the website printed on the first page of this book. Open the Human Design Life Chart program, click on "Select a Folder," then "Create Life Chart."

2. Then enter your name, date, and exact time of birth. If you don't know your exact time, you may input twelve noon as a good estimate for now. However, to make certain you have an absolutely accurate life chart, it's best to consult your birth certificate, hospital records, or a relative to find the exact time.

3. Then click on the "Place" tab and insert the country or U.S. state followed by the city or nearest city of birth. Don't worry about the time zone — that is automatically calculated for you.

4. When you press "OK," your life chart will be created.

Staring back at you is a reflection of your inner being.

When people first lay eyes on a Human Design life chart, it provokes a carbon-copy reaction: a puzzled frown forms across the brow and a bewildered voice asks: "What — that's *me?*"

Yes, that's you, on the inside, the mechanics of your true nature laid bare on the page. All those shapes, colors, lines, symbols, and numbers denote the person you were designed to be. You are looking at the very core of your being — what makes you tick, what makes you function.

The software you downloaded creates the life chart based on two factors: the first, the exact time, date, and place of your birth; and the second, a separate time, *which it calculates*, from a moment three months *before* birth — the instant when the neocortex in the front lobe of the brain turns on and when the spirit is said to enter the body. It's at this time that the soul "tunes in" to the physical vehicle it's been handed in life.

A natal astrological calculation is made based on the time and place of your birth and the planetary influences. Then this calculation is computed and combined with three other ancient wisdoms: the chakra system, the *I Ching*, and the Kabbalah. All this information combines to create a life chart.

One initial question I'm often asked is "Does my design ever change?" The truth of the matter is that during the course of your life you will be exposed to, and perhaps conditioned by, almost every facet and nuance of the different designs of other people. But *your* design is consistent and forever remains your true foundation. It is unique and can always be relied on. There is no need to be anyone other than who you are, because you have everything you need within your design to live a complete and fulfilling life.

This understanding should remove all thoughts of wanting to change something about yourself or trying to be like someone else. There is no "good" or "bad" design, no "better" or "worse." There is only *authenticity*. Once you accept that and start to be yourself, everything around you starts to become clear.

The beauty of what lies within will become clear as we examine you, stage by stage, chapter by chapter, identifying the different ingredients that fuse to create the whole person. So, in order to follow this book, keep your life chart in your hand or posted on a computer screen. I'll be the driver, taking you on a journey. You keep your eyes on the map, because each shape, color, channel, or number tells you so much about your inside story.

Nine Brilliant Jewels

I often tell people to imagine their Human Design as an intricate, precious piece of jewelry — sheer bedazzling craftsmanship as created by the Universe.

We each have nine brilliant "jewels" within us, represented by the square, triangular, or diamond shapes in the illustration. These are the nine *centers* that form the foundation of our design. They are known as the Crown, the Mind, the Throat, the Self, the Heart, the Sacral, the Emotions, the Spleen, and the Root.

These shining stones are set within an intricate framework of thirty-six narrow *channels*. At either end of those channels are numbers denoting the sixty-four *gates* that determine the cut and polish of the jewels.

So each Human Design life chart contains nine centers, thirty-six channels, and sixty-four gates, all with something to say about our true nature and role in life.

The nine centers are effectively chakras, energy centers that, like opening and closing valves, regulate the flow of energy throughout our being. It is not physical energy, but life-energy that has resided within us since birth. Each center, in its own unique way, receives, assimilates,

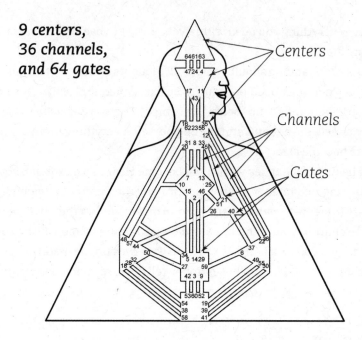

**9 centers,
36 channels,
and 64 gates**

Centers

Channels

Gates

modifies, and expresses this energy, turning it into a human function, perception, awareness, instinct, or behavior. It flows through us, and out of us, every second of every day, connecting us to everyone around us.

Connecting the centers is the framework of thirty-six channels through which the flow of energy passes. These channels, therefore, enhance, shape, and modify energy into more precise qualities, traits, and abilities.

At either end of each channel is a number relating to the sixty-four gates that represent the DNA of your true nature, the imprint left by neutrinos. Each person has the same sixty-four numbers in the same place — the configuration is rigid within each and every design — but some of the gates are "on" and some "off," creating yet more specific components of your design.

We examine all these layers further in the book, as well as the other components that make up your design. For now, just take a look at the symbols and numbers you see in the top left-hand corner of your chart. You will observe many numbers in both black and pink. Each number corresponds to a gate and, therefore, a specific trait, determining whether it's an unconscious or conscious aspect of you.

Unconscious/Conscious

One fascinating truth that emerges from a life chart is that we see in vivid detail the conscious and unconscious elements of our makeup.

The *conscious* is the intentional things we act out, of which we are mostly aware. These are the awake and watchful elements of our personality and way of behaving.

The *unconscious* is our hidden side — the undercurrents that influence the automatic or involuntary behavior that shapes our character. These aspects may not be instantly recognizable to us but will no doubt resonate with the people who observe us. Have you ever had someone say something like "You do that just the way your granddad did," or "Your great-grandmother used to say things like that"? Such statements imply that you have inherited recognizable but unconscious characteristics from various parts of your family tree.

I always say that the conscious is the tip of the iceberg, whereas the unconscious is what lies beneath the surface of our beings. Jungian analyst Gerhard Adler describes the unconscious as "possessing a superior knowledge of our real needs." Psychologists and psychotherapists can spend weeks, months, or years mining and analyzing the thoughts of clients to determine unconscious traits. But now, for the first time in recorded history, there is a system that, at the click of a mouse, reveals what is conscious and unconscious within each individual.

In Human Design, the term *unconscious* represents our ancestral input on a soul level — the combined and collective patterns from our ancestral line, which reads like the DNA of our soul. This imprinting starts inside our mother's womb when there is no access to outside influences. All we can receive is our soul's genetic inheritance, and that inevitably comes from our father, mother, and farther back in the family tree. On a biological front, we receive the genes that determine the color of our eyes and hair, the height we'll stand, and the weight we'll gain, plus a host of other physical characteristics. But, in a spiritual sense, the Human Design imprinting also passes down our emotional, psychological, and behavioral characteristics. In some ways, we might say that the gifts, talents, or issues of our ancestors are echoed in our makeup.

In some respects, this truth within Human Design echoes the theory that, somehow, the experiences of a mother and father are transmitted to their offspring, above and beyond the normal DNA syntax. According to this theory, expounded by a Frenchman named Jean-Baptiste Lamarck, children inherit the traits of parents. Once discredited, it was in fact built on by scientists in the late 1990s when laboratory tests suggested that an experience felt by a pregnant mouse left a physical mark on the DNA in her eggs. It's as if a parent's or grandparent's experience leaves a molecular memory in the child. This is not a mutation, but a transference that science continues to explore, fascinated by the possibility that an experience can somehow alter actual DNA.

Human Design makes it possible for you to become aware of this fascinating genetic inheritance and live a more fulfilling life by becoming aware of the unconscious influences that stir within. It is why, once acquainted with your Human Design, you may suddenly recognize unconscious traits that relatives have already observed about you.

Remember, the conscious influences stem from the exact moment of your birth; the unconscious, from that moment calculated as being three months before birth. It's at this point that your developing fetus is energetically receiving the makeup of your ancestral line.

The conscious/unconscious themes will become more apparent as we go on. For now, simply take an initial look at which parts of your life chart are conscious (black) and which are unconscious (pink). Striped sections of black and pink indicate an overlap of conscious and unconscious traits. This implies that you are actually capable of recognizing these unconscious traits in yourself.

The Planets

In the Human Design system there are thirteen different influences that come to us through the placement of the sun, moon, planets, and nodes at the time of our birth. It is the precise placement of the planets in the neutrino stream at that moment that determines which gates are on and therefore which centers are defined.

On the life chart, these heavenly bodies are indicated by the black glyphs alongside the pink and black gate numbers. Their influences, and what they bring to the table, belong in an advanced form of teaching beyond the scope of this initial presentation of Human Design. But, for your understanding of what you are seeing in that top left-hand corner matrix, I provide this symbolic outline:

☉	The Sun	♂	Mars
⊕	The Earth	♃	Jupiter
☾	The Moon	♄	Saturn
☊	The North Node	♅	Uranus
☋	The South Node	♆	Neptune
☿	Mercury	♇	Pluto
♀	Venus		

Now, to guide you through the basics of a life chart's structure, let's look at an example. Allow me to introduce . . . Prince Harry.

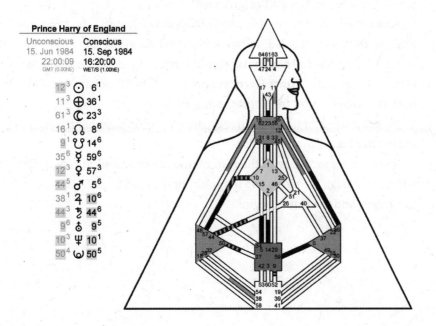

Prince Harry of England

Unconscious	Conscious
15. Jun 1984	15. Sep 1984
22:00:09	16:20:00
GMT (0.00hE)	WET/S (1.00hE)

12^3 ☉ 6^1
11^3 ⊕ 36^1
61^3 ☾ 23^3
16^1 ☊ 8^6
9^1 ☋ 14^6
35^6 ☿ 59^6
12^3 ♀ 57^3
44^5 ♂ 5^6
38^1 ♃ 10^6
44^3 ♄ 44^6
9^6 ♅ 9^5
10^3 ♆ 10^1
50^4 ♇ 50^5

Prince Harry of England, the second son of Prince Charles and the late Princess Diana, was born on September 15, 1984, at 16:20 GMT in London. You'll observe that the software has calculated June 15, 1984, as a period approximately three months before his birth.

These two dates have created the two columns titled "Unconscious" (in pink) and "Conscious" (black). In these columns, you'll note the gate numbers, to be examined later.

All the information in the right-hand column is color-coded black, relating to the moment of birth. These are the aspects that are conscious — sometimes called "personality" information.

All the information in the left-hand column is color-coded pink, relating to that time approximately three months before birth. These represent the unconscious side and Prince Harry's genetic inheritance.

Note that one square center is red. From that center's right side, you'll see a narrow channel colored black leading to the brown triangle center on the far right. On either end of this connected channel are the gates 59 and 6. The meanings of this are incidental at this stage. What matters is that you note the distinction between a center *defined* in *color* and a center that is *white* and therefore *undefined*.

Also note the distinction between a *fully colored channel*, which is *active*, and one that is *white or half-colored* and is, therefore, *inactive*.

It takes just one full channel activation to turn on the connecting centers. For example, in Prince Harry's chart, the active 59-6 channel defines both the Sacral center (red) and the Emotions center (brown).

To recap: a center is *defined* in *color*, depending on whether a connecting channel is *active* or *nonactive*.

You are now armed with the rudimentary basics of what constitutes a Human Design life chart. I've mapped out the road ahead. Now, let the journey — and the fun — begin.

2

The Energy Within

The Nine Centers

Finally, someone has explained what it's all about — who I am, the way I am, and what to do about it.

Rob, London, UK

Life is one long sequence of sometimes dramatic events and introductions. Our days ebb and flow with actions and reactions, meetings and greetings, and it is the nine Human Design centers that assimilate and distribute life-energy around our physical body to determine how we interact with one another. These energies within are what build the foundations of our true nature.

While the centers have familiar names such as Spleen, Heart, and Throat, they are not physical things but internal zones that correspond with the way we function. So your life chart is a map of your "energy body" as opposed to your physical body. In this respect, it is not dissimilar to the chakra system.

The crucial thing to understand is that each center "communicates" and crosses over with the designs of other people, meshing together in a daily dance and influencing all our interactions on a moment-by-moment basis. These invisible energies are forever interweaving by our simply being in the same room as someone else. So, on the surface, our eyes and mouths may well be doing all the obvious communicating, but it's the powerful undercurrents of the nine centers that are doing the real work, pulling our strings on a deep bio-energetic level.

In a basic example, a man could be standing in a room with a woman and their respective energies will interact, drawing them together. You'll be familiar with that feeling when you've been pulled toward someone and yet have no idea why. Or there's something about someone that unsettles you. That "something" is the energy at work within different centers.

Your Human Design, therefore, is *always* affected by the energies of those with whom you engage in love, business, or friendship. It is a system that is interconnected, like humanity itself.

Once you understand how different designs interface, engage, and communicate, you're better able to understand the dynamics and undercurrents running beneath all relationships and associations. It is basic quantum physics — the fact that everything in the Universe consists of vibrations and energy and that we are an integral part of that same energy. I'm not going to indulge in such complexities in this book. All that needs to be understood is something that is supported by science — that the nine centers of the Human Design system interface between the Universe's energy and the energy within all of us, translating it into individual functions and expressions.

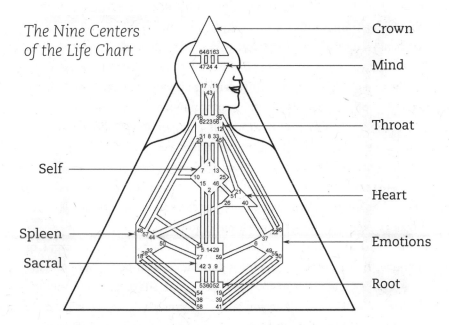

The Nine Centers of the Life Chart

Crown

Mind

Throat

Self

Heart

Spleen

Emotions

Sacral

Root

Defined or Undefined

Knowledge of the workings of the nine centers will help you understand what happens within you on a daily basis, but the first thing you need to find out is: are you defined or undefined?

Take a look at your life chart.

A center defined with color indicates a function or tendency that is fixed and consistent. These aspects are set in stone, a constant part of you. They are the part of your being that you can *always* count on — energy that's available to be harnessed 24/7.

If a center is undefined and white, its specific energy is not consistent, making this part of you malleable and flexible. This means you're open to the influence of those who do have this center defined. When in their company, you effectively adopt their energy and may be swayed or conditioned by it. This is what we call a *conditioning influence*.

But this doesn't mean you're a helpless puppet. Instead of absorbing that energy, you can learn to recognize what's happening, how your undefined center is being engaged, and say to yourself: "This influence is not me; it's them." This will allow you to stand back and adopt a detached objectivity, transforming such an influence into what we call *impassive wisdom*. That wisdom allows you, as an uninvolved observer, to reflect back what you are witnessing, allowing the other person to see the forest for the trees. This is why the white centers provide an opportunity for the exchange of considered reflection, comprehension, and insight.

Please don't think that not much is going on in your life chart if it's not awash with color. If anything, it makes you more empathetic and flexible and less fixed than someone with a more colorful chart.

So, to recap: a *defined* center has *fixed traits and functions*. An *undefined* center has qualities that will be *intermittent*, coming and going depending on what other "designs" are around you.

It is worth knowing that each center also relates to a bodily organ or gland within us, thereby playing a part in our well-being. When living true to your design, you attune to your body's needs on physical, mental, and emotional levels. When you fall out of synch with your design, or go against your nature, you can become susceptible to physical discomfort or illness. Resistance to a center's energy can, therefore, have an adverse effect on the corresponding organ or gland.

THE NINE CENTERS

The Crown
Inspiration

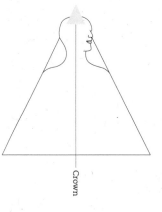

Crown

Sitting at the top of the head is the triangle of the Crown. Kings and queens have always worn crowns to denote an attunement to a higher way of thinking. It is no surprise, therefore, that in Human Design terms, the Crown is the center of inspiration, and the triangle's peak could well be interpreted as the antennae's receptor for the body, receiving inspiration from above. This is the center from which truth, doubt, and possibilities can emerge.

The Crown is unique because it is linked to only one other center, the Mind, where it downloads inspiration to be mentally processed. It is one of two "pressure centers" and its applied pressure is to find meaning in life. Whenever you feel a strain to get your head around something, you're feeling the pressure of the Crown. Or, put another way, the urgency of a problem searching for an answer.

Anatomically, this center relates to the pineal gland, a little-known gland about the size of a pea that sits in the middle of the brain. It relates to melatonin levels, suggesting we are either "awake" or "asleep" in life, either inspired or not.

If Your Crown Is Defined

Rattle, rattle, rattle goes your head, pondering all sorts of ideas, truths, doubts, and possibilities. I suspect you catch yourself saying, "I don't know where the inspiration comes from — it just does!"

When the Crown is defined, it follows that the Mind will be also. The Crown can only be defined through its link to the Mind, meaning you're someone who is always thinking, reviewing, and searching for exciting insights and fresh realizations. You can be of high intellect but need to understand that intellect and intelligence are not one and the same, because you must learn how to *use* that intellect. That's why the CIA should be called the Central Intellect Agency, because until its agents actually think outside the box and process the facts, figures, data, and tips, you can't call it intelligence.

If you have the Crown defined, you'll intrigue others with your mentally active way. That's because you induce deep thought with your take on the world. This can mean you're either received as scintillating company or as ditchwater, depending on how you put yourself across.

The Crown is one place where the sense of spirit can be found within you, whispering, wanting to be heard. It is the nature of the Crown to handle lofty concepts and this can, sometimes, lead to great stress about how to make these concepts practical or communicate them to others in a coherent manner. There is a deep-seated need to understand and explain everything, which, if unchecked, has the potential to send even you around the bend. I always say it can be mentally exhausting to have the Crown defined, and yet highly rewarding when inspiration leads to satisfaction.

If Your Crown Is Undefined

You are open to all sorts of inspirations that seem to pop into your head at odd times. Wherever you go, you find inspiration in all sorts of different company and situations, because you're open to the conditioning of other designs. This is why you love to immerse yourself in inspiring environments such as art galleries and movie theaters and connect with artistic people. You yearn to be inspired in this way.

This can, however, leave your head spinning with a kaleidoscope of thoughts and inspirations triggered by other people. The risk here is that you'll be so influenced by other people's thoughts, issues, and puzzles that you'll act on them. People can end up carrying someone else's flag their whole life and living in someone else's shadow. Ask yourself this question: "Why do I spend so much time thinking about the dilemmas or ideas of others?"

Refuse to get caught up in the highbrow conceptualizing flooding your Crown from outside designs and allow your center to act as a receiving dish to the thoughts of others. This is how you turn a conditioning influence into the impassive wisdom that will give you the objectivity to untangle others' convoluted thought streams and convey them with clarity. An example would be a student understanding a professor's complex take on a subject and writing it out in a more simple way.

Remain wary about committing to flash-in-the-pan inspirations, which can be a waste of energy. Use this openness to remain wise.

The Mind
Thinking

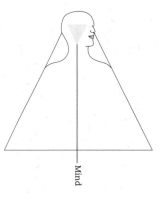

The Mind distills information being pumped in from the Crown and is always filtering and rationalizing to reach an understanding. It's as if the Crown pressurizes it, saying, "Work it out, work it out, work it out."

As one of our three "awareness centers," the Mind is in a permanent state of "work in progress." Worries and agitations can fester within this center. The Mind can trap deep thinkers into an endless loop because the mental wheels never cease as it ponders the past and attempts to relate to the present and future.

This center relates to the pituitary gland, which is located in the front of the brain. Eastern cultures refer to this gland as "the third eye" or as "the mystical eye of knowledge." It is no surprise, therefore, to see it associated with a center that interprets inspiration to make you "see" something you need to learn or grasp.

If Your Mind Is Defined

Your built-in hard drive never stops whirring, processing and backing up its information. Your mind is a human computer, forever comparing, reviewing, and researching. In school or at work, you may have had the sensation that your head was about to burst with all the facts and knowledge overloading you. But when you put your mind to something, you'll work it out and race on to the next thing.

Many troubleshooters and consultants come armed with such a makeup. You can also be a professional worrier and nitpicker, looking for problems that do not exist. Expressions such as "You're worrying about nothing!" and "Will you stop worrying about things that haven't happened yet?" tend to suggest that a person with a defined Mind is in the room. You just cannot turn off your thoughts and worries. Meditation can quiet your mind, allowing you to distance yourself from racing thoughts, but you have a consistent way of thinking and will find you approach an issue or question in exactly the same way each time.

If Your Mind Is Undefined

You can be open-minded and absentminded at the same time. You are open to contemplating anything, but also prone to be forgetful and easily distracted. You might go to your car and forget your keys or leave the house and forget to turn the iron off. I always say that keeping a diary or journal is a good medium for you, because you can make a date or have a conversation and then forget its details within twenty-four hours.

I don't intend to paint you as ditzy. Far from it. The great mind of Albert Einstein had this center undefined, and the reason his mind was so great was that this granted him a detached objectivity that allowed the impassive wisdom of finding clarity amid life's complexities. You, too, must learn to step away from the mental activity of defined Minds. That way, you really can make sense of the thoughts and confusions that others are grappling with. I always tell people with an undefined Mind that they have a gift for resolving other people's issues, for being able to see the forest, not the trees.

You can also walk into a room and sense what everyone is thinking, because you're capable of tapping into the thoughts of others. People may even say, "You always seem to know what I'm thinking." Such is the wisdom of the undefined Mind. Its beauty is that you have a choice: be contemplative and still when alone, or become engaged and thoughtful when interacting with others. The potential of your mind knows no bounds! If you learn to accept this glorious uncertainty, life can be viewed as a mental adventure.

The Throat
Expression and Manifesting

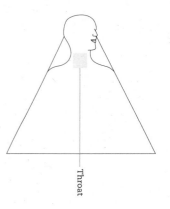

Below the Mind is the Throat, the center that creates and makes things happen with its powers of manifestation and expression. It is both the voice box and the main hub of your Human Design, where all deeds and dreams seek reality and where all voices strive to be heard. It is the center where *everything* can happen.

The Throat has many unique ways of expressing itself through speech, actions, and writing. Its shining qualities are all about teaching, leadership, education, and knowledge. Anything going on within your Human Design is seeking outlet and expression, as words or action, at the Throat.

Anatomically, this center relates to the thyroid and parathyroid glands, which regulate our metabolic rate and sense of well-being. I would say that whatever your nature, being true to it has a lot to do with maintaining wellness.

If Your Throat Is Defined

Here lies the power of expression — but what is expressed, and how, depends on which other defined centers feed into this main hub. All roads lead to the Throat, and so all energies seek a release or voice via this center. For example, a connection with the Mind means you'll speak your mind. With the Emotions, you'll express your emotions. With the Heart, you'll convey your heartfelt wishes. All centers, and their attributes, seek to be demonstrated at the Throat. When that connection is made, an expression comes via an action, creativity, or communication.

You are someone who is consistent in how you communicate, with a voice that carries a certain cadence and confidence. The way you express yourself, therefore, leads to making things happen, catalyzing your goals.

Also, you can be a facilitator for great storytelling, the revealing of personal insight, the teaching of sound education, the authority of strong leadership, and the expression of strong opinions, in either you or someone else.

You catalyze speech in other people, but you need to be aware that they're talking with you rather than at you. People make a beeline simply to chew your ear off, like the person next to you on the long-distance flight who is itching to talk and doesn't care that you've got the earphones on and a magazine pressed to your nose. They want to talk to you — and they will! Your center provides them with a much-needed outlet, magnetizing all their pent-up chatter because, more than likely, *their* Throat is undefined. Take the example of a friend of mine. She has an associate who phones every week and bombards her with forty minutes of constant chat, dumping all their thoughts and issues on her without ever asking about her life and well-being. That's why I encourage you to be aware of this phenomenon and make such people aware of what they're doing. Because, quite frankly, once they get going, they might never stop!

If Your Throat Is Undefined

"I can't seem to find the right words!" I can hear you say. This is the source of much frustration as you struggle to express yourself effectively, consistently, or in the way you'd like. But that won't stop you trying! Once you're in the company of a defined Throat, the silky skills of expression are accessible to you and this can unleash a verbal volley as eager as a greyhound from the traps. The irony is that having an undefined Throat can turn you into a real chatterbox.

I can spot you a mile away. You're the one who can dominate a conversation, sometimes chipping in and interrupting, because so much pressure has stored behind the communicative walls built by your nature. Once in the right environment and up and running, you hardly pause to draw breath.

There is little consistency to your expression, either. Two people can ask the same question and receive two completely different answers. It all depends on the company. This doesn't mean that what you say isn't compelling or interesting. It's just an inconsistency I'm drawing to your attention. What I would be wary about is launching into a conversation that is meandering and without focus — who knows where you might end up?

Speech impediments and anxieties about articulation skills may well occur in people with an undefined Throat. You are, by nature, someone for whom silence is golden, so learn to wait for the right time to say something. The impassive wisdom here is that when you exercise patience, you can speak with a lucidity and poetry that others might not be able to manage. This is because your undefined center reflects the nature of the environment around you, taking the voice of others and transforming it into your own insight. For instance, Bill Clinton, a brilliant orator, has an undefined Throat. He is adept at riding the energy of his audience. But his increasingly husky voice could be an indication that he has a propensity to speak out of turn, thereby straining his voice. He may have insisted on speaking, without practicing patience.

Basically, the ease with which you express yourself depends on the person you're interacting with, as does your ability to make things happen and express yourself creatively.

The Self
Direction, Sense of Purpose, Love

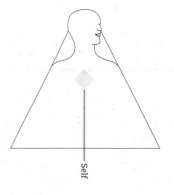

Self

Beneath the Throat is the diamond shape of the Self. This represents purpose and direction in life, as well as self-love. It is like a global positioning system, aligning us with who we are, where we are, and to what we are guided. It relates to our boundaries, determining what is appropriate, what is not; who is in, who is out. This is where we find the answer to the "Who am I?" question. It is a center that provides a consistent connection to the soul.

The energies of love reside here in all their forms: spiritual or fateful love, love as an attraction to the physical form, love of humanity, and love of the journey of life itself. Many self-truths can also be found within this center with the creativity to expand life and the ability to be receptive to all it offers.

Anatomically, the Self relates to the liver, the seat of the soul, where our blood is cleansed. Whether your center is defined or not determines how you filter life experiences. A congested liver raises one's level of intolerance for life and therefore reduces one's ability to connect directly with it.

If Your Self Is Defined

"I know who I am, and I know where I'm heading" is your slogan. You have an assured identity with an equally strong sense of purpose and direction. There is something certain and solid about your character. You seek to be not "just yourself" but also your "best self." If you're not feeling it, start tapping your built-in compass, because it will always guide you home.

Ultimately, you cannot stray for long from a natural sense of self. If you do, you're not being true to your nature and you'll sense an inner angst or frustration, as if you're swimming against the tide. But the majority of the time you are resolute, believing you are who you are and that's not going to change.

The downside is that you can be diverted to shepherd those who feel lost. If you're not careful you could look behind and find an entourage of hangers-on dragging you down. Yet you can be immovable when you find a true path, a pursuit, or a partner you set your sights on, and there is an indefatigable consistency about what you seek. There is a "Nothing is going to stop me" quality about your chosen direction.

If Your Self Is Undefined

"Where I am is who I am right now" is your slogan. You can struggle to find a strong sense of identity and can wear many hats in life. You can be all things to all people, reflecting back to them the truth of who *they* are. This means you derive a sense of self from the environment and people around you. The same could be said for your direction in life — it tends to be a bit changeable, for there is no reliable built-in compass.

There is, of course, a beauty to this flexibility. It allows the compassion to identify with everyone and turns you into something of a social chameleon. In that sense, that's exactly who you are, so your identity crisis is solved!

So, learn to go with the flow and live in the moment. But be wary of succumbing to the conditioning influence of someone else's determination, purpose, and direction — that can lead to all sorts of wrong paths. Your impassive wisdom is to embrace your innate ability to reflect back your observations about someone else's being or chosen direction, even if you don't really know where you're going yourself. You can, in this respect, become an overseeing guide, working out the way ahead for those who are too wrapped up in themselves to see it clearly.

When *you* need to find consistency in how you live your life, draw guidance from those who have this center defined. It's important, therefore, that you trust whom you get your bearings from. If you keep company with, and draw guidance from, people who are personally empowering, you will always have a fulfilling life. If you're swayed by those who are disempowering, you will inevitably make the wrong choices. For example, Britney Spears is someone with an undefined Self, so her stability and direction absolutely depend on the caliber of person she listens to and allows herself to be influenced by. This determines whether she stays on track or goes off the rails! It is crucial for her well-being for her to surround herself with people who have her best interests in mind.

The Heart
Willpower and Wishes

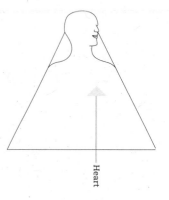

Next to the Self, tucked below right, is the Heart, a center that balances willpower with ego and comes armed with a competitive streak, to either prove a point in business or be top dog in the material world. This is one of three "motor centers" within Human Design, and a motor center pushes us on in life. This one is where our heart's desires are fueled.

The biggest thing to which people aspire is a sense of freedom, and willpower drives us on toward that freedom. The Heart expresses its inherent willpower in one of two ways. One is the use of willpower in accordance with universal and greater good. The other is ego driven, with willpower applied for purely selfish reasons. We are forever caught in this balancing act: do we consider the common good or just look after number one?

All money matters are processed through this center, which filters our material needs and wants as we balance our values: our values of life against our values of money. You may think that making money is all in the mind — indeed, there are mental formulas to assist the creation of wealth — but in actuality, money is an energy form closely related to the wishes emanating from the Heart. Power, prestige, and money are all thrown into this melting-pot center.

Anatomically, this center is related to the organ of the heart, and it is no surprise that the most common disease in the world is heart disease. When people come under intense pressure to "get on with it," "get rich," and "make it happen," it naturally follows that overexertion will lead to complaints from the heart. This center is also related to the digestive process, stomach, and gallbladder. All these organs can function well when you're in natural attunement with your life but can experience problems when your willpower is invested in pursuits that are wrong for you.

If Your Heart Is Defined

It is statistically rare to have a defined Heart, but if you're among the iron-willed few, you can move mountains. You are a potential superhero in terms of Human Design. Your potential to harness raw willpower can accomplish something in five minutes that would take someone else an hour. You are all about throwing your heart into it or following your heart. It is your source of courage, valor and standing in life.

For you, accomplishments are never the question; alignment with what is truly worth your time and energy is more the issue. So you must be careful about to whom and what you pledge this willpower, because the Heart must be respected. You must ensure you're committed, because "your heart is in it."

There is an impressive and consistent assurance about people with this center defined. Classic examples of such powerhouses are Winston

Churchill, John F. Kennedy, Donald Trump, Arnold Schwarzenegger, the Dalai Lama, and Al Gore. These are powerful figures who have put their heart into all they've done and have used their willpower to enhance their sense of values.

Binding themes of this center are the ability to stand on your own two feet, to be bold enough to convince others, to take control of a situation, and to handle crisis. But inefficiency can irk you in a way that makes you want to take on every task and do it yourself. You will want to get your own way and may run the risk of being perceived as arrogant in the pursuit of your goals.

One of the greatest requirements of a defined Heart is rest. Chill. Put your feet up. Take a break! Having the sense to sit down and rest is crucial, even polite — to give everyone else the chance to catch up with you!

If Your Heart Is Undefined

The majority of people have an undefined Heart. In this case, you might yearn to be a powerhouse, but your heart's not designed to be in it. You have nothing to prove and must live your life accordingly.

People may well ask, "What exactly do you want out of life?" or "Where's your willpower?" Having this center undefined does not mean you don't have willpower; it simply means it is not consistent within you. If anything, it is that uncertain aspect that makes you compete with others and work harder. The danger is to compare yourself with others and over-compete, then come up short and struggle with how you value yourself.

That is why it is important to understand that you have *no need* to prove anything — to yourself or anyone else with expectations of you. If you do, you are likely to get caught in the tug-of-war between the universal good and the ego. You can find yourself in situations where matters of ego can be triggered, causing you to be fiercely competitive. This is a conditioning influence. To turn it into impassive wisdom, step away from the ego and allow yourself to be content to mirror back life's intrinsic values to others without having to prove yourself through your actions. You have your own access to truth, so listen to yourself and be good to your heart.

You also have the flexibility and growing wisdom to guide others in what they want out of life. You can put an objective value on the material as well as spiritual aspects of life.

The Sacral
Life-Force and Staying Power

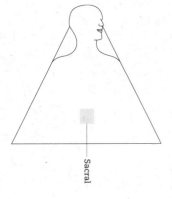

Sacral

The middle square center, second one up from the bottom of the life chart, is the Sacral. Also called the generator center, this is the engine room of the Human Design system, powered by life-force energy. As such, it generates the juice that aims trees toward the sky, empowers baby birds to crack out of their shells, and enables us to endure amazing hardship in life. It is the powerhouse center that fuels growth, expansion, and life. It harnesses an energy that has no awareness — it is just raw power, like a mechanical generator humming away, ready to unleash its stored energy.

Sometimes this center is referred to as the "sex center" because the majority of its gates have a sexual undertone. Physically, it also relates to the testes and ovaries.

The vast majority of the world's population — about 70 percent — has a defined Sacral with the potential to run with this unstoppable energy. Yet, paradoxically, those people rarely know how to utilize it in a way that brings about personal fulfillment. Having something powerful in your hands doesn't necessarily mean you know how to use it, but knowing this energy resides within can be a wake-up call.

Our sexual drive and urges also stem from this center, opening up all manner of human interaction and co-creation. It's important to appreciate that "sacral," "sacred," and "sex" are closely interlinked. This center offers a commentary on the barriers you may or may not establish in your sex life and your approach to intimacy.

If Your Sacral Is Defined

You are here in this world with the natural ability to respond to whatever life offers you. Whether you realize it or not, you have a continuous stream of life-force energy to draw on in order to sustain any endeavor that earns your commitment. But because this is a motor with no "off" switch, once your Sacral energy is unleashed, there's no turning back. Its momentum means it is *has* to be engaged until the experience is complete. Therefore, you must be sure about deciding what and who warrants your time and energy.

The Sacral is where the gut response resides. "I'm following my gut," you might say, and this is a natural reaction within you and a reliable guide. You'll recognize this response emanating from within: either an upbeat "uh-huh" for something that feels right or a frown-inducing "uh-uh" for something that feels wrong. This is your gut, which is *not* to be confused with your emotions. A gut response might also be experienced as a rising or contracting of energy without sound, pulling you to or from someone or something.

It is an ongoing tragedy that people with this defined center often find themselves going through life unappreciated, slogging away as the workhorse, slave, or gopher fulfilling others' projects. There can be a self-perception that that's all they are good for. There are scores of employees out there feeling unappreciated, and countless assistants and secretaries whose powerhouse energy and unstinting effort go relatively unrewarded and unrecognized but who make their bosses shine. There is a saying that behind every successful man lies a brilliant woman. I would make it less gender-specific and say instead: "Behind successful people, look to the person supporting them and see if their Sacral is defined." More often than not, it will be. What *would* they do and where would they be without you?!

Know that you are designed to be a powerhouse. Some of you might say that you don't feel that way, and that can be true if your energy has not been harnessed properly. What I'm pointing out is the *potential* reserves within, waiting to be harnessed.

When you do get motoring, you'll find other people have trouble keeping up, and this can make you feel obliged to take on their tasks as well as your own. But what you'll notice is that throwing your weight behind an endeavor that pleases you will give you a buzz, so it therefore must be right. Intolerance, boredom, frustration, or impatience with an activity suggests you have committed to the wrong thing. Learn to heed your gut response. Wait for that upbeat "uh-huh" or downbeat "uh-uh" as your guide.

With this center defined, sex, for you, is a driving force. This means not that you are naturally a lady-killer or a seductress, but that you have the potential for a sustained and satisfying sex life, provided you make the right connections. This means exercising discipline and discernment rather than just unleashing the energy at every given opportunity. If you're in tune with your gut over sexual partners, you'll find harmony. If you indulge in reckless abandon, then frustration and depression are likely to arise. You may sometimes find yourself overburdened and unsatisfied with partners and projects, and you may ask what you have done to deserve this. The answer is simple: you have committed to people and projects indiscriminately. You have taken on too much. You have promised too much. It is therefore vital to take your needs into account — first! No one is indispensable, not even someone with a defined Sacral.

If you happen to have both the Sacral and Heart defined, you are a positive whirlwind of energy, a nonstop go-getter. Your level of achievement can defy comprehension, but you truly have to find the things you love to do — and find time to rest up, because otherwise your huge efforts and sustainable energy can leave you flat on your back.

If Your Sacral Is Undefined

You will eventually find out that you are not designed to maintain a life in the fast lane. You are not, by nature, driven. You were not born with staying power and don't have consistent access to life-force energy. This doesn't mean you are work-shy, but your best input tends to come in spurts or when you are part of a team. The danger of failing to recognize this nature is that you'll try to keep up with the powerhouses and burn out.

As an example, one woman I know worked in the high-pressure field of sales, in an environment that was relentless in its pursuit of targets, goals, and profit margins. She was not designed to be immersed in such a high-powered environment, yet her job demanded it. She ended up collapsing at work, wiped out by the conditioning influence of the designs around her. Basically, her Human Design couldn't cope. She would have been far better placed being given a team to manage and seeing how that collective energy was best utilized — a situation she now happily enjoys.

The key understanding here is to adopt a more objective view that mirrors the energy of others, thereby turning a conditioning influence into impassive wisdom that strengthens, rather than depletes. You need to learn to pace yourself — to outsource and delegate instead of getting caught up in the dust storm.

When it comes to sexual energy, there is an innocence to your makeup. Your drive and urges will not be as great as those of people with a defined Sacral, and sex won't be such a relentless driving force within you — unless, of course, you tap into a partner with the Sacral defined. Then, you will mirror their energy, and that can magnify matters! Ordinarily, the partner with the defined center will provide the energy for what takes place in the bedroom and you will often guide that energy. Your impassive wisdom is to know when to connect to the energies of others and when to honor your nature and retreat.

The Emotions
Feelings

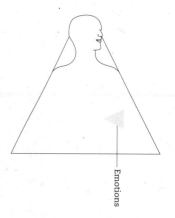

To the right of the Sacral is the Emotions center, which stirs our feelings. It is where life swings between happiness and sadness, pain and passion, guilt and forgiveness. Of all the nine centers, it is the most intense because of what it arouses. It is unique because it is both one of the three "awareness centers" *and* one of the three "motor centers," meaning there is a perpetual balancing act between awareness and the drive to act and accomplish.

Anatomically, this center greatly affects our pancreas, kidneys, stomach, lungs, and nervous system. This is perhaps why countless people will associate heightened emotional problems with a visit to the doctor's office. It is why emotional situations can turn us off our food or make us binge, and why pain can lead to problems within the nervous system. It is also the center associated with addictions, be they to sex, alcohol, food, or drugs.

Although this is the most complex center, it is perhaps the easiest to understand, because emotions are at the core of human nature. But this center is about emotional *awareness*. It is about addressing which emotional experiences are good for you and which ones are not. Of course, it all depends on whether your Emotions are defined or undefined.

If Your Emotions Are Defined

You're a feeling person and yet I'd guess you have little idea about the true scope of your emotions. Chances are that you're the life and soul of the party one minute, down in the dumps the next. Welcome to your erratic emotional wave! You are in this life to fly high and sample the cloud nines and then dive deep and find your nose in the mud. Emotionally, it is your nature to experience the full spectrum of feelings, which, from time to time, may feel like chaos to you and everyone around you. Emotions never sit still for long. They are like the restless ocean, rolling like waves, rising and falling, peaking and dipping. When you feel happy, you want to capture that moment. When you feel sad, you wonder when the blues will end. But there is never a state of permanence to emotion; recognizing these emotional waves and allowing them to pass through you instead of owning you is all part of your evolution.

One lesson to heed is to not get attached to any particular feeling or the expectation of how something might turn out. Emotional decisions made in the heat of the moment are your enemy. So it's all about allowing emotions to pass through you, disengaging from them, and awaiting the calm — like a storm-tossed ship emerging from tumultuous seas spotting the steady beam of a lighthouse that guides the way home.

But here's the main revelation about having this center defined: you are responsible not only for your own moods but also for influencing the moods of people around you. Your Human Design affects people within your aura and triggers their emotions. As daft as it sounds, your emotions are contagious! The moods you experience will be mirrored by the people around you. If you're feeling bummed out, watch others gradually join the despondency. If you're exultant, watch others' exuberance rise. Your lifetime is all about learning to handle, appreciate, and embrace your feelings and how they affect others.

If Your Emotions Are Undefined

You will probably consider yourself an emotional person when, in fact, you are actually riding the emotions transmitted by others. You laugh their laughs and cry their tears. So what you must realize is that your emotions are triggered by the emotional impact of others. Your natural state, when alone, is to be cool, calm, and collected.

What tends to happen when you step outside that personal space is that you get caught in other people's emotional waves. This is a conditioning influence because your design isn't made to cope with such intensity of feeling. People with this center undefined have the greatest trouble in allowing themselves to feel emotions. If you're not comfortable in your own skin at certain moments, it messes with your nature, inducing confusion, temper, or frustration. On the plus side, if you're in the middle of a football stadium being swept away by an air of triumph, you'll feel that glory and celebration. If you're attending a religious ceremony, you'll share the blessed uprising. But you are potentially subject to the emotions of those around you, whether healthy or toxic, so you must remain aware and watchful.

To transform this conditioning influence into impassive wisdom, learn to not react to emotions that are not part of you. Instead, reflect back your clear perception of what is going on, observed from the objective sidelines. Be a witness, not a player.

Put another way, if those with the defined center are flailing in the sea of their emotions, you are someone on the shoreline, observing. This is where you have a choice: you can either dive in and magnify those emotions or stay out of the sea and reflect back to those people what is transpiring and how to be responsible about it.

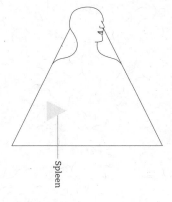

Spleen

The Spleen
Survival and Senses

To the left of the Sacral is the Spleen, another of the three awareness centers, which comes primed with a built-in survival mechanism, plus a feel-good factor that radiates from within. This center is highly sensory, like an inner radar, scanning the environment moment by moment and responding spontaneously based on instinct, intuition, and "taste."

There is no applied intelligence here — it is all about pure survival. This is where the red lights start to flash and the klaxons sound, providing instantaneous warnings of what is right and what might be hazardous in people or situations.

It's also where our deep-seated fears can be found — and triggered. There is the fear of not knowing enough, the fear of the future, the fear of the past, the fear of taking responsibility, the fear of failing, the fear of death, and the fear of authority. Recognizing fear, for both its alerts and its limitations, provides the ability to survive and feel good about life in the moment.

So this is the center of spontaneity and intuition. There is also an acoustic quality, a sense of whether something you're hearing rings true or not. The center literally scans the sound quality of someone's voice or vibe to find out whether something resonates or not. Its theme is all about using its senses to assure survival.

Anatomically, this center relates to the immune system, tackling any foreign bodies, viruses, and potential illnesses. The Battle of Waterloo was nothing compared to what goes on within the body's defense mechanisms. The immune system is fighting on your behalf — it's all about your physical survival.

If Your Spleen Is Defined

You are spontaneous and highly intuitive, designed to react to life on the spur of the moment, always on your toes. You also glow, lighting up a room with your presence because of a radiating feel-good factor.

A spontaneous sensibility scans your environment for any sense of threat or discord, always sensing what's good or bad, but exuding warmth with your touch and manner. You are a curious mix of the alert and ever-watchful bodyguard and the well-being healer. There is a brightness to your presence, supported by a sense of humor that is often sharp and dry. Laughter is, after all, the best form of medicine.

But behind the smiles, you are designed to pay attention to your senses, to disengage the moment your intuition, instinct, or taste warns you. Enter a party where the DJ is playing discordant music or where the atmosphere smells unpleasant, and you'll be alerted. Don't be afraid to turn on your heel and get out of there. These warning signals apply to any environment: someone's home, the workplace, restaurants, and shopping malls. They don't necessarily denote danger; they merely mean there is something there that doesn't fit with your nature. But heed them, however illogical they may seem to others, for they are your true guide. Otherwise, wrong environments can lead to your becoming sick because they put your immune system out of synch.

Your natural — and best — reflexes will come as readily as a click of the fingers. Your whole life is best lived in the moment because of this spontaneity. Yet it also means your antennae are always twitching, and this can lead you to behave like a nervous Nellie. You're liable to be watchful for any conceivable threat and to weigh the risk around every corner. In fact, it is a wonder that you ever step out of the house in the morning! There is a tendency to fear this and fear that, because your survival mechanism is constantly on. This is the mother who is petrified of letting her child go out to play, or the insurance company's dream — the person determined to cover every risk.

The specific fears that can be aroused within you depend on the gates that are turned on within your center, and all this will be examined later in the book. But in order to calm this characteristic, you need to be aware of when this overprotectiveness kicks in and then adopt a more realistic attitude. The Spleen is fearful by nature, so stay alert, but don't allow this to stop your life from happening. Also, a defined Spleen tends to mean a strong immune system, helping you battle illness. If you are constantly sick, it might well be the case that you're ignoring your intuitive senses.

If Your Spleen Is Undefined

Fears don't elude you just because this center is undefined. Indeed, it's very easy for you to get triggered by the conditioning influence of other people and, because you mirror their fears, there's a tendency for them to be magnified. Sometimes you can feel inundated with fears and have no way of processing them. Ironically, fear can overwhelm someone with this center undefined more than anyone with it defined.

What I would say is that those with a defined Spleen are reacting to fears alerted by intuition and instinct, whereas you tend to give focus to fears without a root cause or rationale, and this can be debilitating. Your concerns are likely to be the adopted baggage of those around you or have come from an experience or person from the past.

The way to transform this conditioning influence into impassive wisdom is to view fear objectively. Make your fears friends, not enemies, by becoming conscious of them. For example, a fear of authority can be turned into wisdom by understanding that a position, not a person, carries power. The CEO of your company is not powerful; it's his position that wields authority. Your wisdom grows from shifting your perspective on whatever fears grip you.

You also have an innate ability to diagnose the well-being in others. With an undefined center, you are reflecting the atmosphere around you and will be able to pick up when someone is on edge.

Ironically, though, you struggle to recognize your own well-being. You'll tend to be sensitive to drugs of any sort, so you might try using homoeopathic or other lightweight medicines. Ordinary prescription drugs might well take their toll on your immune system.

Also, be aware that you may have sharpened psychic capabilities because you are open to reflecting the intense undercurrents of life. Many mediums and clairvoyants have this center undefined and thereby pick up the signals being emitted from others.

The Root
Drive

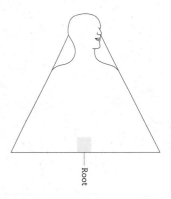

At the bottom of the life chart sits the square center of the Root, the launchpad for all activity in life because it houses our adrenaline and processes stress. As the second of the two pressure centers, it applies the pressure to act.

The Root exists in a condition of stillness and joy, providing a sense of being rooted and grounded. If the other pressure center, the Crown, applies an urgency to rationalize life, then the Root applies pressure to engage with and perform in life. It is, by nature, a center of raw energy, but if it were to have a voice, when triggered, it would scream at you, "Lights, camera, *action!*"

The modern-day world heaps expectation on our shoulders with the pressure to be effective, profitable, productive, brilliant, and able to complete a laundry list of tasks. The Root blindly provides the push to get on with things — and cope.

Ambition is one of nine characteristics of this center. The others are joyfulness, stillness, contentiousness, restlessness, limitation, neediness, provocation, and imagination. These individual characteristics are determined by which gates are on and are explored later.

Anatomically, the Root relates to the adrenal glands, providing us with the stimulus that turns us into adrenaline junkies or provides that adrenaline rush. But, of course, we can also become stressaholics and permanently maxed out.

If Your Root Is Defined

You have the means to handle, withstand, and create extraordinary pressure that calls you and others to perform. All imposed or presumed deadlines are triggered in the Root and you have to gauge whether any goal or time frame is essential or even attainable without losing balance. There is an intense drive from within, almost a compulsion to act. You are sitting on a volcano of energy that could erupt at any moment. Such

57

pressure can blast you, and any person or project around you, into any number of different orbits.

Your natural state is to be living in the eye of the hurricane, finding calm and stillness amid the madness. When you can calmly smile to yourself in the middle of chaos, you've found balance. You thrive on adrenaline rushes, so once you've mastered how to find your poise in any situation, the crazier life gets, the more you enjoy it. You are, by nature, an adrenaline junkie, and as such you can be adept at handling stressful situations.

You may well adopt a classic symptom of someone with this center defined: the inability to sit still. Your leg may be bouncing or your foot tapping, indicating the adrenaline and restlessness coursing through you. You are expert at getting people and things launched, the one who lights the fuse. I would counsel you to marshal the pressure that builds within you. Learn not to jump into something just because it sets off your adrenal glands, because the wrong pursuits or situations can send you off-balance and leave you with stress that not even the Root can handle. The Root is all about finding equilibrium in your life while pursuing your goals and chasing worthwhile ambitions.

If Your Root Is Undefined

Your natural state, when alone, is to be relaxed and unbothered, going through life at your own pace. The problems begin when you're sucked into the vortex of the outside world and start experiencing stress that your center is not designed to handle.

You can probably identify with the expression "getting into a tizzy." This is because a conditioning influence, either in your past or present-day environment, feeds stresses into your system from those with a defined Root.

You can achieve all sorts of goals in your lifetime, but it has to be done on your own terms. Whenever you feel stressed, you've committed to something outside your own integrity. Other people's needs and pressures can send you off-balance and leave you out of sorts if you yield to them. If you've ever been challenged by a statement such as "Get out there and make something of yourself!" that outside pressure alone can lead to your stressing out. You don't have consistent access to the adrenaline needed to carry you through. In fact, you might well be known as a serial procrastinator or someone who does things at the last minute because, to achieve anything, you need time for the pressure to build within. You might be one of those people who pack their suitcase two minutes before the taxi arrives. I would almost bet that you write to-do lists just to be seen to be doing something! You can start millions of things but finish very little.

One likely characteristic people will notice about you is that you'll be hopelessly early or terribly late when running on someone else's schedule. Take the story of a friend of mine who has the Root undefined. She'd promised to take her son, who has the center defined, to an appointment at a designated hour. She was upstairs. He was downstairs, clockwatching. When it was time to leave, he was at the bottom of the stairs, tapping his wristwatch and screaming about being late. With that transmitted surge of adrenaline, she was momentarily confused, dashed from what she was doing, rushed to the stairs, tripped … and fell, landing at the bottom, thankfully unharmed but in a stressed-out flood of tears. That was a conditioning influence in action.

To turn this into impassive wisdom, you need to recognize when pressure is coming at you but note it's not *your* pressure, so remain calm and stay centered and true to yourself. If you constantly get wrapped up in the stress of others, you'll end up exhausting your adrenal glands. So learn to be watchful, find tranquillity, and practice meditation, in line with your nature.

That completes our look at the nine centers. You now have a handle on your inner workings and an overview of the person you were designed to be. But right now we are only at the "getting to know you" stage. What follows is another fascinating truth spawned by the centers — and that's what type of person you actually are.

3

Engaging with Life

The Five Types

Human Design has brought me "home." I have finally been understood. Thank you for opening me up, re-affirming my truth, and providing expert guidance.

AP, New York

What type of person do you think you are? If you had one minute to sum up your nature with a self-appraisal that allowed you to be understood and recognized on first impression, what would you say?

The world is a colorful assortment of approximately seven billion different characters and there are endless descriptions of different types. Sometimes we're identified by our jobs and professions: the executive type, the laborer type, or the caregiving type. Or we stand out by personality: the shy type, the confident type, the thoughtful type, or the reckless type. Some even identify us by hair color: she's a blonde, he's a redhead. Or religion: Orthodox Jew or Southern Baptist. Or ethnicity: African American or Arab. I'm sure as you read those labels, snapshot stereotypes formed in your head. It seems everyone applies superficial labels that really tell us nothing about the person.

Which is where Human Design comes in. It recognizes five types of person, five types that we're designed to be:

- Manifestors
- Generators
- Manifesting generators
- Projectors
- Reflectors

Your type is determined by which centers, if any, you have defined, and to which other centers they connect. Put simply, your type depends on which of the nine centers are in color. It reveals some of the most insightful information about you — and others. I'll go so far as to say that you'll start to view people you have known for decades in a new light. And once you understand people's natural state of being, it allows you to rethink your approach to them. Of course, old habits die hard, and long-established behavioral patterns are notoriously difficult to break. But Human Design encourages us to break down stereotypes, see the real person, and interact in a far more authentic way.

The life chart from the Human Design program actually tells you what type you are. So if you are in doubt, take another look at it, or print it out, and read on. And remember that if at first you don't recognize yourself in your type, this might be caused by conditioning that has made you act in ways counter to your being. So I suggest looking beyond how you act and focusing on your innermost self.

TYPE 1
THE MANIFESTOR

"Making It Happen"

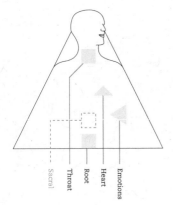

A Manifestor has one or more of three of the motor centers — Heart, Emotions, or Root — defined and connected to a defined Throat. But the Sacral, the generator center, is not defined.

You are one of life's go-getters, born with an ability to make it all happen. People may well observe an air of invincibility about you because you are a catalyzing force who injects tremendous drive and focus into any project or endeavor — and into the people around you. The willpower of the Heart, the intense feelings of the Emotions, and the adrenaline surge of the Root are enough, either in isolation or combined, to surge to the Throat to create a highly motivated person capable of powerful expression and manifestation.

For a Throat connection to be relevant, the channels must be fully in color; that is, they must be active channels. The Root's active connection must find its path to the Throat via the Emotions or Spleen.

Manifestors account statistically for about 8 percent of the world's population, so first appreciate that you are rare with your relentless, compulsive, driving energy that constantly seeks to act, achieve, and do. Your nature is to be a human dynamo, actively accomplishing goals. Such accomplishments, which you might take for granted, can attract either admiration or jealousy from non-Manifestors, mainly because a lot of people hanker for your manifesting ability! You may find it hard to understand why others have such difficulty getting things done, but not everyone can achieve things as quickly or effortlessly as you, so cut them some slack. You are the one type who can go it alone and succeed, needing no one and nothing but your own drive. Indeed, if I were to compare you to a car, you would be the Maserati. You get in your superpowered vehicle, turn the ignition, and you're off! It helps to realize that you are the key and ignition switch missing in others. Imagine how it must feel for a non-Manifestor turning that ignition switch and having nothing happen. You may struggle to understand that feeling, especially if you are an employer, but this understanding alone can lead to a new cooperation that encourages others and enables them to utilize your input.

If you see a stressed-out parent with a child running him or her ragged, you're probably witnessing a non-Manifestor parent struggling with a Manifestor child. You'll recognize Manifestor babies, too — as soon as they can crawl, they're off here, there, and everywhere. Just wait till they learn to walk! I've met many non-Manifestor parents whose children are Manifestors, and they are worn out trying to keep up with their hyper but capable offspring. All these children seek is the freedom to be constantly active; it stifles their nature to be restricted. What their parents must learn is to provide free rein within certain boundaries, such as: "You can stay up, but 8 PM is bedtime" or "You can go outside to play, but the end of the street is the limit." It is the honoring of freedom within limits that strikes the balance here. Also, aim to provide activities and interests that keep their relentless energy engaged. Describe sensible boundaries and let them be!

If, on the other hand, you're the Manifestor parent and your child is a non-Manifestor, you may wonder why she is not more like you. Like mother, like daughter, right? Wrong. It is not in a non-Manifestors' nature to be like you, and you cannot train them to be equal powerhouses.

In relationships, a Manifestor can be hard to live with because of a constant need for action that leads to unpredictability and potential volatility. It can lead to an attitude of "Do it my way or take the highway." Don't even think about trying to control a Manifestor. You might as well lock a lion in a tiny cage and await the roar. But appreciate the gift of an extremely capable partner who, granted freedom, will find a way through anything and be a consummate professional — and forever thank you for understanding them.

The key to understanding Manifestors is to know they are born doers, eager to make things happen. Blocking them, asking them to stop, or nagging them to spend more time relaxing is trying to get them to behave in a way contrary to their nature. You're far better off enhancing this temperament by celebrating it, appreciating Manifestors' efforts and letting them go for it. They *need* to be active. For them, there is no bliss to be found in doing nothing. Be aware that attempts to quiet them can lead to friction or anger.

What I encourage Manifestors to do is to let people know their intentions rather than just rushing off and doing things. Don't just disappear in a cloud of dust and expect everyone to accept it. "But why should I tell everyone what I'm doing all the time?" I can almost hear you protest. Because, in my experience, I've found that Manifestors find immense freedom to be themselves and achieve what they want to achieve *when they cooperate with the people around them.*

Take the case of Caroline. She was traveling abroad with two friends in a country that was unfamiliar to them. They arrived late at the hotel and took separate rooms. The next morning Caroline went to pick up her Manifestor friend Sarah for breakfast, but she was nowhere to be found — she'd just upped and gone. One hour of worry later, there she was, panting through the lobby in her jogging outfit. She had needed to run and it had never occurred to her that her friends wouldn't understand. She found the consternation of Caroline and her "pointless worrying" hard to deal with. But now, when they travel together, this Manifestor has made an agreement to keep her friends informed of what she is doing.

If you do learn to keep others in the loop, life becomes easier. Admittedly, you don't care about being understood — you just want to get things done. But for the sake of peace, if you're working into the night at the office, pick up the phone and inform your partner. If you've gone off to save the world, let someone know what you're doing! And if you have a Manifestor child, educate him or her to inform you before going off and doing something — just dress it up as a request, not a restrictive rule!

As a Manifestor, you must also recognize that your mere presence will push all sorts of buttons in people. Not everyone appreciates a whirlwind. You may rattle people and send them off-balance. This is your catalyzing nature in action, so be watchful of your impact, in the home and socially; recognize who's getting upset and don't take it personally.

The upside is that you do have a tremendous ability to motivate and propel others. You can make people walk on hot coals and bring them through unscathed. You are a truly catalyzing force. But a Manifestor design does not mean you are infallible. You can appear pushy, forceful, and even intimidating, wanting to move "less-able beings" out of the way. Learn to appreciate that people will try their best in your company, and allow them to do so.

There is also a chance that in your childhood you were discouraged and blocked from your natural manifesting. Teachers and parents may not have understood you. "Sit down, be quiet, and stay still" is the worst thing a Manifestor can hear, and this can lead to rebellion or an inner rage building up until it blows. Even worse, you may have shut down and may still be denying your true expression.

Also, be watchful of people taking advantage of you. You might find yourself expected to constantly fetch and carry, fixing everything for everyone around you. You're a Manifestor, not a slave. You're on this Earth to catalyze action, not to perform duties for others.

As a Manifestor, you have a big responsibility to be clear about to what and whom you lend your manifesting abilities. When you're clear, or moving forward, you're a sight to behold. When you're unclear, or blocked, you're liable to tear the world down around you. Once you understand that the world doesn't necessarily operate on your level, you'll find it easier to engage with others and their slower way of getting things done.

What I will say about life with a Manifestor is that it can be fun — because who knows what's going to happen next?!

FAMOUS MANIFESTORS

Jennifer Aniston, Neil Armstrong, Al Gore, Paul McCartney, Jack Nicholson, Arnold Schwarzenegger, Donald Trump, and Liv Tyler.

I think it's fair to say that the common thread binding these people together is the indefatigable, nothing-is-going-to-stop-me, must-keep-manifesting theme. It is somehow apt that the first man on the moon was a Manifestor who had to find his meaning in life by going into orbit, and that Al Gore's life commitment is to change the world.

TYPE 2
THE GENERATOR

"Listen to Your Gut!"

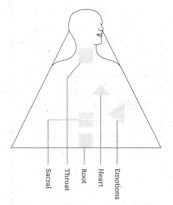

A Generator has a defined Sacral, but neither this center nor any of the other motor centers — Heart, Emotions, and Root — are connected to the Throat by an active channel.

You are a workhorse with endless life-force energy radiating outward but don't find it that easy to make things happen. Some effort is required before you get into your full stride and reach your potential. You are designed not to initiate but to *wait*. Your motto is: "Wait, respond, then get going!"

Being a Generator makes you relatively one paced but highly effective, and your momentum is a joy to watch because it is Sacral powered, therefore remarkably enduring. You are the Duracell or Energizer battery that keeps on going and going when others are fading. Your challenge is to know how and where to best apply this enormous energy.

Waiting for the right projects, opportunities, and people and honoring your gut response are your keys to finding fulfillment. When you chase or initiate without waiting, life can go wrong. It's when you *attract* opportunity or respond after exercising patience that things tend to work out.

We live in a time when everyone wants to act now, get going, waste no time, achieve ASAP. This expectation may taunt you into getting a move on, but don't be misled into thinking you must launch great initiatives. You first need the energy to generate within you; only then is it capable and effective. So sit down, be patient, and master the art of *waiting to respond.* View yourself as a magnet and let people and openings seek you out. And they will. It is an energetic law of life that magnets *attract*.

So if you are wailing something like, "Why does everything I start or chase turn out bad?" or "Why can he make those things happen but I can't?" my answer would be: "Because you haven't learned to wait and attract." Don't initiate. Wait.

Your mistaken self-perception is that you have so much energy that you can automatically make things happen. That's probably fueled by people describing you as purposeful and dedicated. You walk into the workplace and your life-force energy radiates, lifting everyone else. Here comes the real worker, the real juice — the Generator. You can save the day — and you even believe this yourself. Whether it feels right or not, you have a tendency to wade in and answer the call. Hours later, you'll be head down, hard at work, and look up to find everyone has gone back to sleep. Then you'll have a quiet word with yourself and ask: "Why does it always fall to me? Why did I ever get involved?"

What you must realize is that the only things that prove fulfilling are those that duly arrive after you have exercised patience — openings or possibilities that arrive at your door or make your phone ring.

Then what's crucial is your *response*. This response is governed by a built-in guidance system, the Sacral gut response, signaling who and what warrants your commitment. This is the core secret of your inner being, one that opens the doorway to what's right for you.

You'll recognize this gut sensation in the form of an involuntary reflex or sound, or the rising or contracting of energy, pulling you to or pushing you away from something. The sound is that familiar "uh-huh" which says "yes" or that "uh-uh" that says "no." You need to attune to this sensation because it is, quite literally, your built-in indicator.

You'll sense your gut in response to questions that people ask of you: "Can I ask for your help?" "Do you want to go on a date?" or "Are you hungry?" But it also kicks in with much more profound questions that life asks. Test yourself the next time someone asks you something, but be aware that you might be waiting for an instantaneous gut response and, half a second later, the Mind will get involved. Don't allow it to distract you. That's not where your answer lies. Listen to your gut.

Also, observe inner musings that don't require a direct question. If you are sitting in a restaurant, looking at a menu, going through the entrée choices, your "uh-huh" or "uh-uh" will kick in. Listen to your gut.

Your process is played out thus: wait for what life offers, listen to your gut response, then get going.

Gayle is a Generator and has learned more and more to tune in to her gut response. She was once being pursued by four potential suitors and was torn about to whom she should commit. After a Human Design reading, she needed to distance herself from the fog of her fears and presumptions, none of which played a part in a natural gut response. She stood in her bedroom, looked in the mirror, and created a yes/no question for her gut to answer. One by one, she named the four men. "Should I go out with Doug?" She felt that "uh-uh" for no. "Should I go out with Marshall?" Again, she felt "uh-uh." "Should I go out with Michel?" Once more, "uh-uh." Finally, she came to Nick and felt a clear "uh-huh." There was her "yes" answer. Somewhere in her being, Nick resonated with her, and this was her clear guidance to give him a chance.

The mistake Generators can make is to think too much, allowing the Mind to override the Sacral. When this fog blurs the gut response, you find yourself committing to all kinds of wrong people and wrong pursuits. And then, the trouble for the Sacral is that once it is committed, it has to follow through and complete the experience, however inappropriate or ill-fitting. Quitting is a poor option — and this is one thing that requires understanding — because once your energetic momentum gets going, it's engaged. Your nature builds up such a head of steam by waiting and waiting that it doesn't know how to stop the momentum. It's like asking a thundering express train to stop at a moment's notice.

As a non-Generator, you might see people running toward disaster but you'll be powerless to stop them. You must wait for them to return to their senses in their own time — exhausted, unfulfilled, and ready to try again.

Generators must be wary of other people seeking to harness their energy, to take advantage of them. A lot of them are found in the service industry, on the factory floor, or as assistants, secretaries, and personal trainers, with a treadmill-like momentum that keeps things ticking like clockwork. That's because Generators provide the juice for most things.

If you are a Generator, you represent 37 percent of the world's population and appear to be someone with enough power to raise the dead. Your energy turns heads when you enter a room. You're viewed as capable and unflagging. I bet you're someone who rolls out of bed, cooks breakfast, drops the kids off at school, goes to work, gives your all, fixes other people's stuff, works out at lunchtime, impresses the boss some more in the afternoon, goes home, does the laundry, fixes the dinner, bathes the children, puts them to bed, then turns to your partner — and collapses in a heap. No one, except other Generator types, can hope to keep up with you.

The problem is that you can arrive at the end of your days feeling you've accomplished a lot but still feeling unfulfilled. That's because, in large part, you've just been going through the motions. Life is not just about ticking boxes and keeping others happy. Herein lies the key to a Generator design: *only engage with people and activities that resonate*; otherwise, you'll discover the flip side to your type and become the pure couch potato who has given up, exhausted with life and fed up trying. Or you can become someone who is wiped out, prone on your bed, waiting for energy to be regenerated.

I would also advise everyone not to throw too much, all at once, at a Generator. However capable and energetic they seem, there's only so much responding they can do. You'll know they've reached their limit when their hands go up and they say: "Enough!" Or when, feeling overwhelmed, they simply ask for space.

As parents of Generator children, your task is to clue them into their gut response if you want them — and you — to avoid tears and frustration. There is no point in handing a child a trumpet and expecting him or her to master it if it doesn't resonate with the child. It's a waste of time for dads to coach their boys in baseball or football if this fails to excite. Parents need to understand the distinction between their expectations for their children and what actually resonates with those children.

Likewise in relationships, it is asking for trouble to declare to your Generator lover that you've decided what you're doing for the weekend

FAMOUS GENERATORS

Muhammad Ali, Fred Astaire, Beethoven, Bill Clinton, Madonna, Margaret Thatcher, and Oprah Winfrey.

The common theme here is the bundles of energy that sustain prime ministers and presidents and artistes. Plus, there is a perseverance and unstoppable momentum about them. Whirlwinds in their own right, many of these greats, I suspect, nevertheless needed to wait and allow the Sacral energy to build before releasing themselves into full flight. And I would love to know how much gut instinct played its part in the decision making of Thatcher and Clinton!

and drag your partner off to the beach for a picnic without first sounding out his or her gut response. Partners should learn to ask Generators questions that start with queries such as "Would you like to do this today?" or "Do you think it's a good idea if we . . . ?" Don't worry about being "man enough" and taking control; honor the Generator nature, not the ego. These people require consultation if your relationship is to work.

Over the years, I've met thousands of Generators and have tried to point out what makes them tick. Some of them get it straightaway, but far too many have fallen prey to conditioning and are slogging away as workhorses in situations where their unstinting efforts are taken for granted. It is indisputable that wrong people and projects will fly high because of a Generator's input, but that's not the point to their life. They need to find where their amazing source of energy is best directed and appreciated.

Geraldine is a hardworking mother with three delightful but extremely demanding children. She saw it as her duty to fulfill any demands they asked of her at any time. However, despite the pleasure she derived from this, she was exhausted and more than a little frustrated that she rarely had the time and energy for anything else. In a classic Generator situation, the attention and demands of others were depleting her. Since she could not afford a nanny, there seemed no solution and she gradually found herself getting more and more worn out.

At my reading for Geraldine, she had no idea she had such a bountiful Sacral. She just assumed she was being run ragged and operated on autopilot. When she learned that she had an infallible built-in indicator system capable of letting her know which activities worked best for her, she immediately began changing the way she lived.

She actually saw the importance of educating her children to approach her in a different way. Instead of "I want" demands, she coached the children to ask questions that required a yes/no response. She was savvy enough to disguise this shift into a playful set of new rules. To her delight, the questions elicited a reliable gut response and now she only commits to the activities that resonate. This, in turn, has empowered the children to be more resourceful, and they're delighted to see Mom having more satisfaction — and energy — in her life.

I tell all Generators to acknowledge the blessing they are. As a Generator, you may well be harboring fears that you'll miss the boat if you don't act now or that everything will go wrong if you don't jump in and seize control. But trust your nature. Trust the person you were born to be — and wait to respond.

TYPE 3
THE MANIFESTING GENERATOR

"Moment of Truth"

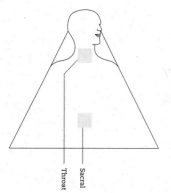

Throat Sacral

A Manifesting Generator has a defined Sacral connected through any sequence of active channels to a defined Throat. Alternatively they have a defined Sacral and at least one of the three motor centers — Heart, Emotions, or Root — connected through any sequence of active channels to the Throat.

You are a potential powerhouse and bundle of energy combined but require the tight rein of patience before you can release your considerable resources effectively.

You "MG types" make up an estimated 33 percent of the world's population — a twinning of the two previous types, yet distinguishable with your own unique markings. I call you the MG because you're a classic human vehicle in your own right, impressive in motion when you've found your speed.

You have the built-in guidance system of the gut response (as described in the Generator type) but the subtle distinction is this: you *can* initiate and make things happen, but only after honoring that Generator gut response. In effect, you are a Manifestor in waiting.

The vital difference that sets you apart from Manifestors and Generators exists in the *moment of truth* between a gut response and actually manifesting. I call this "being in the gap." It's in this gap that you first need to taste the action to confirm an initial gut sensation. In a basic example, if you're an MG type and a friend asks if you want to go for a walk, you get an "uh-huh" positive response and get up from your seat. This is where you enter the gap between response and manifesting, because it's when you get to the front door (tasting the action) that you actually find out the walk isn't happening for you (moment of truth) and give up on the idea. Whereas if you were a Generator, once you'd decided to leave that seat and head for the door, you'd be committed and on that walk whether you liked it or not, carried by momentum. This is the subtle but significant difference in action.

So what I tell Manifesting Generators is to view the process like this: respond by listening to your gut, find the moment of truth by putting your toe in the water, and then, if there is clarity to your conviction, make it happen.

When you do make it happen, when you're off and committed, you're powering forward with Manifestor zeal. You've a faster gear change than a Generator. You can go from 0 to 60 mph in four seconds and leave burning rubber on the road. You actually have many speeds and, unlike Generators, you can stop once you've engaged your energy because your manifesting side allows you to correct course midstride. You'll also be constantly looking for the next challenge, forever on the lookout, forever restless. I wouldn't be surprised to find you trying to keep several plates spinning, but your focus is best applied to one project at a time.

I always have fun imagining a Manifestor, a Generator, and a Manifesting Generator in the same room. This is not typical, but it's a likely scenario:

> *Whooooosshhh, there goes the Manifestor, out of the door, telling no one. The Generator looks up from his seat, wondering quietly about when things are going to start happening for him while flipping through a magazine. But the frustrated MG is all antsy and pacing the room, waiting for the red light to turn green. When it does, and when he gets a clear gut response and affirms his moment of truth, there's no seeing him for dust. The Generator, seeing the same green light and having his clear gut response, looks in the mirror, checks he has everything, starts to build his momentum, and then goes out there to give it his all.*

My experience of Manifesting Generators is that they are always restless, fidgeting, tapping their feet, ready to engage with anything at a moment's notice. If this is you, you're an intense fusion, torn between a compulsion to manifest and waiting for the right moment, torn between the need for all-conquering action and the surrender of having to wait. Once more, you must learn to wait for the green light from life itself.

John, my friend of thirty years, always got into relationships that didn't work out. He'd fall madly in love and have passionate affairs, and then the next dramatic step would be an inexplicable separation. John is a Manifesting Generator and would view his role in relationships as being the one to make the first move. With his natural urge to manifest, he'd fail to wait and would jump in with both feet. In that respect, he'd act like a pure Manifestor.

I explained to him the process required for a Manifesting Generator in all things, including relationships, but he seemed to think that persistence would ultimately pay off. So he lurched from one disaster to another until, after a failed marriage and costly divorce, he was ready to give up on everlasting love.

One evening, on his way home from work, he detoured to a health food store, but he'd left his reading glasses at work and found himself squinting at the labels on the shelf. That's when fate sent an attractive woman shopper to his side. "You seem to be having trouble. Can I help?" she asked. John was able to feel his instantaneous gut response as a "yes." It was while she was reading the labels to him that he applied his moment of truth in the gap between response and action. As he chatted and laughed (tasting the action), he felt the clarity to proceed. One thing led to another and they are now happily ensconced in a partnership of real strength.

John responded, then manifested the relationship. From the Human Design point of view, he was not seeking any intervention at the vitamin shelf section and so he was able to respond naturally. I'm pleased to say that he is now happier than I've ever known him to be.

The temptation within relationships for you MG types is to break the ice and make things happen. But you're going to get it right only when you've not done the chasing and you're with a person who elicits a clear gut response from you. Now I can hear all the men — and the women who like to be wooed — moaning that this can't be right. I'm not advocating that all men deliberately avoid women, waiting for the vitamin shelf woman to enter their world, but I am imploring you to listen to your inner guidance system. So, men, if you see a woman across a crowded room, check out your gut response. If it's a "yes," make the approach and start chatting (tasting the action) and then you'll know (moment of truth) whether to proceed. A relationship founded on that clear beginning will bring about settled harmony.

You can always observe MG types hovering on the sidelines, determining their moment of truth. When they allow themselves the patience to find inner certainty, there is no one more determined, unstoppable, and fully committed. They are a blessing to have on your side, manifesting without the volatility and unpredictability of a Manifestor.

In the workplace, a Manifesting Generator is striving to find that balance between the Manifestor and Generator aspects. The Generator part enjoys committing to projects that require huge, sustainable energy. The Manifesting part likes to forge into new territory and launch new projects. You MG types must be given freedom and flexibility to break new ground and reach new heights. You are, in that respect, a tricky employee to understand, a hybrid of workhorse and pioneer. Ideally, you'll be a respected high-flyer, an executive, or someone who has the independence to operate freely.

MG children are a potential handful as they grow, struggling to find the balance between their lawless manifesting wants and sustainable generating power. They are as torn as the elder MG types and really do need parental advice on exercising patience in their restlessness. Parents are best advised not to scold them for the chaos they are liable to cause as they flit between this and that. It can be easy for a child to escape the Mind and understand the Sacral response. I've seen it happen with parental coaching, quieting temper tantrums.

It can be confusing for parents. Don't be surprised if you ask your son or daughter if they want to go to the cinema and they scream, "Yes, yes, yes!" in gut response, only to sit grumpily in the backseat of the car as

---

FAMOUS MANIFESTING GENERATORS

David Beckham, Simon Cowell, Jimi Hendrix, Paris Hilton, Elton John, George Lucas, Salman Rushdie, Britney Spears, and Mother Teresa.

A common theme here is high achieving combined with great sustainable energy and, no doubt, peppered with an indecisiveness about what is and what isn't right. I wonder how many songs Hendrix and Elton wrote and then ditched. Or how many program ideas Simon Cowell has devised and then abandoned.

you pull up outside the local Imax (tasting the action/moment of truth) and say: "I don't want to go now!" Such infuriating indecision comes with the territory and needs to be understood.

Such episodes happen not just with children but also within the work-place and relationships. Manifesting Generators must be tired of hear-ing the complaint: "You said you *wanted* to do this twenty seconds ago!" That was then. This is now. Know that when they commit to something, there is always the prospect of a change in direction when that moment of truth dawns.

That moment between response and manifestation means every-thing for these types. It is the confirmation or rejection. But, mark my words, when there is absolute clarity and they're marching forward with purpose toward the right relationships and right openings, they are quite, brilliant at all they do.

TYPE 4
THE PROJECTOR

"Recognition and Inclusion"

A Projector has an undefined Sacral, and none of the motor centers has an active connection to the Throat.

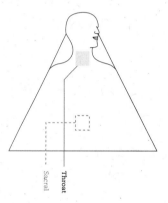

Waiting in the wings. Waiting for the spotlight. Waiting to be invited. This is the essence of a Projector's life — yearning to be included and for their contributions and abilities to be recognized. Then, when working from a position of appreciation, they are an assured performer, contributor, director, organizer, manager, guide, visionary, and conductor of affairs. If you are a Projector, there is no doubt you have abilities and gifts in your own right, but your true nature requires them to be recognized *first* if you are to shine, and this awareness is essential for your personal fulfillment.

I'll let you know that I'm among the estimated 21 percent of the world's population that make up this type. Whereas the three previous types are self-driven people, a Projector can often be an observer, waiting to be asked for his or her involvement. So I can empathize with the feeling that it's sometimes a struggle to be "seen," understood, or valued for all you offer before getting the chance to act and contribute.

There is no life-force energy generating within you and no motor center connected to the Throat providing any manifesting drive. There is a chilled, easygoing nature about you, something that can appear lightweight yet assured, firm but fair.

When you walk into a room, the first impression is that you seem keen to connect with everybody, wanting to plug into others, yearning — and sometimes struggling — for recognition. Be watchful that such enthusiasm doesn't translate into trying too hard. Being noticed is intrinsic to who you are, but only when it arises naturally. You have nothing to worry about, either. It's a natural law that people *will* find themselves being drawn to your innate "projection field." What they are being drawn toward are specific qualities within your centers, not to mention your serene, all-knowing calm. You are potentially an ideal networker who can link up that person with this person and matchmake to your heart's content. Likewise, you can also hide out, not wishing to engage.

I often tease Projectors that it's important to have a comfortable armchair to fall into without guilt or shame when nothing is happening. You must learn to enjoy the lulls in life and embrace the part of your nature that makes you more spectator than chief player. You are born guides and managers and make ideal leaders, organizers, coaches, and administrators, overseeing everything. You come into your own when steering, shaping, and driving the people and energy around you. The truth is that some people don't know how to use their energy without your objective assistance.

This doesn't mean you can't get drawn into the thick of the action yourself, but for that action to be fulfilling you first require recognition in the form of an invitation. This is the chief component in your nature. It's important that you first receive recognition if you are to be effective. Then, and only then, can you walk into your arena to quiet applause and obvious admiration. Recognition and invitation light up your being, and it is important for non-Projectors to understand this.

What, precisely, constitutes an invitation? Well, it can range from a gold-embossed card with an RSVP instruction to an invitation cloaked as a question, an aside, or a glance. It can even be an inner sense that you are being drawn toward something, like having a calling. It is anyone or anything seeking your involvement while genuinely recognizing your qualities.

This doesn't mean that you should fall prey to overt flattery and sycophancy. An invitation will not resonate if someone recognizes your "tremendous ability to lead" when in actual fact you've no aptitude for that role at all. The recognition needs to be authentic and respect your worth. It is not about ego but about appreciation. Your true nature absolutely requires this.

Take Rolling Stones Projector Mick Jagger. He'll wait in the wings, relaxing in his dressing-room armchair, waiting for the scene to be set and the tempo to build. This is when he gets his invitation to go center stage, where the recognition of his talents resonates with him. Without that recognition-invitation process, it could be argued, he "can't get no satisfaction." With it, he'll entertain a sell-out audience for ninety minutes.

You could argue that no one is more energetic than Mick Jagger, so how can he possibly be a Projector? But what he's actually doing is riding the energy of his bandmates and fans. He's utilizing a conditioning influence of his environment, allowing the energy of others to flood his undefined centers, triggering him. This is what Projectors do — they tap into, ride, and guide the energy of others . . . then flake out after short bursts.

Projectors need to be careful about how much borrowed energy they run through their system. Fatigue and exhaustion are your Achilles' heel. In a high-pressured, high-energy environment in which you adopt the "go, go, go" of everyone else, there's a danger you'll blow an internal fuse. Be wary of trying to keep up with Manifestors, Generators, and Manifesting Generators and bowing to the commitments of others; otherwise, you'll exhaust yourself to the point of near collapse. Be open to taking breaks and having siestas and catnaps. Remember where your armchair is! These energetic limitations require attention.

One mistake I made as a Projector was to override my inner resistance and convince myself to do things or join in with others, pretending to be naturally that way inclined. I sought to be one of the crowd and forced myself to jump into the fray. Then, when I was snubbed, unappreciated, misunderstood, but still embroiled in obligation, I'd wonder why. Nowadays, I'll await the recognition-invitation process. In this respect, we Projectors are always hanging around waiting for our cue. But it makes a world of difference to how comfortable I am in certain surroundings. It must boil down to honoring a sense of belonging.

FAMOUS PROJECTORS

Tony Blair, Princess Diana of Wales, Queen Elizabeth II, Mick Jagger, JFK, Nelson Mandela, Napoleon, Barack Obama, Pablo Picasso, Brad Pitt, and Steven Spielberg.

Look at how many statesmen and stateswomen are among that list — all people who are masters of manipulation and stirring and arousing energy with whatever they do. Blair and Obama are great orators, Princess Diana and Queen Elizabeth great royals, JFK and Nelson Mandela legends for different reasons. But all of them are or were sustained by the energy of the entourage, environment, and institution around them, organizing and inspiring in their Projector-style way and knowing where the energy in life is best applied.

As a Projector, you'll be able to identify with an inner pressure to be recognized for your gifts and abilities. You can quickly develop a sense of gloom or despair when you appear to be passed over or ignored. You'll often ask yourself: "What do I need to do to get noticed?" or "Why do I keep getting overlooked?" Some of you can travel through life frustrated by a sense of untapped potential, but if you learn patience and the humility to concede that not everything requires your input, the frustration can ease. The good news is that Human Design readings impact Projectors immediately because a reading recognizes their true nature and they feel celebrated!

As a Projector in the workplace, you may feel overshadowed by the achievements of more energetic types. But if I were the CEO of a company, I would want my Projectors heading up the planning and management departments because, as natural guides and without the Sacral's impetus, they have a good view of how the whirlwind energy of others is best harnessed. Projectors are also versatile because, not being tied to the Sacral, they can change speed and focus on a whim.

In relationships, Projectors cannot abide being taken for granted or being told how to act. Recognition and invitation are vital here. As a partner, you like to be recognized for your worth and invited to do things, even when it comes to household chores! Your partners also need to honor your need for rest and replenishment. You might well be accused of being lightweight and lazy, but you were not born with natural reserves of energy. The benefit for you is that you can help steer your partner's energy and support him or her in becoming a power for good. You're expert at guiding a relationship and suggesting ways to improve and enhance relations. You provide the balanced perspective that can see the forest through the trees. Projectors bring great variety and freshness into a relationship; they are the natural connectors and organizers.

The first thing you'll notice about Projector children is that they're not necessarily energetic. Don't think of them as lazy or lethargic. You'll also notice them doing things, from activities to gestures, "just to get noticed." See through the act and read its subtext — they need recognition. It's important to honor their every attribute, skill, and good turn, however small. There is nothing more upsetting to Projector children than not being recognized or earning parental pride.

The need for recognition can sometimes play itself out as neediness, too, as it can in adult relationships. No one is being clingy — they just want to have their love, feelings, and position recognized. Very few Projectors wish to walk through life alone because they need someone else's energy to tap into to fuel and nurture them. They can function but cannot thrive in isolation.

As a Projector, what you achieve in life tends to depend on being drawn into the right company and right environment. When your gifts and abilities are truly recognized, you'll feel empowered. The difference between being recognized and not recognized is day and night to you and essential to your sense of well-being and satisfaction. Recognition means everything — and brings out your best.

TYPE 5
THE REFLECTOR
"Clear Vision"

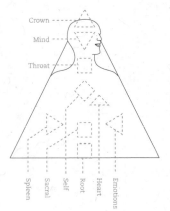

A Reflector's entire life chart is colored white, with all nine centers undefined.

You are as white and as clear as the moon and constitute an estimated 1 percent of the world's population, making you the rarest of all types. The first thing to appreciate is that you live your life in a novel way, yet everyone expects you to view the world and act the same way they do. Actually, I should make T-shirts for Reflectors that say: "I'm nothing like you, so let me be!"

At first glance, it looks as though nothing is going on in your life chart. There is an apparent emptiness about you, but you are *anything* but empty by nature. This lack of activity means you are a receiving dish drawing in everyone else's energy and constantly reflecting back to others who they are, what they're about, and what life is about. You absorb and brim over with the qualities and energies you receive from other Human Design types. Someone's defined Heart fills your Heart. Someone's defined Emotions flood your Emotions, and so on and so forth. Nobody is affected by the designs that surround you more than you are.

Consequently, this makes you empathetic because, under these conditioning influences, you experience all the passions, fears, thoughts, emotions, and ambitions that are transferred onto you. This makes you, by nature, extremely sensitive, vulnerable, perceptive, and potentially wise, because an innate objectivity allows you to witness the energies passing through you and what they all mean to everyone.

Reflectors reflect, like mirrors. People see themselves in you. This is a gift, but this can also be frustrating because when is someone going to see *you*? You're no doubt tired of listening to everyone else's achievements and problems, smiling politely and then giving your viewpoint. What about *you*?

The eternal struggle for you is when to engage and when to detach, when to become distracted by others and when to focus on yourself. Reflectors often find themselves being leaned on, absorbing everyone and everything into their lives and not knowing where the boundaries lie. You will find that many people off-load onto you and sound you out. Indeed, this can be burdensome and you may struggle to know your own identity because it's tangled up in the energies you're getting from other people. You Reflectors cannot escape being impacted by other designs, and it's understandable that you can become overwhelmed, and sometimes deeply disturbed, by the thoughts, chaos, and nonsense of others. No wonder you seek your own solitude, needing to escape for your own sanity — and inner reflection!

My advice to you is to understand how impressionable your design is by nature and then learn to disown the energies thrown at you. This is how to transform a conditioning influence into wisdom. Stand back, observe, appreciate what's happening, and reflect back your take on everything. If you do this, others will often seek out your insightful perspective. "You always understand me," "You're always good at working it out for me," and "You always seem to grasp what's going on" are some phrases you might be able to identify with. This is all well and good, provided you filter who gets access to you and who does not. You need to know when to draw the line and to be disciplined with your time to prevent being swamped.

Imagine living in a world where 99 percent of people seem to be power brokers and you're the 1 percent exception to the rule. You're bound to feel different in some way. You're bound to feel like a cork on the ocean, bobbing and bouncing around in the currents and waves of others' lives. Until you learn how to bring stability into your life. Until you learn to reflect and not absorb. So view yourself as the go-between for different people's energies, as if you're passing the ball from one to another, not holding on to it. And with each pass, you can add your detached perspective as a gift of wisdom.

Betsy had always sensed something was different about herself but hadn't been able to quite put her finger on it. She had been through all manner of situations where people had dumped their problems, aggression, meanness, and bad behavior on her and had often found that she was completely powerless to do anything about it. At work, everyone cried on her shoulder, and at home, friends unburdened themselves over the telephone. The collective agreement was: "If you have a problem, Betsy will fix it." Even her managers found her to be a natural troubleshooter when it came to resolving entanglements within company policy.

As brilliantly as she was able to make sense of it all, she never really felt that she was getting what she needed in life. She was deeply contemplative and her moods were up and down. She didn't seem able to nail down who and where she was in life. She would just sit and absorb the problems like a sponge. After a while, she actually began to believe that this unhealthy attraction was, in some way, her fault.

But when, in her midthirties, she discovered her Reflector nature, things changed. She learned to unhook herself from the auras that had become dependent on her. Somewhat drastically, she moved to a quieter neighborhood where she could start again and lay down her boundaries. She cleared space in her calendar for exclusive "me-time" each day. At work, she gave people fifteen or so minutes for their problems, then called time. She wasn't, she pointed out, a full-time Dear Abby. She started to respect her own needs and found assertiveness within her newfound knowledge. Human Design had enabled her to see where she had been going wrong and what she needed to do if she was to honor her true nature.

These days, Betsy is enjoying a newly enriched life in which she receives the love, acknowledgment, and appreciation she cherishes. She has learned the ultimate Reflector lesson: to receive as much as she gives and to guard her time and space as if they are the most precious things in the world.

In Human Design experiential workshops created by my wife, Carola, I invite someone to stand quietly before a Reflector and be open to the experience. What often happens is that the non-Reflector is moved to tears, arising from a deep sense of being "seen" and having their true nature profoundly reflected back to them. When you witness this happening, it is the power of the system speaking for itself. The non-Reflector comes to appreciate how benign, passive, and unconditionally loving the Reflector is. I tell these people to embrace Reflectors because, as our mirrors in life, they're a source of great knowing and wisdom.

As a Reflector, you don't need to get someone to stand before you to know your impact. You draw others toward you in a quiet and noninterfering way. You are a soothing, calming influence, and those people who engage with you quickly appreciate your innate wisdom. The quiet, wise owl sitting serenely in the corner of a room is likely to be a Reflector, as is the person who wanders off from the crowded picnic to find solace on the riverbank. If you do this, don't be surprised if you find a cluster of Manifestors, Generators, MG types, and Projectors scurrying after you to off-load and then listen to your advice. Just show them your hand and say "no" — you need your time alone.

In times past, Reflectors would often find themselves in hermitages, in the remote countryside, or in spiritual communities, indulging their need for privacy, nature, and solitude. Being at one with nature is what a Reflector's nature is all about! The frenetic pace of life and crowded places tends to freak you out. I also suspect that small social gatherings are your thing, as opposed to manic parties. Such upbeat environments can lead you to go haywire because your type is not designed to soak up and sustain the energy coming at you from all directions. Overstimulation to your sensitive being can leave you depleted and disheartened.

The beauty is that once you're removed from the chaos, you find it easier than most to switch off and find a deep place of inner reflection. I always tell Reflectors that having their own space is fundamental to their nature. If it's practical, live in a house with your own wing or lots of garden space, or in a home on its own land. The receiving-dish Reflector finds it uncomfortable, to say the least, living in a center-city apartment block or a crammed housing development where they're impacted

FAMOUS REFLECTORS

Sandra Bullock, Richard Burton, Rosalyn Carter, Fyodor Dostoyevsky, Uri Geller, and H.G. Wells.

You'll note how different and diverse these people are, reaching into varying fields of expression. Sandra Bullock and Richard Burton, as actors, are classic Reflector types because they can capture any role in life and be fully immersed in the part. And take Uri Geller, tapping into skills that go beyond the comprehension of most, using his design's receptivity to reflect back his skills that push the envelope. Basically, a Reflector can be all things to all people, often defying imagination, and, as the above examples illustrate, they are sensitive, perceptive, different, and wise.

by the volatility of modern-day life. When overloaded, stand under a shower to wash away any borrowed burdens; sit in meditation to regain your center.

The one question Reflectors always ask is "If I have no consistent design, how do I find my way through life, and how do I make consistently right decisions without being influenced by everyone else's input?"

Well, the recognition of your sensitive, malleable nature is the first step, because this allows you to access the company and environments that resonate with your nature. The second is to understand that the moon is your mainstay, ally, and timekeeper. Just as the moon has a regular twenty-nine-day cycle each month, so do you. Other Human Design types experience consistency via active channels and defined centers, but your nature is ever changing because it is largely dependent on where the moon is in the sky. If you watch closely, you will notice that your moods are in exact correlation with wherever the moon is. It will pull you in different directions at different times. This is explored in greater detail for you in the next chapter.

Reflector children are going to impress with their extraordinary grasp of life, seeming wise beyond their years. Yet they are very gentle, sensitive beings who can find themselves overwhelmed by peer pressure to fit in, to be someone other than who they are. The last thing a Reflector child needs is a parent who doesn't understand this social reluctance and says things like, "Go on, what's wrong with you? Join in and play!" In the playground they can quickly feel like the odd one out, swamped by the energies of other types. There is something about retreating and being alone that appeals to them. It's important for parents to acknowledge this difference and explain that it's not an oddity but a uniqueness.

These children will ride the energy of others like a Projector child but can become exhausted far more quickly. Some Reflector children can appear withdrawn or shut down, unable to cope with life's pace and bombardments. They will tend to remove themselves from trouble and chaos and will feel at home in more serene environments. So allow them alone time in their bedrooms, just chilling out or listening to music. These kids have a tendency to float through childhood, not tear through it, and adolescence can be quite a trial for them. Nature is a good ally for them, so I would encourage living close to nature and going to parks instead of football games.

If you're a Reflector parent, you'll always be stretched to the limit trying to keep up with the boundless energy of your child. So learn to limit your doses of activity, and encourage your child to be more resourceful. Also recognize that the child will grow to appreciate your wisdom — even if that's not always apparent! He or she couldn't have a better teacher in life.

In relationships, Reflectors are very dependent on the clarity and loving-kindness of their partner. There is a complex dichotomy to them in that they need you but then need space away from you. There is a constant shuttling between independence and dependence. And somewhere in the middle of those two natural states lies the balance of their perfect relationship.

There is no one more sensitive, vulnerable, yet potentially wise than a Reflector partner. Reflectors are searching for those people who appreciate their unique nature. One of the best setups I've seen is where the husband is the capable, breadwinning Manifestor who zips out the door each morning, leaving his Reflector wife with the house and garden to herself. Even when he's at home, she literally has her own exclusive part of the house to which she can retreat whenever she feels overwhelmed by life. Her Manifestor husband has recognized her true nature, honored it, and struck a balance that works for them both.

There is an enormous difference between the perspective that a Reflector has on life and that of everyone else. Everybody knows the experience of walking around a garden during the day when sunlight lights the surroundings. But Reflectors know what it's like to walk around that garden by night, when everything appears completely different, under moonlight. The moon lights them up and provides their true and unique perspective.

Meditation, prayer, and deep solitude will feel good for all Reflectors. If you are one, these will help bring you into your true self. This is a special process unique to you. But then you are a unique being, one of the brightest, most loving, and wisest people on this Earth. With your openness and availability to life, you bring some of the greatest wisdom to the world.

If you have a Reflector in your life, know that you have literally found someone special, so honor them and recognize the very particular way they need to live their life.

By way of review and recap, here are the key phrases that describe how each type engages with the world:

- Manifestor: *"I am; therefore I do."*
- Generator: *"I respond, then I do."*
- Manifesting Generator: *"I respond and wait for my moment of truth, then I do."*
- Projector: *"I am recognized, invited, and available, then I do."*
- Reflector: *"I am called, I reflect, then I do."*

Knowing your type and how you're designed to operate is vital in aligning yourself with your nature. It also provides a more accurate snapshot identity. The revelations contained within type alone can be potentially life changing, as this real-life account bears testimony. Angel from L.A. is a former model with a young daughter. She told me:

> *The thing that Human Design helped me the most with was being a parent. My daughter is a Projector and I am a Manifestor, and the two could not be more opposite. It had been difficult for me because I expected her to do things as quickly as me. Understanding type has given me a lot of ability to have faith in her timing and the way she does things. Personally, I don't let any parent cross my path without recommending this system because it allows you to actually understand your children on a different level.*

People undeniably experience relief when the insights gained through knowing their type hit home.

Remember, there's no great advantage in being one type or another; the most important thing is to look for all the openings life offers and then honor your type in the process.

Once you've grasped this aspect of your design, you're ready to dovetail it with the next stage in understanding: how to make wiser and better decisions.

4

Honoring Your Authority

Making Wiser Decisions

Your insights clicked on so many levels. I've since seen how my life works when I follow my Human Design and release resistance.

SL, Nebraska

In life, most of our wrong turns, frustrations, and pain can be traced back to the bad calls we've made. Knowing when to say a clear "yes" and when to assert "no" is how we effectively navigate the choices and dilemmas before us. Life's rich palette of choices knows no end and I wonder how much time we must waste deliberating the best course of action. Everyone I know shares the same determination to get it right, but the stories I hear bear testimony to a disappointing reality: that a lot of us get it wrong!

Yet there is a way of finding out exactly how to make wiser decisions, and this is where we find the second key to unlock our true nature: within our "authority." This provides a strategy that steers us toward a better, more reliable decision-making process that is specifically tailored to individual designs.

"Authority" is the ability to take charge of *your* life. It allows you to trust your decisions, removing hesitancy and installing confidence.

The problem is that many of us have been wrongly conditioned in how to reach decisions. In our formative years, parents, guardians, or older siblings made them for us — decisions that were "for the best." Then, as we emerged into the wider world, multiple factors kicked in with media and advertising pressures to feel like this, look like that, do this, be sexy, be cool. Society often makes decisions for us, without our even realizing it.

But the biggest conditioning factor is the belief that we should "think" our way through life. For far too long, humanity has labored under this misapprehension. I remember teachers and elders who stabbed a finger to their temples and told innocent children: "Use your head!" or "God put a head on your shoulders so you could use it — so use it!" If only people would just stop giving the Mind such power!

One look at a Human Design life chart tells us all we need to know. The Mind has no direct connection to the motor centers of the Heart, Sacral, Self, and Root; it is, therefore, devoid of the power to move us forward. The more it gets embroiled in our decisions, the more chaotic and stressful everything becomes. It might well be an incredible data bank, but it's lousy at making decisions. In fact, it is incapable of doing so. It is designed to *process*, not *decide*. It is split into two hemispheres and therefore has two diverse ways of viewing the world. It is indecisive by nature, so a mental decision becomes as reliable as flipping a coin. Getting your mind around this truth is the first step on the path to wiser decision making.

People also fall into the misleading trap of relying on other people to make decisions for them. This is often seen in subtle pleas like "What would you do if you were in my shoes?" It is an impossible question because another person always has a different makeup and authority. What's right for them would not be right for you.

Your best decision-making process depends on your design. The truth is that the best decisions come via either the Emotions, the Sacral, the Spleen, the Heart, or the Self or, for some people, from outside the Self. All will become clear as you read on.

Which decision-making process works best for you depends on which centers, if any, you have turned on. So check your life chart, because the Human Design software automatically spells out your authority for you.

THE EMOTIONS AUTHORITY

"Be Emotionally Clear."

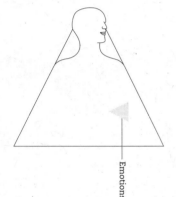

Emotions

This is your strategy if the Emotions center is defined in color.

Whether you are man or woman, feelings rule your life and you're here to surf them. Regardless of any other centers that are defined, the Emotions rule.

Earlier I used the analogy of a storm-tossed ship in tumultuous seas to describe what it can feel like to be you. Your correct decision-making process, therefore, is to find lasting emotional clarity in spite of the storm.

Such clarity isn't easy if your emotions are particularly intense or confusing. When something is sending you into a tailspin, the easiest option is to make a decision, any decision, just to bring matters to a head or to end the pain. Conversely, if you're experiencing huge pleasure, you might want to hang on to that feeling and let yourself get carried away. That would be equally rash. Few decisions will work out if you are emotionally spontaneous or reckless; your natural authority demands that you seek emotional clarity before you make decisions.

True and reliable decisions will form in the clarity that arrives when that storm-tossed ship suddenly finds itself at rest in the middle of a still lake. At that moment, everything becomes clear. Admittedly, it takes time and practice to recognize this, but the more you allow yourself to *witness* your emotions, the more quickly you'll begin to find an emotional balance, which, in turn, will foster clarity.

Have you ever agreed to do something one day, only to wake up the next morning groaning with regret because you're absolutely not in the mood anymore? Or how about making a fundamental switch in direction, only to rue your haste some days, weeks, or months down the line? Rash decisions tend to be attached to some emotional expectation of hope or fear about how things will turn out. Heightened emotions, therefore, paint a misleading outcome and cannot be reliably followed.

Take the following two real-life examples:

> *If I marry him, that's it, I'm trapped, there's no way out. What if he's wrong for me? I might fancy someone else when walking down the aisle . . . (Panic, panic, panic!)*

In this state, the bride-to-be is in a heightened state of anxiety and fear and is painting expectations on a canvas before her.

> *I can't believe it; he's offered me the job! Loads more money — think of the car I can buy, the house I can have, the girls I can attract . . . (Joy, joy, joy!)*

In this state, the job candidate is in a heightened state of excitement, and joy is painting expectations for him, too.

In real life, I'm pleased to say, the bride eventually walked down the aisle and now she couldn't be happier. And the job candidate ultimately rejected the post despite the trappings of wealth because, he said, "It wasn't for me in the end." Those two people recognized the emotions rising within them, refused to be attached to them, sought clarity, exercised caution, and gave it at least a night's sleep.

In some cases, it can take days before such clarity dawns. In the case of the bride-to-be, it took months, but she finally got there! Sometimes, though, you don't need to sleep on anything. You've already set your sights on a new car or a fashion accessory you've seen advertised. The emotional clarity is already present, waiting for that specific item to show up. But if you act in haste, be prepared to feel that inner frustration and resistance that is your true self's way of saying: "You got it wrong again!"

Your decision-making process hinges on finding that still point that Buddha calls "the middle way," "neither this nor that." Picture a frequency sine wave where the signal, like your emotions, makes swooping peaks and dips on either side of a central line. It appears dramatic but, essentially, nothing is happening except the rising and falling of waves. The frequency is only captured at the constant still point in the middle. Likewise, your emotional clarity exists at that still point.

Emotional clarity is when something *feels* right — the most peaceful, natural thing in the world. It is a clarity that resounds in your very being. Feel it, don't think it.

Sometimes this process requires enormous patience in a life that can seem hurried and urgent. But seek clarity — crystal clarity to the point of absolute knowing. Allow it to happen. *Patience* is your watchword, clarity is your authority, and stability can be carried within you, no matter how wild the emotional waves become.

One Important Note

If you have both the Emotions and Spleen defined, you'll be aware of instantaneous alerts within you, coming from the Spleen. But wait. Emotions still rule and you must seek emotional clarity. Sit with your senses and "feel them out" until it all becomes 100 percent clear. Then you can make your decision.

If the Emotions, Spleen, and Sacral are all defined, your alert senses (from the Spleen) and gut responses (from the Sacral) may well be jumping up and down. But wait. The Emotions still rule and emotional clarity will enable you to determine what feels clear and right.

THE SACRAL AUTHORITY

"Follow Your Gut."

This is your strategy if the Sacral is defined and the Emotions are undefined.

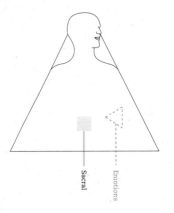

Your correct decision-making process is about "following your gut" — and trusting it.

Am I seriously telling you that your best decisions in life will stem from that sensation in the lower belly? Yes, I am. Indeed, you were born with a natural inclination to follow the gut, but this was quickly drummed out of you by well-meaning parents and teachers who provided the conditioning to use the Mind instead.

The most important thing for anyone with Sacral Authority to appreciate is that this inner guidance system is only ever effective when in *response*. It is not proactive; it is *responsive*. Thus, your authority is designed to wait until there is a clear response that speaks from the lower belly with an "uh-huh" for "yes" and "uh-uh" for "no," or that sensation of being drawn toward or repelled by something. If there is no response, this in itself implies a lack of interest at the time.

This authority needs to be applied to everything in life. It is not healthy for you to commit to, or engage in, anything without first waiting and then receiving a gut response in agreement.

You've got to be careful not to be tempted into making decisions just because of conditioning or the people around you. An emotional friend with a contagious excitement could make an idea sound like the best thing since sliced bread; an iron-willed colleague could make a persuasive argument to commit your vast life-force energy to an important project. At such times, your authority demands that you sit and wait for your gut response to make its voice known. Because, as we already know, once you commit, there is no stopping your being carried onward by the Sacral's relentless momentum.

Learning to get out of the head and into the gut is how you'll learn to make wiser decisions. Many people with a defined Sacral struggle to differentiate between gut response and emotional reaction. A response is patient, relaxed, and measured, whereas a reaction is an unconscious reflex and hasty. With practice, you'll learn to notice the difference and hone this authoritative skill within you.

With that in mind, I will now give you something to ponder. Consider a time in your life when you made an important decision that turned out to be one you regretted, be that a decision to get married or let someone go, sell your house or buy a car, move to another country or move down the street. Now recall *how* you made that decision. Were you over-analyzing and thinking too much? Did the influence of another person convince you in some way? Were you feeling obliged to commit? Rewind and review it all. Look at what unfolded when you made that poor decision.

Now consider an important decision where everything turned out favorably and you felt an inner harmony. How did you make that decision? Did you, perhaps, wait, trust your gut, and then go for it?

Your golden key to making correct and consistently better decisions lies in identifying the answers to these questions.

One Important Note

When you have both the Spleen and Sacral defined, your gut response becomes greatly enhanced by the Spleen senses. This means that your gut is fast-tracked into an instantaneous split-second response.

THE SPLEEN AUTHORITY

"Instant Decisions"

This is your strategy if the Spleen is defined and the Emotions and Sacral are undefined.

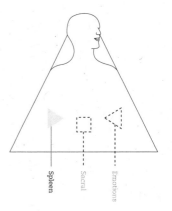

Spleen Sacral Emotions

Your correct decisions are made in the blink of an eye. You are designed to seize the "now," deciding instantaneously, without hesitation. It is a snap decision in every sense.

If an Emotional Authority is based on watching the entire movie and experiencing the drama's ups and downs, the Spleen Authority is all about being decisive in a freeze-frame, snapshot moment. This might seem like a frighteningly rash process, but it's the only way your decisions can be trusted.

This is because your intuition senses whether something sounds right or wrong, genuine or insincere. Your instinct senses whether something smells fine or fishy. Your taste knows whether something is suitable, whether it be food or "tasteful" people or surroundings. All these senses view the end result in an instant and alert you in a split second. The process can be impressive when you learn to trust it! You either pay attention to your lightning-quick authority or let the moment pass — and your fortunes with it.

If you find yourself hesitating or pondering, you've disappeared into the Mind and are not being true to your nature. This, then, is not the time to make a decision. Spleen impulses come only once and you either live by them or ignore them. There is nothing to think about!

The use of this authority may well alarm others around you. "Take your time. Think about it," they will urge. Don't listen to them. Stick to your guns. Your snap decision is not ill-considered or impatient; it's right for you. So trust this reliable Zen-like "now" process. You cannot afford to base a decision on a past premise or a future reckoning.

With this authority, your senses are naturally sharp. It can mean something as simple as walking into a restaurant and finding its noise, smells, or décor jarring to your inner being. Take the following real-life case when the Spleen Authority was seen in action:

> *A friend had booked a table at a well-known restaurant in Santa Barbara, California. He and his girlfriend sat down and he started to scan the menu. He looked up and his girlfriend was scanning the room, looking distracted and bothered.*
>
> *"What's wrong?" he asked.*
>
> *"I don't like it here. Can we leave?" she said.*
>
> *"But we've only just sat down!"*
>
> *"I know, but something's not right. It's the ambience and I don't like the smell," she said.*
>
> *And with that, they got up and left and went elsewhere.*
>
> *Here the Spleen Authority's inner radar had been scanning the environment and alerting her that it wasn't right for her. Had she ignored that alert or been swayed by her boyfriend's insistence on staying, then the chances are that the night would have been grim, possibly ending in an argument or food poisoning. Her Spleen had given its signal to exit an environment it had deemed unhealthy for her sense of well-being.*

Be alert for that feeling that something is wrong — or right. Out of the three awareness centers, the Spleen is the quietest of them all, almost whispering its decisions. So wherever you go, whomever you meet, and whatever offer is put before you, keep an ear peeled and a nostril flared for that inner radar.

Let's not forget that the Spleen's hunches also point out who and what is right to pursue. "I smell money in this venture — yes!" or "That sounds right to me!" or "This cheap bottle of wine tastes fantastic!" There is nothing necessarily reasonable about following your nose, something sounding right or something seeming tasteful, yet there is an irrefutable reliability about these senses as they instantly indicate whether you're on the right track in life.

THE HEART AUTHORITY

"Do What You Want."

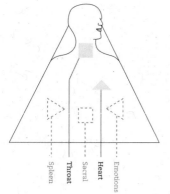

Spleen Throat Sacral Heart Emotions

This requires the Emotions, Sacral, and Spleen to be undefined and the Heart defined, connected to the Throat.

Your decision-making process is all about attuning to your heart's desire. What you want is what needs to happen.

This authority is dependent on an active connection between the Heart and Throat via one or more active channels. It is the most straightforward authority to have and can be the most direct by nature. In its rawest form, your decision lies in your heart's desire and is expressed as something like: "I want it, so I'm going to make it happen."

The consequent accomplishment is never the issue, because of your inherent iron will and powers to manifest. The issue is whether you'll allow yourself to be deflected by the pleas or indignation of others. Protestors will stand in front of your steamroller because your look-after-number-one strategy can run against society's expected consideration of others. How can you handle this? Look back at what I said about being a Manifestor: be gracious enough to inform others of your intentions. But once you've set your heart on something, your natural drive is not to be stopped.

When you need to make a decision, tune in to your heart. The reliable "yes" or "no" can be found in what your heart is drawing you toward or pulling you from. It's a very personal, subjective process, but extremely powerful. If your heart's not in it, there's your decision. If your heart soars at the mere pondering of something, go for it. Just be careful to commit your manifesting powers to those people and projects that accord with *your* heartfelt wishes. Otherwise, you will exhaust yourself fulfilling everyone else's wishes as if it were a duty. So, when making a decision, be clear that the "yes" or "no" comes clearly from *your* Heart, be it for the universal good or a selfish pursuit.

THE SELF AUTHORITY

"Be True to Yourself."

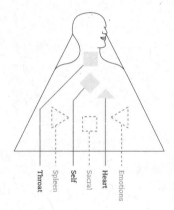

Throat | Spleen | Self | Sacral | Heart | Emotions

This is your strategy if the Emotions, Sacral, and Spleen are all undefined, and either the Heart is defined to the Self, which is not defined to the Throat, or the Heart is undefined and the Self is defined to the Throat.

The Self Authority is quite different from the authorities discussed previously. It provides a subtle inner guidance as delicate as a butterfly's touch in the way it alerts you, and yet it's as robust as an ox in its execution. That's because it's all about inner knowing.

If you have this authority, your correct decision-making process is rooted in a "knowing" which only you can begin to comprehend. It is, perhaps, the most difficult authority to grasp, until you get the hang of recognizing its signals, accuracy, and rightness. It arrives, gently and sometimes unannounced, as a realization that should not be suppressed. It is an innate sense of knowing that could not be associated with any other authority. Quite simply, it just "knows" what is right and what is wrong in uniquely personal terms.

Where does this knowing rise from? I tell those with the Self Authority to move their attention to the sternum, the midcenter of the rib cage. It is here that a physical sensation brushes you, emanating from the Self. Those who have it will recognize it — and must trust it implicitly.

Your decision will be heard as something like: "I just know it. I can't explain it, but I just know it." The key is not to be dissuaded from this knowing because it can come across as woolly and is susceptible to being bulldozed by the emotions, gut responses, intuitions, and willpower of others. It's as if they have a greater authority than you. But start to trust your inner knowing as the most reliable of confidantes.

With this authority, you have the design of Barbra Streisand, Mick Jagger, or Steven Spielberg, who are Projectors as well as natural-born leaders. You provide leadership, according to the recognition-invitation process that you require. As a leader, you need to exercise your Self Authority with caution, though, because it is easy to get swept up in others' endeavors that you don't have the energy to complete. What you commit to has to have meaning to *your* life. But this requires you to trust in your true nature more than any other authority.

THE OUTER AUTHORITY

"Accessing Intelligence"

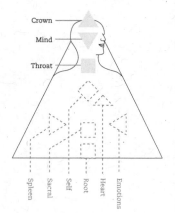

This is your strategy when either the Crown, Mind, or Throat is defined and all the other centers are undefined, or when the whole chart is undefined.

This is a unique authority, because rather than having an internal prompt, you go through an external process to discover your inner truth.

This authority must not be rushed into making decisions. It is slow, deliberate, meticulous, and measured. It weighs and balances, thoroughly researches, checks, and double-checks before reaching any sort of conclusion.

With this authority, you will be either a Reflector type or a specific Projector with only the Crown, Mind, or Throat center defined. You don't have an internal filter to rely on, but don't despair — you still have the means to make intelligent and accurate assessments; it's just that you must exercise great patience and take an expanded, open view of all the situations confronting you.

All the white space within your life chart means you're able to access everyone else's perspectives, concepts, and ideas and turn them into your own wisdom. Your correct decision-making process, therefore, relies on consultation with other people, directly or indirectly, over a period of twenty-nine days. Those twenty-nine days are in accord with the movements and phases of the moon. This is why it's called an Outer

Authority, because it is consultative by nature and takes the lunar cycle into account. It may well sound crazy at first, but just as the moon is responsible for the coming and going of the tides, so it relates to your shifting perspectives.

When you are faced with a choice or dilemma, the usual tendency is to start mulling it over and going inward for the answers. But it's necessary for your nature to look *outward* and sound out the world around you. If I were you, I'd buy a lunar calendar and familiarize myself with the moon's movement in the sky. Mark down "decision day" twenty-nine days hence, then turn back to the present and begin your inquiries. Do research. Read books. Search the internet. Allow your empathetic nature to pick up on everything and everyone involved. Most things will get written off in the first few days of your decision-making cycle.

While it is not always practical to make a decision over twenty-nine days, be aware of this cycle and try to apply it as much as possible. Once accustomed to this tie-in with the lunar cycle, you'll often be able to anticipate your process and decide preemptively. But for major decisions, it really is worth waiting those twenty-nine days.

Joint decisions with others require practice and patience, and a lot of times you might find yourself being usurped in the hurry to reach a decision. That will require great trust in your partner, friend, or associate. This can be an extremely difficult — and testing — strategy to both adopt and understand, but if you have it, and your cycle is allowed room to breathe, you can end up the wisest decision maker of them all. In many respects, the Universe is your co-decision maker. With this kind of ally, you will find not only that you're a walking lexicon of knowledge but that your level of intelligence can outstrip that of most people around you. You will begin to appreciate the opportunity to find your own place within a huge arena of opinion, experience, and possibility.

You now have an overview of your Human Design through the centers, type, and authority. You could, at this point, start using the information to transform your way of interacting with the world. If, for example, you have discovered you are a Generator with Emotional Authority, you will know that you must listen to your gut response and then make better decisions in accordance with an emotional clarity. Just using this knowledge could start to change your life.

But there is so much, much more to your nature we've yet to discover.

In the next section of this book, we delve deeper and start to mine the real gems within you. This is where we start to examine the nitty-gritty of who you are as an individual. We examine the unique fingerprint you leave on this world. Here, self-recognition is taken to an even more amazing level.

Just who are you?

5

Uniquely You

The Thirty-Six Channels

I still consult my Human Design chart and reading as if it were an ally. Your reading was like being instantly "known" and recognized for who I was.

SA, Cheltenham, UK

Scattered around the life chart are narrow channels that "spider web" between the nine centers. There are thirty-six of them, containing the stuff we are made of, the finer components of our being. These thirty-six channels, inspired by the ancient wisdom of the Kabbalah, act as conduits between the centers, running life-energy back and forth.

On your life chart, you'll note that at either end of a channel there is a number. This number correlates with one of the sixty-four gates that also shape our design, as explored in the next chapter.

What needs to be noted is this: if the channel between two centers is colored, it is an active channel, taking qualities from each of the gates it connects to become an entity on its own. It is like a wire in which two "charges" meet in the middle in a rush of color and energy. These are the channels that will have consistent meaning in your life.

If a channel is white or only half colored, it is an inactive channel. This means it has no consistent meaning for you. However, other people may have that channel activated, and so this will intermittently light up your channel as they come in and out of your company. This is another example of how different designs mesh and merge.

This is also the first time in your design that you'll start noticing the conscious and unconscious themes emerging—what you're aware of in yourself and what's hidden within.

The color of an active channel is informative on its own: black denotes a conscious trait, pink signals unconscious, and a striped combination means it's a mixture of both. What will tend to happen — if my experience of readings is anything to go by — is that you'll recognize the black-colored channels and their meanings as conscious elements of your personality, something you already know you act out or do, whereas the meanings of the pink-colored channels are not so readily obvious because they're unconscious elements. These characteristics are what your parents and grandparents have handed down. I always tell people that the unconscious elements are stirring within, whether they are recognized or not.

The beauty of Human Design, and this treasure trove of information, is that once you know something is part of your makeup, you become more conscious of the fact it exists — and can start to appreciate and harness its influence. A channel of black and pink stripes simply means you've a better chance of becoming conscious of these unconscious parts of yourself.

So when you look at your life chart, find the active channels and locate the corresponding channel numbers in the following pages. Each channel has two numbers and a name that sums up its combined influence. For ease of reading, I've deliberately started with the lowest number first.

Remember, a channel has to be completely colored (defined) for it to have a relevance to your design for life. If only half of it is colored, this means you have a gate that is activated, ready to make a connection to the other center through interactions with other people but not always doing so by itself. This is something we will examine later.

If you have no active channels at all in your chart, you are a Reflector who will easily perceive the active channels in other people's charts and how they impact your life.

THE THIRTY-SIX CHANNELS

1 Channel of Inspiration 8

From the Self to the Throat

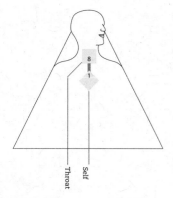

You are a creative role model with an empowering influence, here to be recognized for your leadership and guidance. As the channel name implies, you are a walking inspiration, automatically knowing how to take charge of situations and lead by example. You have a strong sense of identity and are someone others trust and on whom they can rely. You can motivate people and make things happen.

You succeed when others bow to your leadership and are sufficiently inspired. You sense an inner resistance and frustration when your decisions are unappreciated or when those you lead sit on your coattails.

I would caution against volunteering for anything because you are an individual whose nature sings when recognized by a personal invitation, not just because you've stuck your hand in the air.

There is an acoustic quality with this leadership channel, the 1-8, meaning you have an ear for what sounds right about people, projects, places, and music. You're forever tuning in to your environment, working out the best direction in which to head, based on the quality of what you hear. If something doesn't sound right, you won't proceed.

When you are certain about taking a specific direction or lead, be alert to the tone of your voice, because that tone affects the outcome of the guidance you give as much as what you say. If, for example, you're feeling nervous as you speak, your audience will detect it. When you speak with clarity and assurance, like all effective leaders, everyone listens and takes note. Recognize that you have a gift to empower other people.

2 Channel of the Alchemist 14

From the Self to the Sacral

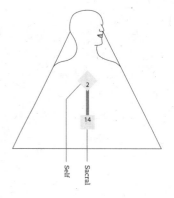

According to mythology, the alchemist turns lead into gold, and so it is with this channel, denoting the transformative power and creative potential locked within. The 2-14 is capable of innovation through plugging into the Sacral's life-force energy.

As an agent of transformation, you empower with the creativity, contribution, and potential improvements you bring to a situation, accomplishing feats that can defy the odds. There is something of the genius or wizard about you. Give you raw material and you'll make it shine. Show you an ailing company and you'll turn its fortunes around. You know the direction things need to go in and can put projects and people back on track. Your conviction and energy are contagious to those working or living with you.

The 2-14 is an individualistic channel, meaning you march to the beat of your own drum, unstoppable with your self-thrust. You also happen to be an expert at handling finances, steering resources, and managing property.

This is one of four "tantric channels." Although *tantra* is a word often associated solely with sex, it actually denotes the potential for transmuting energy from a lower to a higher form, hence your transformative touch. Of course, we can't ignore its influence in the bedroom, either, because it can transform the physical act of sex into an experience of super-consciousness.

Because this is a Generator channel by nature, the power contained within it is best operated and most effective on the back of an affirmative gut response. When applied correctly to the proper endeavors, it will render you capable of impressing everyone who witnesses you in action.

3 Channel of Mutation 60

From the Sacral to the Root

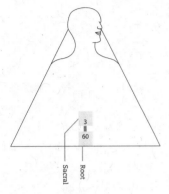

Sacral
Root
3
60

You might already be aware of how dramatically events can change around you. Join the 3 and the 60 and it becomes symbolic, because your life is always doing a 360-degree circle. Partners who travel with you in life must be adaptable and prepare for an erratic but rewarding experience of change and growth. Expect the unexpected.

Everyone I know with this channel has a life made up of a sequence of quantum leaps from one place to the next, forever changing direction and relying on nothing more than blind faith — and an affirmative gut response from the Sacral.

The 3-60 is one of three "format channels." A format channel has an overriding impact on your entire design, dictating how your life *will* be lived out, regardless of whatever else is going on in your life chart. With the 3-60, your Human Design has the ingrained motto "Dramatic changes and transformations equal personal growth." Your process is bringing about renewal, but don't expect a fanfare everywhere you go — because not everyone welcomes upheaval.

Have you ever watched moving events lit by an erratic strobe light? That is similar to the way in which you operate: the light hits you and everything is seen clearly. But then the light darts away, leaving you in darkness. When it hits you again, everything has changed and you and everything around you are moving in a new direction.

The strobe light's randomness also matches the cosmic timing that governs your life, pulsing on and off in an irregular pattern. Likewise, dramatic change has no sense of timing. Things happen when they are *meant* to happen and this is a natural law that all 3-60s must learn to accept. This in itself can be limiting, especially if you've set something in motion and things stall. This can induce a melancholy that is hard to shake. At such times, your best allies are music and nature. The acoustic quality of this channel needs to tune in to sounds that match your mood. Then exercise patience. If life is teaching you anything, it's that things don't remain stuck for long. Trust this channel's mutative energy, and the frustration over temporary inertia can ease. Throughout your life, you'll come to see that the transformations you bring — to your world and others' — are immensely empowering.

4 Channel of the Logical Mind 63

From the Mind to the Crown

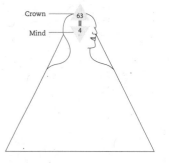

You have a logical mind with a critical perception that scans tomorrow's world for improvements but also worries about the future. Your logical thinking follows consistent trains of thought that are coherent and realistic, weighing up probabilities. "If this happens, that will happen..." and on goes the sequential process. There is a consequence to everything — and you're working it all out!

The ability to think logically has practical importance but can also mean you're plagued by doubts and worry. So consider these phrases: "If it ain't broke, why fix it?" or "If you can't change it, why worry?"

Your great task is to determine how much attention you give to your problem-seeking thoughts, knowing the delicate balance between being concerned all the time and actually enjoying life. You are designed to think and worry. Accept this and you can start to step away from more troublesome thoughts.

Your mind is a great asset and is better trained to find solutions in the lives of others rather than in your own. It finds rational and sound solutions that bring about improvement. There is no doubt that you have marvelous solutions for all sorts of problems, but wait for a real problem to arise or for when something really does need fixing, then come in with your step-by-step thought process and astound everyone with your logical, grounded perceptiveness.

5 Channel of Rhythm 15

From the Sacral to the Self

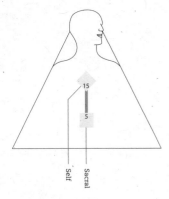

You are in the flow of life and have an inexplicable knack for the right timing to be somewhere or to introduce something new. You are the same as the turtle that knows exactly when it's time to head for the beach and lay its eggs — your timing and rhythm are a heartbeat ticking in synchronicity with Nature's time and seasons, guided by the Sacral's gut response. So nothing drives your true nature crazier than being with clock-watchers who demand punctuality. You need to be unhurried and measured — in step with your unique timing.

I have a friend who can be dashing around the house, running late, while her punctual partner is desperate to leave for a function on time. They both eventually get there, to find that the event is delayed by thirty minutes. The person with "rhythm" has just proved how in tune they are with the Universe's natural timing.

It's not all about literal timing, though. It's about knowing when to introduce something or someone into your environment, when a product, concept, or invention is ripe for the times. It's also about knowing when to switch direction in your life.

The 5-15 is one of four "tantric channels," and *tantra* means transmuting energy from a lower to a higher form, instigating change in others, encouraging them to access and trust the flow of life. You establish order amid chaos. You organize the headless chickens running amok. You're like the river sweeping everyone else along, swirling between the banks, sometimes moving gently, sometimes rushing through rapids. But whatever the pace, the transmutation you bring urges everyone to go with the flow.

When you are in that flow, life seems effortless and natural, but when you step out of rhythm or are forced into someone else's timing, life can become chaotic and unhappy — out of step, out of time. When you experience such difficulties, pause and re-examine whom and what you're committing to, because it's not conducive to your well-being. Listen to your gut response and you will always be reacquainted with your natural flow. You just need the time to realize this!

6 Channel of Connecting 59

From the Emotions to the Sacral

This channel forms potent bonds with people and projects, making connections where sexual chemistry sparkles and creative juices flow.

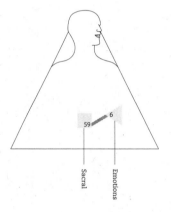

This sole activation between the Sacral and the Emotions creates the "sex connection" and carries an intense charge. It makes you alluring, but the 6-59 is not all about the act of pleasure; it's about the two halves coming together for the basic biological need to procreate. Others' genes are not concerned with personalities — they just want a genetic match. This channel carries a high degree of fertility and if you have it, people will be drawn to you like bees to honey. Your key is to practice discernment. Only then can you find an inner sense of satisfaction and balance, instead of being a slave to sexual energy. Your true nature requires deep spiritual connections.

But this channel is not all about sex and mating; you have a huge potential to give birth to new creative projects, concepts, and movements. When you get passionate about a project, there's no stopping you. So you are a cocreator in every sense of the word.

You also have strong feelings, sensuality, and desires, powered by the Sacral. This means you penetrate the emotional auras of everyone around you, just with your presence. A friend with the 6-59 started noticing how her mere arrival at a social scene could almost stun the ambience. It's not her, of course; it's her penetrating Sacral-Emotional aura impacting on everyone.

You, too, might wish to observe the effect you have on people around you. Of course, some will feel at ease, but others can wish to step away or sometimes withdraw. The force field of the 6-59 reaches in and touches the most stoic individuals. What is actually happening is that you're triggering old unresolved emotional upsets in them. Your nature might feel a responsibility to bring about resolution, but you'd be wiser to realize these triggered issues have nothing directly to do with you. You're just catalyzing them. If you do get sucked in, the Sacral's momentum will mean you'll have to see it through . . . to the bitter end. So when it comes to selecting potential projects and mating partners, listen for a gut response but, even more crucially, then seek emotional clarity. As the poet Lord Byron once said: "There is nothing so amiable as discernment."

7 Channel of the Alpha 31

From the Self to the Throat

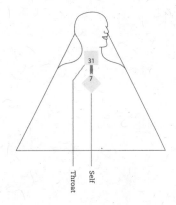

31
7

Self

Throat

"Logical leadership" could be a name badge you wear. You are a born leader who can march with purpose into an uncertain future, knowing the way. Whether you hear yourself saying it or not, what others hear is "I lead toward an assured future . . ."

"Alpha" is the highest rank in the social order of wolf packs, and you, as an alpha male or female, stand out as the leader of any pack. People regard you as an obvious candidate for leadership, so prepare to be nominated, selected, or, better still, elected. Public recognition makes your soul sing!

There is something logical and authoritative about your style of leadership, which is why people follow you and defer to you. People automatically pay attention when you walk into a room; your arrival brings about governance and brings everyone onto the same page.

But you will appreciate that it is one thing to suggest something needs to happen and quite another to get involved in doing it. Like a general, you may stand back, leaving the job to the foot soldiers working to your instructions. This need not give you a false air of superiority; it's just that *alpha* means being first in the order of things.

Being a leader brings many responsibilities, and perhaps the greatest is to be true to yourself. You do not have to lead everyone just because they look lost or seem in need of guidance; leadership is an ability, not an obligation. The wrong company and wrong situations can lead *you* into a role that is unfulfilling and meaningless, but when your true leadership is recognized and invited, you bring about radical and positive change.

9 Channel of Concentration 52

From the Sacral to the Root

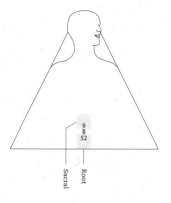

You have the ability to focus your determination and concentration to bring about improvement and success. Focus, focus, focus — that's what your life is all about.

There is a tenacity about the way you pinpoint targets, goals, and visions and set about accomplishing them. In all ventures, particularly with business, you are a great asset, especially for companies with future-oriented goals. You arrive at the starting point of any project armed with the determination to make things work — even in relationships. You can have incredibly fulfilling relationships, but only when you know everything is perfect, ready, and in place. You find it hard to commit until every flaw has been ironed out and every "imperfection" tackled.

As with all channels stemming from the Root, there is an intense adrenaline-filled pressure to get things moving. But the Channel of Concentration knows how to keep a tight rein, hold back, and ride the stress, keeping the horse on the bridle but never losing sight of the winning post. You allow the energy to build and only drop the reins when everything is ready to be propelled. It frustrates you if things are set in motion before all your resources are assembled and a great plan is drawn up. Nothing drives you crazier than something that feels ill-prepared, without focus. This is why you make an excellent planner.

An affirmative gut response will tell you the correct things to focus on. Then there's no stopping you.

The 9-52 is one of three "format channels." A format channel has an overriding impact on your entire design, dictating how your life will be lived out, regardless of whatever else is going on in your life chart. So your Human Design has the ingrained motto "Before moving, picture the arrow in the bull's-eye."

America's Olympian swimmer Michael Phelps and golfer Tiger Woods both have this channel, and focused determination is the hallmark of everything they've achieved in life.

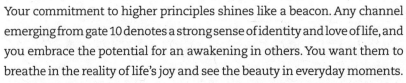

10 Channel of Awakening 20

From the Self to the Throat

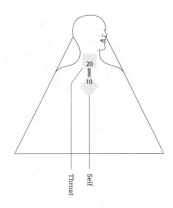

Your commitment to higher principles shines like a beacon. Any channel emerging from gate 10 denotes a strong sense of identity and love of life, and you embrace the potential for an awakening in others. You want them to breathe in the reality of life's joy and see the beauty in everyday moments.

The 10-20 stems from the Self then does a dogleg up to the right, finding expression in the Throat with phrases like "I am being true to myself right now." I would wager that this is something you say, or wish to say, quite often in life. "Just be yourself" is the hallmark of this channel, and your "awakened" state finds its voice through an assured self-expression that leaves no doubt about who you are and where you stand. This empowers others to be more like you, bringing them into alignment with their *own* integrity. But should anyone challenge what you say, it can feel like a personal assault, so be aware of this sensitivity. The test is to detach from such criticism and find assurance in self-appreciation.

You cannot abide people who are untruthful and situations that appear dishonest or unjust. You demand unabashed candor and that people be upfront at all times. You want to meet people on a higher level, so integration with kindred spirits accords with your nature. No one entertains the possibility of the world becoming a better place more than you do.

The 10-20 is one of four "leadership channels," but this form of leadership can, to some, appear as though you're standing on the moral high ground, trying to lead people toward finding their higher purpose. Of course, such principled leadership does not appeal to everyone, but you'll go it alone if necessary. For those who do follow, it will be a profound experience as you open a doorway to a higher spiritual level. Life, for you, is all about the "now" and embracing your days moment by moment.

People with the 10-20 rarely grasp this channel's meaning. That's because they are so involved with the higher purpose that they really can't be bothered with the mechanics. "I am who I am, so why concern myself with this channel's meaning?"

And so you prove my point, just by your state of being.

10 Channel of Exploration 34

From the Self to the Sacral

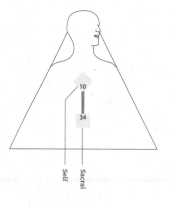

It is imperative that you have the courage of your convictions in all you do. Any channel emerging from gate 10 denotes a strong sense of identity and a love of life. For you, happiness lies in doing something you love, regardless of anyone else. There is a supremely selfish aspect to the 10-34, because you *must* get your own way. You shouldn't feel guilty about it, though, because this is being true to your nature. Besides, others may quietly admire you for being a true person of conviction.

You'll notice in the life chart that this channel stems from the Self and goes on a tangent to reach the Sacral: it's a perfect illustration of this quality in you — shooting off to follow a unique path. Make no mistake, when engaged with your convictions and supported by an affirmative gut response, you will be on the right track. It doesn't matter if others disagree or believe you're being impossibly selfish or stubborn. Always follow through, regardless of the madness around you. Your happiness hinges on self-approval, not eliciting approval from others. It truly matters to your sense of well-being that you love your life, where you live, and what you do. If swayed from your path by others, you'll start to feel lost.

The 10-34 is one of four "tantric channels," and the word *tantra* means the transmuting of energy from a lower to a higher form. This transmuting is personally applied, powering your convictions and nothing else. If other people get you and feel empowered, all well and good, but the main thing is that you stick to your guns!

10 Channel of Survival 57

From the Self to the Spleen

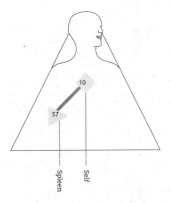

You have an intuitive interaction with life on the edge — dancing with danger, toying with risk — and yet you always seem to survive. That's because you can rely on the Spleen's intuitive survival mechanism, which, somehow, guides you through life's minefield. You are someone who could jump from the Eiffel Tower and somehow land on your feet!

There is, therefore, a sense of the indestructible risk taker about you. The 10-57 seems to bless you with an invisible protection shield in the activities you undertake and the decisions you make. Without doubt, you are better protected than most in life.

This doesn't mean that you should take silly risks, but you'll discover you have an inexplicable knack for dodging danger and getting out of trouble. "How do you get away with it?" people will often say. You'll be the one person who is fine when the rest of your table is down with food poisoning, or the person who sidesteps a falling piano in the street. There's nothing logical about this channel. It just happens. I always joke that the safest — and luckiest — seat in life is the one next to you!

You must learn to trust this automatic intuition rising from the Spleen. It's a visceral intuition based on what "sounds" right. Your being detects vibrations every second of the day, pointing out which people, environments, and choices are right. It makes you as alert as a lightly sleeping cat, twitching at the slightest noise or change in environment and then awakened to instant alertness.

Any channel emerging from gate 10 denotes a strong sense of identity and love of life. For you, that shows up as living life to the fullest. You can entertain fears about the future but this is balanced by knowing that everything will work out just fine...somehow. You will tend to feel the fear and do it anyway, whether it's about a pursuit, project, or relationship.

11 Channel of Curiosity 56

From the Mind to the Throat

You are forever seeking life's meaning, then yearning to express it so that others are stimulated by your findings. Your insatiable curiosity never stops in its pursuit of finding something out or obtaining new information to share with others.

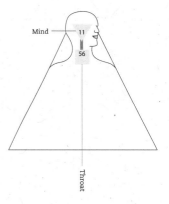

In many situations there is the inclination for you to "speak your mind" because of the activation between the Mind and Throat, and this emerges in phrases like "I believe what you'll find is..." Then you'll be curious to see how your audience reacts and will ponder the meaning of that reaction.

Your excessive interest in anything and everything means you dip in and out of life's belief systems, flitting from one stimulating idea or concept to the next, collecting knowledge along the way. To those witnessing your behavior, it's as if you're chasing butterflies, trying to keep pace with their erratic dance, tasting each flower to find flavor and meaning. You devour philosophies and wisdoms, investigate concepts, and probe all kinds of new beliefs. You like nothing more than seeing the results of your curiosity stimulate others. You will also take on all sorts of trips and travels as a means to satisfy your curiosity, always wondering what's around the next corner, always sensing that there is nothing quite like firsthand experience to stimulate your ideas and beliefs anew.

The Biblical phrase "Seek, and ye shall find" is applicable here, except that for you, the search continues until your last breath. It's as if your mind cannot rest until it has come to grips with everything there is to experience in life. For you, truth cannot be known through having preconceived ideas. You must seek out the experience and sample it for yourself.

12 Channel of Openness 22

From the Throat to the Emotions

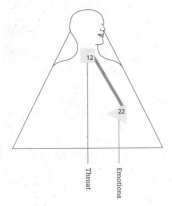

Throat   Emotions

You are someone who can find yourself at the mercy of your emotions. There is a depth and openness to you that makes you empowering, vulnerable, and unpredictable all at the same time. You arrive in situations armed with an intensity that fuels a passion to make great things happen. In many regards, you tend to take the path less traveled, opening doorways — for yourself and others — with innovative interactions that most would consider off-limits.

En route to your achievements, you may appear calm and assured. But under the surface, there are all manner of emotional waves pulling on you. Man or woman, you have no difficulty expressing emotions, from exuberance to rage. Indeed, this is an outlet that brings relief. But be wary of who shares your emotions, because they can arrive with an impact some people struggle to understand, let alone handle. You can be extremely passionate about what you do, but also hot-tempered. Indeed, others may wonder, "Where on Earth is all this emotion coming from?"

I always tell people with the 12-22 to be clear with themselves and others before expressing emotions. This helps foster understanding. Emotions that are dismissed become pent up and block your manifesting abilities. Emotions that are recognized allow you to maintain a balance and chase the stars. En route to outer orbit, you just need to keep checking in with your feelings and honoring them. That way, you remain open to whatever life throws at you and can empower others with the social and business links you forge and the accomplishments you attain.

Always know that you'll forever lurch between emotions, experiencing huge swings, but you will be driven to succeed and be passionate about all you do. Also be aware that even if you're not expressing emotions, your auric field is so intense that it can affect everyone around you, without your saying a word! If you're feeling up, others are up. If you're down, everyone else is down. So knowing when to socialize and when to retreat is important. And emotional clarity will always guide you — wherever your feelings take you.

13 Channel of the Prodigal 33

From the Self to the Throat

You are the chief witness, called to the world's courtroom to bear testimony about all you've seen, felt, and tasted in life's real dramas. Others can learn from your notes and observations, failures and pain, success and joy. You are the prodigal son who endures all manner of experiences and returns home to be celebrated by a father who insists that all your stories be recounted to a wider audience, so that others can learn from them. In this respect, you are a reporter on life and perceived as a fount of all wisdom.

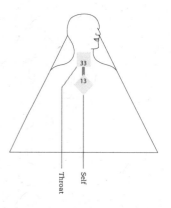

The 13-33 is a "leadership channel," providing direction, creative guidance, and a sense of purpose for others. You can steer people and projects beautifully. Your history helps guide and reassure others through an uncertain future. It finds its voice via the Throat with expressions like "I remember when . . ." or "In my experience, what happens is . . ."

You are a great listener as well as a talkative witness. Your strong sense of identity is fortified by each life experience you absorb and so you become the perfect confidante — and magnet — for everyone's agonies. Friends will cry on your shoulder, seeking reassurance and wanting you to recognize and identify with their dilemmas or challenges. Even relative strangers will off-load problems and then say: "I've no idea why I'm telling you this but . . ." You must fall back on your authority to know when to help and when to steer clear.

In your own life, you take painstaking care to assimilate everything that happens, processing every detail before transforming it into wisdom. That wisdom is your balance and understanding in life. More happens to you in the course of a day than can be processed in a single night's sleep, potentially leaving you open to intense dream patterns. In the waking hours, you'll need to seek opportunities to recuperate, refresh, and meditate.

I wouldn't be surprised to find an archive of journals in your loft, tucked away so that your grandchildren can draw insight and lessons from them. This can breed a certain nostalgia and sentimentality.

You have the ability to read people like a book, sometimes viewing their situations on a much deeper level than even they can grasp. You can startle people with your profound perception and empathy. Thus your wisdom becomes an indispensable counsel. Being around you allows people to know who *they* are and injects purpose into *their* life.

16 Channel of Talent 48

From the Throat to the Spleen

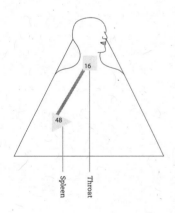

You are a natural-born talent whose creative flair can lead to mastery. Whatever your skills and dreams, you strive for artistic expression with integrity in all arenas — arts, business, or sport. What you come to learn is that true mastery depends on continual practice, training, and repetition — and, just as crucially, having the right support network around you.

The activation with the Spleen means you get a taste for what is right for you in life. There is great depth and skill to your being, and the 16-48 digs deep to mine talent that will ultimately flower, sometimes after months or even years of dedication and commitment.

The question asked by most people with this channel is "How do I sustain myself on the way to mastery?" That query gives voice to a real fear, injected by gate 48, of not having done enough or not knowing enough to get where you want to be. This anxiety then looks around for allies who can inspire you and help fuel your goals with *their* support. Support and encouragement from others, therefore, become your source of sustainability.

The dangers with this channel are twofold: one, you can divert your talent to assist others to make it big; and two, you become a lifetime student, chasing one degree or qualification after another. By all means, keep on developing, researching, refining, refreshing, and practicing, but also know when to trust the completeness of your abilities. You have a talent for almost anything in life, even something as mundane as washing the dishes. You can carry it out perfectly! You come armed with the diligence to get everything absolutely right. Even when it comes to personal relations, you'll keep honing your skills.

Your yearning to turn life into a perfect symphony means there's no need for pointless diversions. There is something clinical about the execution of everything you do. You are always cutting to the chase, getting to the point, wanting to get it right — a cool operator if ever there was one. And, boy, when you do get it right, you are poetry in motion!

17 Channel of the Organizer 62

From the Mind to the Throat

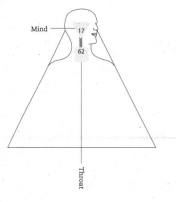

You are an organizer and strategist who expresses logic, someone who absorbs all the facts, details, and politics of a situation and then threads them all together to form your own concrete opinion or recommendation. You will be so well informed that few will doubt the convincing arguments you put forward.

Futuristic think tanks, managerial positions, and any campaign would benefit from your methodical mind, which is forever looking into the future to find solutions for systems, projects, and people. The activation with the Throat emerges as an expression that may sound something like "I think this should happen..." or "I think we should do this..."

Of course, this mind-set means you can be highly opinionated and adopt a forceful debating style. The activation between the Mind and the Throat brings an urgency to speak your mind. So be wary of expressing untimely and unwanted opinions. If you're not selective in this regard, what you have to say may well lose its impact.

I knew a man with this channel who could sit for three hours on end giving his opinions, spouting forth on every facet of life. His captive audiences would sit in awe of the power of his arguments. Then, three days later, he'd return with a modified view, completely undermining what he had set in stone previously! This is typical of the 17-62, because even when you've stated your case, it doesn't mean you won't retreat into your mind once more, review your own argument, and embrace completely different conclusions. You are someone who will continue to investigate everything that confronts you, and your mind is a great asset to you, because it's capable of seeing the way ahead.

18 Channel of Judgment 58

From the Spleen to the Root

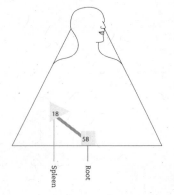

Armed with a perfectionist streak, you scrutinize society, looking for ways to improve everything for the benefit of everyone. You sit in impartial judgment, pointing out what is and what isn't working. It is a continual assessment with the goal of enhancing the social, working, and living environments around you.

Everything from the health service, education system, and economy to the local supermarket and neighbor's garden could and *should* be improved — and you know exactly how! It's an instantaneous judgment that is never considered, because of the spontaneous signals from the Spleen. But there is a tendency to challenge everything and campaign for change for the sake of it. Your intentions are well meant but can lead to misunderstandings, especially if your judgment is misdirected into your personal life. If you don't restrain the 18-58, great conflict can arise in relationships because you'll be viewed as being overcritical. Learn to reserve judgment for the public sector rather than applying it in personal relations.

Your ability to point out where things can be improved is a great asset within companies or communities. You are the consummate consultant, troubleshooter, overseeing authority — and art or restaurant critic, but you can also be your own worst enemy, turning the ever-critical eye inward. You can be needlessly hard on yourself, so I always tell people with this channel to cut themselves some slack and appreciate that not even they can be perfect. Instead, realize that you have the gift of correcting and improving society's failings with your spontaneous recommendations, appraisals, and rulings. Fall back on your authority and make sure you're applying your abilities in the right direction and then you'll feel fulfilled.

19 Channel of Sensitivity 49

From the Root to the Emotions

Compassionate, tactile, sensual, and supersensitive, you naturally feel everyone's wants, needs, and emotions — and know how to meet them. This tends to result in a hands-on approach to everything you do.

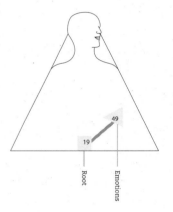

Your emotions are so sensitive that you could wear a blindfold and earplugs and still detect what everyone was feeling around you. Nothing gets past your built-in "feelings antennae," bringing goose bumps to your skin and tears to your eyes. But this also makes you compassionate, fair, and supportive of others.

Pressure from the Root means you feel obliged to reach out, whether requested or not, to assist, encourage, or soothe. This makes you a tower of strength, one of life's pillars holding up the community temple, where you also happen to have organized an event to bring everyone together. A sense of community is important to you in this harsh, insensitive world, so you foster unity and togetherness.

Your test is to balance your own needs with the needs of others. When this is effective and you've honored your own space, it's a win-win situation. The 19-49 puts you and everyone else back on track. But you will need emotional clarity before knowing to what projects and people to attach.

You've also got to appreciate that you will be wounded by the slightest criticism. Sometimes you just need to roll up like a hedgehog and wait for the harsh traffic to pass by.

Your sensitivity is like a magnet of its own, radiating its unique quality with an almost seductive pull. People feel safe in your company. In relationships the 19-49 brings a sensuality that seeks close contact with another and needs to be tactile. The lightest brushing of skin holds its own electricity. That's why your sensitive touch can make you a natural healer, masseur, or Reiki specialist. It probably explains why you also like to hold hands and prefer handshake deals, conducting calm business meetings over food, breaking bread together. You also have an innate affinity to animals. Everyone and everything comes to appreciate your sensitivity!

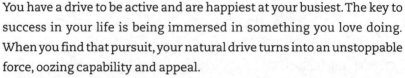

20 Channel of Keeping Busy 34

From the Throat to the Sacral

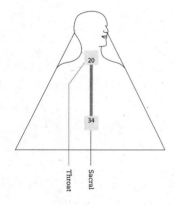

Throat

Sacral

You have a drive to be active and are happiest at your busiest. The key to success in your life is being immersed in something you love doing. When you find that pursuit, your natural drive turns into an unstoppable force, oozing capability and appeal.

Keeping busy, busy, busy — that's what your life is all about, and your charisma shines forth when it finds its joy in the right pursuits, projects, and people. You are a bundle of energy who rarely sits still because a "to do" list covers the deeds that need doing, the mountains that need climbing, and the people who need helping.

This is a Manifesting Generator channel that expresses its power by keeping active 24/7 and doesn't wish to be distracted. Anyone who travels with you in life must be prepared to keep up with your frenetic pace. Walk into a room and your charismatic capability empowers everyone else to become busy. One hour in your company tends to be the required shot in the arm for others. Your mere presence can get things moving.

You are always on the go, from one project or endeavor to another. So the inevitable question is, "Is it enough to be busy for busy's sake?" Absolutely not. It is vital that you be engaged with people and projects you love. Don't succumb to flattery or the fact that people need you on their team. If you are continually jumping from one activity to another without discernment, you'll become an express train without brakes — and will eventually derail. An affirmative gut response will advise which express trains you should drive.

You can nail certificates to the wall, put lots of money in the bank, and collect trophies for the shelf. But *none* of it will matter if the activity doesn't marry with your vision. What matters to you is what you love doing. I can't say it strongly enough, so I'll repeat it again: be aligned with your vision in all that you do!

20 Channel of Involuntary Impulses 57

From the Throat to the Spleen

You are an intuitive, expressive live wire whose impulses guide you through life. You are one step ahead of most people, scanning what's in the present, and unseen future, with an almost X-ray perceptibility. Your acoustic senses detect what sounds truthful about people, projects, and the way ahead. It is an intuition that penetrates most auras, piercing social smokescreens, hidden agendas, insincerity, and risky pursuits. Your senses get to the core of matters because they "hear" what's really being said or offered in any moment. There is no pulling the wool over the eyes — and ears — of the 20-57! Your intuition is too smart, arriving instantly like brain waves, keeping you alert in any environment. As a result, others may observe a "twitching," forever-on-your-toes manner, but it's just the survival mechanism of the Spleen working overtime.

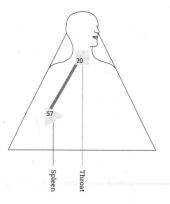

The activation to the Throat means there is an involuntary impulse to your voice and so there is a scattergun tendency in your conversation. You can be in midconversation and suddenly you'll sense an internal jolt or twitch alerting you to something somebody has said or to a situation going on around you. Then you'll launch into a conversation about that instead! Often, what you perceive is completely hidden from everyone else until you relate it to them.

Having involuntary impulses means you must be wary of constant interrupting and talking over people. When you speak out of turn, you can quickly alienate others.

You can also appear anxious, worried about how the future will turn out. Your sense of survival needs to know that you and loved ones are going to be secure and safe. This is what is really motivating your constant reappraising of the world and your role in it. But if you keep your feet on the ground and a sensible restraint on your intuitive gift, your future will always be bright.

21 Channel of Money 45

From the Heart to the Throat

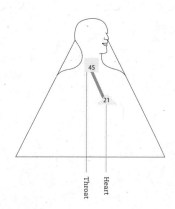

Don't get carried away! Having the money channel does not automatically mean you're going to be a millionaire, but it does mean you have an immense capability to make money.

You are designed to be at home in a material world. When your heart's desire sniffs money, your willpower becomes a driving force to make things happen and generate wealth. Your environment tends to revolve around money matters, positions of power, and prestige. They say money makes the world go round and yet love of money is the root of all evil. Your aim is to strike a balance between the two as you weigh material value against your core values.

You have two choices within this channel: you assume the regal nature of Queen Elizabeth II or you are her prime minister. In other words, to make money happily, you have to differentiate between times when you receive the benefit of allowing others to carry out resourceful work and times when you need to get your hands dirty. Take billionaire Donald Trump, who has this channel: he forever has the option of overseeing his empire or micromanaging it.

Your nature, like his, finds harmony when hard work makes profits for your company, family, or community. You have a tribal value that aims to look after number one but also wishes to financially look after everyone else. You demand a freedom and autonomy to make money in line with your wants and wishes. If you're held back, or in a position without autonomy, you will feel deprived and frustrated.

The flip side is that you can sway toward greed, but if that happens, you'll feel less than wholesome. Your greatest fulfillment and self-esteem come when you are a force for the common good and are recognized for what you manifest.

A classic example of someone with the 21-45 is actress Angelina Jolie, someone with great wealth but immense goodwill. No wonder the UN appointed her its goodwill ambassador to assist in the distribution of resources for millions of refugees.

Oscar Wilde once said that the cynic knows the price of everything but the value of nothing. I would specifically re-word that quote for 21-45 people and say: "You know the cost of everything — but can also know the value of everything, too."

23 Channel of Structuring 43

From the Throat to the Mind

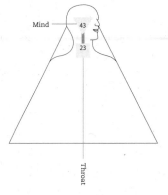

An individual expression gifts you with an insight that breaks new ground and can change how others view the world. You paint the bigger picture for everyone, bringing increased structuring to their lives. Your world is built on a succession of perceptive mental assessments and observations. It's almost as if you have a third eye.

Out of all the thirty-six channels, this is one of the most empowering, because you're forever fizzing with flashes of insight that have an urgency to be articulated because you are, quite literally, someone who speaks your mind. The activation between Mind and Throat brings a need to express your knowing and demonstrate your insights for the awareness of others.

The quality of your expressed insights means you can blow people out of the water — provoking all sorts of reactions! That's because your lucidity can be light-years ahead of most people's. The great task for the 23-43 is to get the message across in a simple, tactful manner.

When an insight is accepted, you are considered a genius, and this chimes with your nature. When people start frowning, you're suddenly viewed as a freak. What appears obvious to you may seem off the wall and incomprehensible to someone else. So first ask yourself: "Is this something people are ready to hear?" and "Am I speaking in turn?"

Oddly enough, the tone of your voice is your greatest ally, and people with the 23-43 have a unique-sounding voice. The tone is always as important as the words you express because it can convey authenticity, confidence, and knowing.

Your test, once you've fallen back on your Human Design authority, is to know the right time to share your transformational insights. Otherwise, you can blurt things out and this can become a social handicap. When unrestrained, you simply blurt out the first thing that comes into your head, be it an insight or a thought. If your mind "sees" a bad haircut, a fashion faux pas, or a terrible mistake at work, it's in constant danger of expressing that truth. But when you learn restraint, speak in turn, and show tact, your thoughts will seem like the considered insights of a genius. You can spark significant paradigm shifts in your working and personal environments, and nothing is more satisfying than knowing you're getting through and transforming the lives of others.

24 Channel of the Thinker 61

From the Mind to the Crown

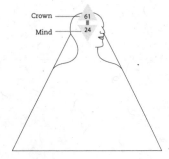

The French would call you Le Penseur, a person carved out of bronze and marble and captured in deep thought in the Musée Rodin in Paris. And just like that famous sculpture, you seem to be frozen in time in intense contemplation, mentally refining everything and anything to find truth.

Auguste Rodin's stunning work was intended to depict a man in sober concentration with an internal mental struggle, just like people with this channel. You are a deep, intellectual thinker who can exhaust yourself, and others, by trying to rationalize everything in life.

The antennae of the Crown are always detecting new inspirations and you want to work it all out in a tireless pursuit of knowledge. I get exhausted just thinking about what goes around your head, over and over in constant review. You think so hard that people can almost hear the wheels turning! There is a pressure to capture an inner truth, but this mental exertion can send you into a maddening whirl. Yet you find it impossible to release your thoughts from the revolving door that traps them inside your head. You have glimpses of truth and knowing, but these rarely become absolute realizations because you insist on returning to the start to review it all over again. It's why you find it hard to switch off at night.

The first thing you must realize is that this is your nature. That acceptance by itself can ease frustration. The second is to practice not becoming a slave to your mind. Enjoy times of silence and quiet reverie. Immerse yourself in soothing music. When the Crown's wheels start spinning, step back from racing thoughts, allowing the Mind to chatter away without your direct participation. This is the first step toward meditation and it's where you'll find great refuge and solace. There is no point believing that the more you think about something, the sooner "the ultimate answer" will dawn. Instead, divert your attention onto the challenges in the lives of other people, or society itself. Your constant reviewing and rationalizing are a great gift when they inspire other minds to join you in thinking outside the box.

25 Channel of Initiation 51

From the Self to the Heart

You are an indomitable force, initiating fresh experiences to propel you and others into new arenas. You know *exactly* where you're heading: toward a bigger and better life.

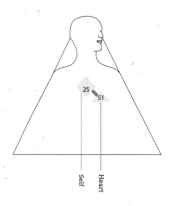

The combination of your heart's desire and self-love means you are determined to penetrate new frontiers, leaping into the unknown and gambling with fate. This attitude instills a tremendous focus in anyone sharing your journey or working with you. The 25-51 also leaves you seeking rewarding, invigorating experiences to satisfy the hunger within your heart and soul, and to become first in all that you do. This makes you fiercely competitive, roaring with displeasure if denied or crossed. In its rawest form, the 25-51 can come across as arrogant, elbowing its way to the front to be first, first, first. Your strong sense of purpose means you seek the highest seat in the chamber and the pole position in all pursuits.

There is also a tendency to act as if people must listen because you come from an all-knowing higher plane. You are highly individualistic by nature and have a mystical air about you. That's because you are a bridge between the material and spiritual worlds.

You are also a great proponent of universal, unconditional love. This more transcendent view of love is sometimes difficult for partners to understand because it's more of a spiritual than physical love. In fact, the incidental matters of romantic love don't necessarily concern people with the 25-51. You don't mean to come across as cool, though those who entertain the drama and movielike notions of romantic love might misinterpret you as such; you just believe that the spread of unconditional love is the only way for the world to grow.

You are someone who can open doors to new possibilities, movements, and organizations, instigating opportunities for the personal and widespread renewal of others. You want to shake up everyone's world as much as yours, believing people can better themselves. You also entertain a sneaking suspicion that everyone else is asleep and you're wide awake! But remember that not all people wish to leave their comfort zones with the same wild abandon as you.

Of course, there is a contradiction between the concept of universal love and the desire to be first all the time. Therein lies the duality within you, caught between the heart's desire and the highest values of the self, someone who stands with one foot in the West and one foot in the East. You might well be described as gutsy and pushy, but then you'll hear: "Your heart's in the right place!"

26 Channel of Enterprise 44

From the Heart to the Spleen

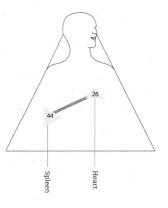

Enterprising by nature, you are someone whose communicative skills and desire strive to improve everything in the world by conveying creative concepts. You are the enterprising salesperson, the enterprising persuader, the enterprising investor, the enterprising messenger. Whatever situation you face, you're innovative in your negotiation and execution, forever cutting your cloth to suit the needs of the moment.

You believe that what you bring to the world can make a difference. You can be the architect who improves a building's design, the salesperson whose product changes the world, or the charmer whose mere presence will rock someone's world. You are a creative being, master manipulator, and charming messenger rolled into one, driven by willpower, seeking to be the best.

Your communication skills, which can sometimes be masked by a court jester attitude of not taking life too seriously, can get to the heart of the matter within seconds. You're able to defuse a conflict, get a message across, or find the tender words that someone is struggling to express. But all your communication, whether it is in the service of diplomacy, sales, or love, can be compelling and persuasive, because what you say comes from the heart. That's why you're great at making the pitch for a project, opportunity, or relationship.

Entrepreneurial by nature, you are instinctive in changing situations, guided by the senses of the Spleen to follow your nose into the right ventures, projects, and company. Once something smells right, you can work your magic to ensure your skills are recognized, your self-interests rewarded, and money made.

Anything and everything you do and receive must be "new and improved." You can even enter personal and business relationships with this mind-set and exit them with choice remarks such as "You won't do better than me!" You are, in your own eyes, the greatest thing since sliced bread. But you'll find that your self-pride will glow more when you're *invited* to make a difference.

You will always be asking yourself whether you're engaged in something for your own gratification or the common good. The moral tussle is played out between the feel-good factor of the Spleen and the ego potential within the Heart. Either way, you're striving to be a facilitator of improvements and believe that people need what you have in your possession, be that a truth, a product, or a creative skill.

27 Channel of Preservation 50

From the Sacral to the Spleen

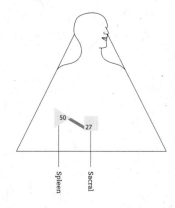

You are a natural caregiver and caretaker, born with a sense of duty to protect and serve. Don't be surprised to find a lot of service people, health givers, nannies, hospital administrators, executive secretaries, and massage therapists with the 27-50 quality. You are always engaged in caring for members of a community by promoting or providing nurturing and the preservation of a way of life.

Your humility will go the extra mile for anyone in need, guided by an instinctive response to nurture, care, and protect. Your impulse in life is to take care of everyone and remain open, and to work for the preservation of humanity. It's as if you've entered into a social contract with yourself to put your needs secondary to those of everyone else.

Friends and family will no doubt observe how you're always mothering someone or forever wanting to look after people. But you derive great satisfaction when your duty and care nourish or protect people. It is a tribal instinct. It even stretches to the caretaker whose job is to preserve a caregiving institution or community club. In some cases, the preservation of a way of life and community projects is just as important as the nurturing of citizens themselves.

The Spleen's alertness and your gut response will tell you what situations and people merit your doting attention. Tuning in to your senses and confirming them with a gut response is where you'll derive your satisfaction. Otherwise, you risk being taken for granted.

Indeed, there is a risk that you'll overreach by putting others before yourself. In relationships, this can lead to an imbalance with partners, so you must ensure that you receive as much as you give. You're always catering to the well-being and happiness of others, even when it comes to sex. Be wary of turning yourself into a workhorse, running around trying to care for everyone; otherwise, you can become spent and frustrated. Preservation is an essential quality for any community, and people around you are lucky to have your trustful and considerate presence.

28 Channel of Struggle 38

From the Spleen to the Root

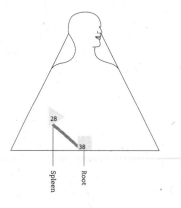

You are a champion of individuality, standing up and fighting for what you know to be right, regardless of the odds and rules against you. A stubborn individuality means that life can seem like an eternal struggle as you rail and campaign against the world and its unfairness. I would almost describe you as a rebel without a cause, except you do have a cause: it's the empowerment of the individual.

Stubbornness is a rough old word that conjures up the image of a stubborn mule. But for you it is a gift, empowering you and others to fight for fairness and stand your ground, no matter what the odds, or the antagonistic forces opposing you. It's almost as if the best thing you can hear is "It can't be done." Nothing will make you dig your heels in more and get you moving toward the accomplishment of mission impossible, as you mumble to yourself: "You just *watch* me!"

Have you ever been in a gale that is so strong it almost knocks people off their feet? Now imagine walking into such a wall of wind. That is an illustration of what life can feel like for people with the 28-38. It requires poise, balance, and determination to keep moving forward, step by steady step.

Fortunately, you have an intuitive sense that knows what things and people are worth fighting for. Indeed, you are someone who could walk into a foreign country, see the rights of its people being denied, and want to start a resistance movement, banging your campaign drum as loudly as you can. There is something of David in you, always looking to take on Goliath, and this can lead to a tendency to fight everyone and everything. It's a level of inner resistance that people around you may well struggle to understand. "It's always you versus the world!" they might say as you thumb your nose at convention and rule systems. But you can be deaf to others' input as you attune to what sounds right for you.

This is simply your individualistic nature. You'll swim upstream when everyone else is heading downstream, and you'll climb in the window when you could have used the front door. It's just you demonstrating your individuality and saying: "I do things *my* way."

The difficulty is that your standards in life might not be realistic. Your fulfillment comes from knowing which battles to take on and which to leave alone. Otherwise, the indefatigable spirit of the campaigner may well be taken advantage of, leaving you frustrated and depleted. In your personal life, leave your struggles on the doorstep — don't invite them into everything you witness in the home. And then you can sit back, fish out the old Frank Sinatra album, dig in your heels, and start singing "My Way!"

29 Channel of Discovery 46

From the Sacral to the Self

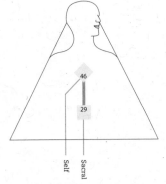

"OK, here comes the whirlwind. Life's going to get interesting, so fasten your seat belts and hang on to your hats!" When someone says this, you can bet that a 29-46 has just entered the scene, bringing the potential to embrace success.

You are someone who is here to immerse yourself in the discoveries of life — if only you can ditch the attached expectations. These days, everyone wants guarantees of success before committing, but with this channel, you're designed to dive in without thinking and derive the value of the experience itself. And then you'll find something magical happens: success naturally finds you. It's as if the Universe hears that you're in it for the value of the experience and wishes to reward you for what life intended. It also knows there is a natural potential, locked within the Sacral, for you to succeed where others fail. Post that motto on your door or desk: "I succeed where others fail."

The truth of this channel is that if you commit to the right people and projects, the sky is the limit. But therein lies the key: the activation to the Self means it's vital that you have clarity and passion for what you're doing. Then the potent mix of life-force energy with love of the physical dance of life generates such a whirlwind and such dedication that failure is out of the question. Once you receive an affirmative gut response to engage, the clock goes out the window as you become an all-consumed embodiment of what you're doing, losing yourself in the experience. Nothing can distract you, and the Channel of Discovery is intended to embrace success, because with that rare combination of energy and passion motoring within, you're the one person who can make it happen.

It is a sight to behold as you dissolve into the totality of an experience, and partners must learn to appreciate your all-consumed nature. I compare it to watching the mystical dance of a whirling dervish. It starts slowly but, as the tempo and music quicken, the dervish spins so fast that the dancer disappears, becoming the whirl.

The 29-46 is one of four "tantric channels." Although *tantra* is a word often associated with sex, it actually denotes the potential for transmuting energy from a lower to higher form. With the 29-46, you turn the ordinary into the extraordinary. This is why you'll have countless people seeking your input to launch their own rockets. Use your gut response to commit correctly and selectively, and immerse yourself in one experience at a time. Do this, and a life of fulfilling discovery and success is within reach every time.

30 Channel of Recognition 41

From the Emotions to the Root

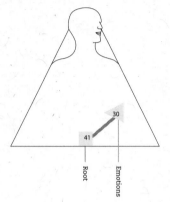

Root   Emotions

A focused imagination makes you one of life's pioneering visionaries with a passion to build a better future in the interests of everyone. Visionaries are often pushing forward concepts that go beyond the reach of collective foresight, but you believe your dreams for the future can become reality and you're passionate about figuring out the way ahead. Mission statements fill your life. You have a clear vision of how things should be.

Such visions usually reside in people who work in social, political, artistic, or spiritual fields, constructing a new future, regardless of whether it seems realistic at the time. There is an urgency for others to see what you see and share your passion to make it a reality. Such recognition becomes your empowerment.

It's extremely hard to get your attention at times because you are so wrapped up in your own world that nothing else matters. Nor can people easily read your moods because you are engaged in an internal struggle to determine whether your glass is half full or half empty. As you entertain great visions for the future, you can also experience dramatic changes in mood. It's why most people with this channel need a steadying hand nearby. But you know that the story of human experience is not complete and want to write the new chapters, so you will thread together pieces of your imagination, dreams, and visions and set about the task with intensity.

Your fulfillment comes from having the emotional clarity to follow through with your dreams, detached from expectation. Giving your best is all you can do. Just put your dreams out there in the Universe and seek a collective interest, and you never know what fascination you could attract. With sufficient backing, you can wait to see how the dreams work out, learning to enjoy the experience of making others believe and painting a future that invigorates them.

It is no surprise that U.S. president Barack Obama has this channel. He puts his dreams out there for the world to capture and hopes everyone sees what he has long before envisioned. Anyone who backed his dream in the election in November 2008 will have seen something of his visions and joined in to keep him on the right track.

32 Channel of Transformation 54

From the Spleen to the Root

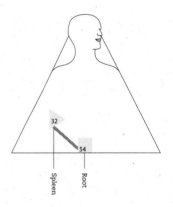

You are immensely driven and determined to succeed through applying yourself — and finding the right people who can help you climb the career ladder. You sometimes sense a power greater than yourself thrusting you forward and upward.

Your motto is almost "I'll make it to the top—no matter what it takes!" Material or spiritual success matters to you and you're forever scouring your environment to find the allies and connections that can help you get there.

This fierce ambition is fueled by a fear of failure, injected by gate 32, and this means there is a tendency for you to become a workaholic. You can be the last out of the office or putting in overtime, determined to impress the boss or hit the latest sales or performance targets.

You're here to expand and compete to be the best in life. The 32-54 is the Channel of Transformation because it can shake up your life and all those around you once your advancement kicks in. You have a compulsion to succeed, and your contacts book is brimming with connections to those who can assist your ascent into a position of power and wealth. You are all about power meetings in the boardroom and behind-the-scenes chats that can fast-track your life. But, as a result, the one question you're forever asking yourself in business and social circles is "Can this person help get me where I want to be?" In this regard, you follow the senses of the Spleen and follow your nose. If you trust those senses, you'll be guided to the right connections.

You bring transformation into the lives of everyone you meet and can find yourself in great demand. That's because people know you'll work all hours and schmooze away to make things happen. So make sure you engage in all situations from a well-adjusted win-win perspective and not from a need of selfish gain. When you find this balanced approach, you will discover that everyone willingly gathers to support your causes.

34 Channel of Power 57

From the Sacral to the Spleen

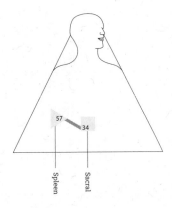

This channel is all about embracing the power of now — and acting on it. You are a true force with the potential for greatness — and the power to bring about change.

The connection between the raw energy of the Sacral and the survival instincts of the Spleen mean you are a born powerhouse with an empowering intuition. When responding correctly to your senses, you are awesome in your swift and decisive actions.

No one is better at getting things done in a crisis than the 34-57, because the spontaneity of the Spleen's senses means you're jumping into action in an instant to save the day, galvanizing everyone else's activities as you go. It is a power drawn to taking action to help others in distress with senses as alert as those of a superhero. Your intuition responds to cries for help and wades into action in the interests of the survival of yourself and everyone else. It is a power capable of resurrecting the lives of anyone living in a disempowered way, down on their knees. You can also give systems, situations, and companies the kiss of life if the purpose resonates with you. If you start a new job at 9 A.M., you'll be starting the revolution by 9:05, as you hit your stride.

The unique combination of mighty energy and gentle intuition means you wield your powerful hand in a velvet glove. Your energy gets everyone upstanding and moving toward the achievement of great things, propelled by your voice yelling: "Go, go, go! Now, now, now!"

You already know that your considerable abilities and energy are sought out by others, but realize the need for discretion in how to use them. Bringing healing and well-being into the lives of those around you can be a naturally wonderful sensation, but remember to look after your own needs first!

Former British prime minister Margaret Thatcher has this channel, and look at the power she wielded to bring about the "Thatcher revolution." Whatever you think of her decisions, the "Iron Maiden" felt Britain had its nose in the mud when she took power in 1979 and wanted it back on its feet. So she set about making it happen, with an eye on bettering its future. This is a natural response of the 34-57, taking action for the long-term good that might even become a lasting legacy.

35 Channel of Versatility 36

From the Throat to the Emotions

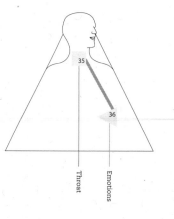

Get ready to experience everything! You have an insatiable thirst for life's experiences and are probably walking around in a T-shirt that declares: "Been there, done that!" There is something transient and short-lived about all that you do because an urgency to live life to the fullest leaves you in a constant search for stimulation. It's an insatiability that covers all areas: living locations, relationships, jobs, travel…and sex.

You may well be described as a "jack-of-all-trades, master of none," because this quest for fresh experiences turns you into a very versatile and highly charged being. You are a passionate individual with something of the thrill seeker about you as you challenge your own beliefs about being able or allowed to do something. In this respect, you are often torn between being driven and feeling trepidation. The value and importance of an experience won't even be considered until you've thrown yourself into it and emerged out the other side to consider what it all meant. You're not interested in the final destination — it's the enjoyment of the journey that counts, taking each day as it comes and keeping it fresh. This is what makes you feel alive! Sometimes you even invent crises just to feel the thrill of drama and change.

You are driven by an urge to cram as much into life as possible because there is a desperate urge to keep progressing. But there is also the fear that time is short and you don't want to miss out. This makes you a barrel of fun to be around but can lead to confusion and pain in your private life as partners struggle to understand your need for new horizons and challenges. You'll be forever hearing "I thought you loved this job" or "I thought you liked living here" or "I thought we had something going between us." You'll need to maintain honesty in your relationships, keeping people continually informed of your intention to be a constant wanderer.

You must also learn to trust your emotional clarity before jumping into new experiences for the sake of it, because a great sense of anticipation can lead to huge disappointment when an experience doesn't meet expectations.

Recognize that you have a great talent to play out all things human and you can be a leading light for anyone seeking to experience life's varied intensity. But know that the greatest wisdom to be gained is finding the patience and contentment to live out only the experiences that resonate within you. Then your thirst for progression will be satisfied. Well, almost...

37 Channel of Community 40

From the Emotions to the Heart

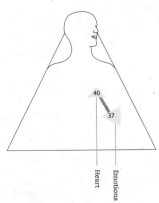

Heart

Emotions

Your word is your bond and you wish to live in a community called Trust and Fairness, viewing the world as a large family. As you seek purpose in life, you need like-minded allies who support your goals. You build bonds on the foundations of trust and honesty, where everyone pitches in and pulls his or her weight. These values underpin all your relationships and associations. This channel is tribal, and you need the right company if fulfillment and success are to be achieved. If you fall in with the wrong people, life tends to go pear shaped.

Your aim is to bring everyone onto the same page, using the same values, desires, and emotions to build a strong, interconnected family, marriage, business, or community. You are the parent whose heart swells when everyone gathers together for a family dinner or when a marriage is built on a mutual sense of give-and-take.

Some people might describe you as touchy-feely because you are naturally tactile — shaking hands, sharing hugs, and throwing arms around friends and family, being inclusive. You also have a distinctive winning smile — a smile that literally wins people over, brings reassurance, and makes everyone feel included. It wins friends — and influences people!

You need to know you can trust the people around you. That's why you prefer a handshake deal before a written contract, so you can look the person in the eye and sense their sincerity. You prefer a friendly discussion over dinner to the austerity of a boardroom. In fact, you seek to make friends with the people you work or conduct business with, forever seeking true allies.

You have zero tolerance for people who renege on a deal, sometimes banishing them from your life. If people let you down, you can freeze them out. You are someone of your word and expect others to be the same.

People like you are the glue of communities and can often be found rallying the troops at the local church, village hall, town hall, or sports club. When projects run like clockwork and people are working and laughing together, your nature sings. You, in turn, then bring reliance, honesty, and stability, which is warming in today's world.

39 Channel of Emoting 55

From the Root to the Emotions

"All the world's a stage" is how the melancholic Jacques begins Shakespeare's play *As You Like It*, before going on to say: "Sighing like a furnace, with a woeful ballad." It is a monologue illustrating the different stages of

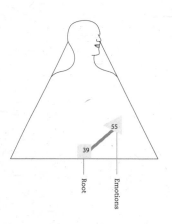

life, from infancy to old age, with all the associated emotions. Shakespeare could have written it with 39-55 in mind. Your life can sometimes feel like a great tragedy or a great joy — and all the roles are delivered with passion.

So dramatic are your mood swings that you can sometimes struggle to get a handle on matters. Whereas the 12-22 has an ability to *express* emotions via the Throat, you don't have that natural outlet. Instead, your emotions are stirred by pressure from the Root, driving them nowhere — except inside you! It's not so much an emotional wave you experience but an emotional spike, like markings on the Richter scale. And yet this intense drive means you are passionate about anything you do, digging deep to give your all and best. It is two sides of the same coin: emotions that take you to deep, dark places and yet provide access to the highest levels of creativity.

You are acoustically tuned, so soothing music will be your greatest diversion and solace, something to hang on to.

When you're down in the dumps, no one can help you feel better, regardless of their best efforts, and this can be distressing for partners, who may struggle to understand. That's why I tell people with this channel to find a space all their own to which they can withdraw. Your mood will shift when it is good and ready. These are the seasons of your emotions you must learn to accept.

The sooner you accept that life is going to be profound, the easier it will become. Honor your emotions. Make them your friend. Celebrate your emotional depth as the unique gift of a fully experienced life. And recognize that when you are down in the dumps, your creativity will shine. Just as the brightest stars shine in the highest sky, so the brightest diamonds come from the deepest mines.

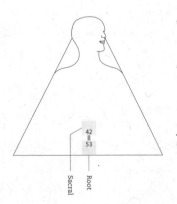

42 Channel of Cycles 53

From the Sacral to the Root

Just as the moon orbits the Earth in a lunar cycle, so you travel through life in a personal cycle that results in progressive growth and wisdom.

Everything, from career and relationships to living situations, requires a beginning, middle, and end and needs to be a fully completed experience.

This is the third format channel, and it implies that everything in your life happens in cycles, ranging from days to weeks to years. Some lives are ruled by five- or seven-year cycles. If you were to look back on your life, you, too, would be able to identify a sequence of cycles. One friend with the 42-53 had a Human Design reading and noticed that all his relationships, job changes, and house moves fell into five-year cycles. They were, he said, "the changing seasons" within his life.

These cycles mean it is vitally important that you know which cycles to commit to. Once you are committed, the Sacral energy will lock you in until matters have gone full circle. It is like a motorized wheel. You can't throw a stick in its spokes, and if you do, you'll just have to go back to the beginning and start again because the cycles of your life experience *have to be* completed to find their meaning and propel you to the next level. So you cannot afford to waste time spinning in wrong cycles. An affirmative gut response will guide you to the correct people, projects, and places.

The inherent propulsion within this channel also means you are good at getting other people airborne with projects. Viewing life in cycles yourself, you always encourage new beginnings and advancement for others. So anyone seeking a change in direction or wanting to take his or her life to the next level can get great energy from your launchpad. Of course, if committed to the wrong people and projects, you spend far too much time propelling others into the stratosphere while remaining earthbound yourself. Again, rely on your built-in gut response mechanism to ensure your own evolution is not ignored.

The Channel of Cycles is like a book: it has a beginning, middle, and end, and you only want to select it from the bookshelf if you're going to complete it. There's no point getting halfway through and losing interest. And so it is with the story of your life — careers, locations, partnerships, and marriages. You will feel a pressure to perform or get involved in many things, but only select those that resonate clearly with you. Then, don't fret about *how* the story ends; just enjoy the journey. That way, you'll derive fulfillment, happiness, and abundance from all the cycles you've properly engaged with.

47 Channel of Abstract Thinking 64

From the Mind to the Crown

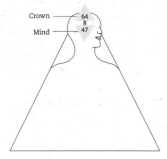

If a tree falls in the woods and no one is there to hear it, does it still make a sound? Many would say, "Who *really* cares?" Well, you do, because it's a question that can give your abstract mind hours of fun.

Your mind loves wrestling with the abstract to try to make sense of everything in life. You consider shapes, colors, textures, and intangible concepts. You immerse yourself in a great pondering of history and philosophy. You become absorbed by theories and past cultures. You want to work out what it all means in order to help mold and update systems and beliefs in the modern world. Life is one great mystery that you are determined to solve.

If the 24-61 is about rationalizing and tracking down reason, the 47-64 is about making sense of the sometimes incomprehensibly profound, with questions such as "What is the meaning of life?" You could quite happily lock yourself away with great texts or tomes and devour every page to find nuggets of truth that bring about *meaning,* but this can lead to either crystal clarity or tying yourself in knots.

The ideas you emerge with may risk being incoherent to others and can sound ideological, but you are driven by the belief that a mental realization could transcend everyday understanding and turn on a giant lightbulb for humanity. And yet you also derive pleasure and solace from the thought or theory itself, whether or not it comes to anything.

Abstract thinking, by its very nature, tends to happen during moments of quiet solitude. Sometimes realizations happen just before bed or in the middle of the night when the bulb turns on inside your head and you suddenly comprehend something you'd been pondering for weeks.

Often you are able to resolve issues for others but less able to solve your own. But always know that you are a great thinker with the potential at least to inspire — and that's what keeps you going!

Uniquely You

All thirty-six channels form the pathways linking the energy within all of us, the inner wiring that makes us individual. Some people can have no active channels, or just one, and others can, theoretically, have up to seventeen. Quantity is unimportant. What matters is the information that makes *you* uniquely you.

Also remember that, because our designs are forever interacting, your inactive channels will mesh with the active channels in others, so you'll intermittently feel their varying influences. Just remain aware of what is consistent within *your* design.

How our designs interweave and fit with others is one of the fascinating aspects of Human Design. And such potential synergy becomes even more relevant as we examine those channels where the color runs only to a halfway point. Because this means we're starting to open the sixty-four "gates of truth."

6

Gates
of Truth
The Sixty-Four Gates

E mpowering, mesmerizing, and amazing...

Rachel, Brisbane, Australia

There's a $64-million question at the heart of this chapter relating to the sixty-four "gates of truth." The question always centers on what gates you have turned on, and the answers reveal the individual attributes, predispositions, and attitudes you'll carry through life. Here's where we get to examine more of the nitty-gritty and minutiae of the person you are.

These sixty-four gates are inspired by the sixty-four hexagrams of the *I Ching* and stand at either end of a channel, each representing a trait, emotion, or tendency that you are conscious of (when colored black), that's a hidden characteristic (when colored pink), or that you are both aware and unaware of (when colored black and pink).

What is particularly fascinating here is that research has already informed the world that there is a direct link between the sixty-four hexagrams of the *I Ching* and the sixty-four genetic codons, a discovery made by a German physician, Dr. Martin Schönberger, who explained his findings in his 1973 book, *The Hidden Key to Life*. He demonstrated, by drawing specific parallels, the similarities between the structure of a hexagram and the syntax of DNA.

Schönberger was not alone in chipping away at this breakthrough. Six years previously, a doctor named Marie-Louise von Franz had speculated that there might be some credence to the belief of a structural link between the *I Ching* and DNA codons.

Such research was the beginning of the realization that DNA holds information that, even today, has probably not been fully tapped. It shone light on the fact that the sixty-four hexagrams, and now the sixty-four gates of the Human Design system, are an accurate description of human nature. There is no better illustration of science meeting spirituality.

What needs to be noted is this: the numbers scattered around the body within the life chart represent gates 1 through 64. Everybody's design has these numbers in exactly the same location. If there is a colored section running from a number to halfway along the channel, this means that gate is activated, representing an embedded part of your makeup. If there is no color emanating from a number, that gate is not activated and is not an embedded part of your makeup. So remember half-colored channels are not defined but the colored gate is activated and has the potential to connect with the gate at the other end of the channel in someone else's design.

What's particularly interesting is that as well as showing our individual distinguishing marks, life charts can illustrate what differentiates us from others and what connects us. Once you have singled out the messages contained within your gates, you can set about discovering the gates of truth within your nearest and dearest, or potential love interests, to discover the common ground, the dynamics, and compatibilities in any relationship or association. Then you can draw parallels between your gates and those of friends, family members, partners, and business associates. What I'm particularly drawing to your attention are what we call electromagnetics and friendships.

Electromagnetics

It happens when meeting certain people that you get a sensation of sparks flying between you. This comes about when one person has the gate activated at one end of a channel and the other person has the gate activated at the other. So, for example, you have gate 59 on and your partner has the opposing 6 — welcome to sparks flying in the bedroom!

In Human Design, we call this an "electromagnetic connection" because it is seen as an interaction where there is a magnetism. It can feel like a rush of energy in an otherwise quiet part of your being. The more of these connections there are in a relationship, the more intense the chemistry. What I would say is that no relationship would want too many of these connections, though, because they can cause an overload of electricity leading to blowouts that are not conducive to long-term love. It's a bit like having too much ice cream — too much of a good thing. But, of course, it's all subjective. So much depends on what else is going on within your design, and the detail of these connections is a subject for another time. For now, simply appreciate that these connections are a positive sign and enjoy the electric charge!

Friendship

When you share the same activated gate, or indeed the same defined channel, with someone, this suggests harmony and common ground within your relationship. That's why it denotes "friendship." It is as though both parties are looking through the same window at the same view in their lives.

I always say that shared gates provide the essential glue that holds a relationship or friendship together when the going gets tough. It suggests the compatibility and strong foundations on which any association can thrive. So if you ever ask yourself, "What do we have in common?" these are the areas that provide the clearest answer. I would suggest that a sound partnership is when there is a healthy mix of both friendships and electromagnetics — then you really are on a firm footing.

Conscious and Unconscious

If any gate is colored black to halfway across the channel, it indicates a conscious trait in you whose meaning and influence should be readily obvious to you. If it's colored pink, the trait is unconscious in you and probably more recognizable to friends and family. The striped combination of pink and black signals unconscious aspects with a conscious overlay; you are part aware, part not and have the means to observe and utilize your unconscious attributes consciously.

Extra Dimensions

If you have no gates turned on within a particular center, check out the "Extra Dimension" notes at the bottom of the relevant section. When no gates are on in a center, that center is referred to as "open" as well as undefined, bringing an extra dimension to its meaning. This also makes it extrasensitive to the conditioning influences of other designs. Each footnote, therefore, will explain what each open center means.

Now, look at your life chart to determine what gates you have turned on and explore these additional facets of your nature.

You will, inevitably, find parallels between the traditional descriptions of the *I Ching* hexagrams and some of the Human Design interpretations I present here. We'll now dissect those meanings one by one, center by center, starting with the lower numbers and moving to the higher each time... because each gate tells its own story about you.

GATES WITHIN THE CROWN

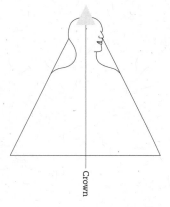

Crown

Gate 61
The Gate of Inner Truth

Your urgency is to determine what is authentic in life and ensure that everything remains on a genuine path. The Crown's pressure demands that all you deal with be true. Inner Truth is like the pointer on a compass; it indicates itself to you as a sensation where you "just know" something is right and to follow it. This gate filters what is truth and what is nonsense, what is genuine and what is fake. There is no conning someone like you!

Inner truth often arrives in a flash of inspiration during a moment of inner stillness. Becoming familiar with this sensation helps guide you toward integrity. It doesn't matter what chaos surrounds you; this gate is all about knowing what is authentic and true.

Some of the inspirations that come through gate 61 may have a lasting impact on the lives of others, bringing them epiphanies, penetrating *their* minds with *your* knowing. Trust that truth will reveal itself as you consider and contemplate, for your own benefit and that of others. You can rely on this resolute "sword of truth" to provide inner reassurance in all situations.

Gate 63
The Gate of Doubts

You are constantly surveying your environment to work out what doesn't appear right. You are, by nature, a doubting Thomas. "Is this right for me?" "Will this work out?" "Did I do that job right?" The Crown's pressure streams doubt into your head and you are constantly questioning the validity and effectiveness of things, and even yourself, attempting to be forewarned of any pitfalls or shortcomings in concepts or projects. You will question something until you are satisfied that doubt can no longer exist. Sometimes, this can make you overly hesitant or uncertain.

In terms of assessments for business and safety issues, this can be a great asset, but know that such critical perception will not be so appreciated in your personal life. Having doubts about everything and everyone can become irksome, so understand this gate is *collective* in its perception, not personal. You are often just providing a viewpoint from which others can qualify their life circumstances.

Also appreciate that not every apparently logical outcome needs to be entertained. This will provide a clearer view of the future, with all its potential pitfalls, to help you and others navigate a safe way through life.

Gate 64
The Gate of Diverse Possibilities

As with all the gates within the Crown, this brings the pressure to examine life, and you will find yourself poring over the countless constellations of Diverse Possibilities. It's like looking into the night sky, reaching for a star, taking it in your hand, dissecting it, and attempting to find profound meaning. You'll take anything apart and turn everything inside out to grasp its significance or value.

This gate dwells in possibility, pondering all potentials and "what ifs" in search of advancement. So you can find yourself trapped in a constant quest to examine everything — religions, histories, philosophies, belief systems, and previously recorded truths or scriptures — seeking a breakthrough or new understanding. Some people with this gate can become overwhelmed by life's possibilities, forever working out what is relevant to them and whether further exploration is required. Your inquisitiveness is endlessly inquiring.

Remember that life is a mystery you'll never solve, so don't tie yourself up in knots, grappling with the conundrums you've set yourself. Acknowledge your mental pressure, cast off from the shore of expected certainty, and move into the currents of the unknown and unknowable, for it is there that you will find yourself and discover the *meaning* of the wondrous journey of life.

Extra Dimension

With no gates on, the Crown center is open as well as undefined, making you open to all kinds of influences and requiring you to be wary of getting swept away by flights of fancy and other people's inspirations. It also makes you a medium for all things inspiring, and you'll no doubt feel energized when surrounded by rousing people, art, music, and wildlife. You'll recognize the correct inspirations to follow by trusting your own authority.

GATES WITHIN THE MIND

Gate 4
The Gate of Mental Solutions

This gate will attempt to fix anything, anytime, anyhow, any way. Perhaps you are described as a Mr. or Mrs. Fix-It, but you can sometimes find solutions to problems that don't even exist! With this gate on, your mind *must* be kept active and *must* have something to resolve, be it a crisis at work or a drama in someone's life. You love nothing more than someone handing you a problem to solve, even if it's a crossword! But when your mind cannot grasp something, you can become anxious.

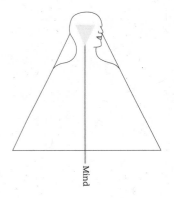

With such pressure, there is a tendency to get overly fixated about the worth of your solutions. So learn to lighten up. A brilliant mind can be a great gift or too clever for its own good. "You seem to have an answer for everything!" is not necessarily a compliment. Sometimes, people don't seek a solution; they just want to get something off their mind.

What the solution mechanism within gate 4 needs is the fuel of problems, be they real or perceived. So what you need to do is sort the wheat from the chaff and focus on the relevant matters in life. What solutions do you really need? This is your pathway to increased satisfaction.

Gate 11
The Gate of Harmony

This gate is rich with imagination, cultivating ideas capable of bringing about social harmony. It is involved with the promotion and teaching of peace and consideration between people, always seeking new ways of bringing everyone into agreement in the home, the workplace, relationships, or the environment.

You are forever thinking of new ideas to keep things fresh and evolving. You easily dispense with outdated methods or concepts that no longer seem relevant. In your eyes, the power of consensus is far greater than the power of an individual. That explains why your ideas tend to be in the interests of the collective, as opposed to only yourself.

You're also someone who will remind the individual of their responsibilities to everyone else. Conservationist Al Gore has this gate on, which is why he has been banging his drum about individuals contributing to the well-being of the Earth by being more environmentally responsible. With a balanced view of the bigger picture, you, too, are capable of pushing ideas that can strengthen the world around you. The motto of this gate is "Change for the better."

Gate 17
The Gate of the Following

Life is a stream of agreements and disagreements and requires a certain degree of flexibility if we are to find accord in social environments — and there is no better diplomat or debater than you! Gate 17 is not afraid of being strongly opinionated but also entertains a broad spectrum of views about all aspects of life. So you love nothing more than your opinions being tested and can encourage fair debate that hears both sides of any story. This logical thinking allows a fostering of cooperation and understanding between all opposing sides and foes, be that in your own circles or the world at large. And in all situations you can be both forceful and fair.

You're likely to entertain opinions about almost everything and to ponder them while always remaining alert to the input of others. The flip side is that you sometimes become dogmatic and fixed in your views. But your mind just needs to remain open without attachment to any strident views.

There is a natural inclination within you to be fair, balanced, and impartial. What matters to you is the quality of the life you envisage and you're quick to follow the views of anyone who can show you a way of enhancing it.

Gate 24
The Gate of Returning

This gate returns to rake over old ground in a bid to rationalize everything. It is engaged in constant rewind and review, like a spool of tape playing over and over until continual refinement leads to the ultimate answer. You have an intense, preoccupied, forensic mind that always insists on returning to the starting point of a situation to determine its worth, find a missing clue, or understand a key message. Maybe people complain, "Can't you just leave it alone?!" You are the detective who can't crack the case and repeatedly revisits the same old avenues, conceptualizing and theorizing and eliminating all erroneous matters until you get it.

This means you can become set in your ways, holding on to old perspectives because you know them so well. What you must realize is that the Mind is a thought-process factory and should be kept open to process new materials and new possibilities. Otherwise, your mind will forever spin in circles and get nowhere.

As your thoughts revolve, this gate does offer potential bursts of insight. It is designed to rewind and review to find such moments. So eliminate old ways and ideas and see the fresh turning points in life. Embrace them and, as with cleaning a dirty window, you'll get a fresh view of your life.

Gate 43
The Gate of Breakthrough

It's as if you have a voice inside your head, always ready to deliver deep insights that will constitute a breakthrough capable of making a difference to a work project or to people's lives. You receive brilliant flashes of pure knowing, but often it seems that no one around you understands matters on your level. You can be one step ahead of everyone else and yet unable to express your insights clearly. As a result, you can find yourself challenged in converting them into coherent language. At such times, trust your authority. When honoring your authority, you'll be able to naturally convey your breakthroughs without thinking about it and access profound wisdom with universal truths capable of shifting people's entire perspective.

You don't suffer fools gladly. What you'll find, when you're interacting with different people or situations, is that insights will arrive. The wisdom comes in knowing whether it's timely to communicate those insights.

This gate can actually become stubbornly wrapped up in its own insights and unconcerned with the thoughts of others. The point here is that your insights cannot be swayed; they just need to be appreciated. So staying resolute to your own truth and being patient is the way to nurture your nature.

What you must appreciate is that your insights are novel and it may take time for the penny to drop with others. It's as though your inner ear tunes in to things that others cannot hear.

Gate 47
The Gate of Realization

This gate leaves you thinking, thinking, thinking, trying to work out life's great puzzles, seeking realizations that turn lightbulbs on inside your head. It is the story of that great thinker and mathematician Archimedes, who was given the task of determining if the king's crown was pure gold or cheap alloy dressed as gold. With that puzzle on his mind, he eased into a full bathtub and noticed that his body weight made the water run over the brim. Thus came the realization that he could solve his puzzle by dropping the crown into water to determine whether its weight matched that of pure gold. He had the realization and went running naked through the streets shrieking, "Eureka!"

Such inspiring moments are your ultimate quest because you are a born problem solver. You tend to think in an abstract way. I suspect colleagues or partners often hear your mind working overtime before you punch the air with the words "I've got it!" Finding relaxation is your key to such breakthroughs. So take a leaf from Archimedes' book and step aside from your thoughts into a place of calm. It's like trying to find a sensible solution on the end of your nose using a telescope — you need to step far enough away to see it. For you, relaxation can lead to pure ingenuity.

Extra Dimension

With no gates on, the Mind center is open as well as undefined, making you, quite literally, the most open-minded person of all. You can sometimes feel overwhelmed by everyone else's thoughts and you're always picking up on a thought or idea that is thrown your way and deciding whether it is worthy of investigation. This openness means your mind is capable of profound reflection on what everyone else is thinking about. But you need to be wary of getting sucked into other people's mental chatter. Fall back on your authority to determine which ideas are worth exploring or expanding on.

GATES WITHIN THE THROAT

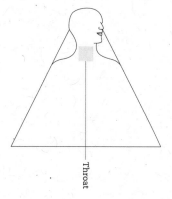

Throat

Gate 8
The Gate of Contribution

You are someone constantly looking to make a valuable contribution to a cause or project, either through your involvement, inspiration, or a marketable promotion. The inherent honesty of this characteristic always asks, via the Throat: "Can I help?" or "Is there anything I can do?"

You don't like sitting around doing nothing or occupying the sidelines with incidental matters. You need to be in the thick of the action. You always seek to make a difference with your contribution — and galvanize others through cooperative input. That's why there is a tendency with gate 8 to take charge and direct people into new territory. It's a voice that expresses possibilities in an empowering direction.

Of course, it is one thing to constantly donate time and energy, but it is quite another to follow through and commit. This gate is not necessarily about involvement but is about pointing the way ahead. So be wary about volunteering your services as a matter of course. Sometimes, if others are not ready for your novel and creative approach in life, you could put a few noses out of joint. Yet you are often the glue that holds projects and relationships together, reminding everyone of the great vision you are working toward and fostering both loyalty and respect.

Gate 12
The Gate of Standstill

This gate makes you naturally cautious or sheepish about most things in life. It emerges as a voice that expresses concern as "I'm a bit cautious about this…" or "I'm not sure about that…" and you will sometimes appear reticent about striding forward in life. You often have to stand aside from the mad rush to work out your next move. Are you here to trudge through life and focus on all the hazards? Or can you be allowed to dream and aspire to greater things? Generally, you will always err on the side of caution, sometimes unsure what it is that you are feeling.

There is a strong but cautious tone when you speak, and this can frustrate some people. That's because from your place of standstill in a world that's running around in circles, you get a sense of what is coming, making you wary about things that might appear unproblematic to everyone else. Conversely, it can make you chase things that go beyond the bounds of ordinary imagination. Gate 12 dares you to dream, sometimes unrealistically, of a fairer, more idealistic world.

From Standstill comes the potential to make great leaps in the evolution and expansion of human endeavor — and the equal potential to dither and procrastinate because your vision can extend farther than you sense you can jump. You know, though, that when you do speak, what you can say can move people and inject confidence in them, because they know you've exercised caution and discrimination before saying your piece.

Gate 16
The Gate of Selectivity

You have a high degree of selectivity and foresight, spotting potential in projects, pursuits, and people. Gate 16 affords you the skill to see the way ahead and to harness an innate enthusiasm to make things happen. Expressed via the Throat as a voice, it brings backing and praise but can also be quick to withdraw or criticize both yourself and others. This expression is collective in nature, so you will comment out loud about what issues, goals, and projects are worth pursuing. That way you can awaken the latent enthusiasm in others, but you will expect their dedication to match your own.

People will always notice an enthusiasm about you — and a canny eye for what is worth chasing. You know how good it feels to devour something worthwhile and how uncomfortable you become when coerced into working on something unappealing or assisting someone who is ungrateful.

In life, everyone has brilliant ideas or crackpot schemes for which they require backing. Gate 16 gives you the selectivity to choose those endeavors that will promote an assured and successful future. Your enthusiasm can then attract eager assistants and helpers or unify everyone to make all goals possible.

Gate 20
The Gate of the Now

Gate 20 could almost be a literal gateway, like the temple gates of China and Japan that denote the exit from the city and the entrance to a holy place, from the maddening to the sacred. Sitting in such a gateway, you are in neither the city nor the temple, but in the here and now. This Human Design gate is marked with the words "Be in the Now."

People with this gate often ask what that actually *means* in a practical sense. It is all about bringing yourself into the present moment, harboring no regrets, resentment, or stress about what has passed, and letting go of expectations and hopes for the future. Being present. This gate is all about sitting, watching, and being in contemplation.

Your thoughts and visions are simply shaped by what the past and future have made of you, and mean for you, in the moment. The question that is most likely to arise within you, therefore, can be "Is this relevant to the moment?" Your nature wants to feel fresh in the reality of the present.

Meditation proceeds in three stages — from concentration to contemplation to being. So, gate 20, being in the now, is the sanctuary where you find yourself, in the present, here and now.

Gate 23
The Gate of Assimilation

What you say and do can bring dramatic change to your world. Gate 23 tends to shake life up and instigate new perspectives. Indeed, your grand statements can often come right out of the blue and make everyone sit up and take note. Imagine a landslide that breaks loose from a mountain and, as the rocks and earth tumble away, exposes previously unseen views of the mountain. That is what it's like sometimes when you express yourself. You are a proponent of radical measures and are eager to see people thinking in new ways and embracing new approaches. The question is this: are your contributions timely and appreciated?

Assimilation gets right to the point, sometimes impatiently stripping away what is not apparently useful anymore. You can bring about an entirely different view of the world with your authoritative manner. As a voice, gate 23 speaks with the forthright and clipped tone of "I know something...," keen to bring about change or add a fresh dimension. It can sound very knowledgeable and factual when actually its "knowing" may not be based on anything relevant at all!

Many would call you forthright, direct, and blunt, and this can sometimes lead to great misunderstandings. So choose your language — and timing — carefully. It is almost always preferable when your comments and view of the world are invited by others. When they are relevant to the needs of the moment, you are able to express profound insights and truths in a way that can be easily assimilated by others.

This is the gate that gives voice to received insights. It expresses itself as a voice that says, "I know...," regardless of what that knowing is based on.

Gate 31
The Gate of Influence

You are a highly influential person with an authority to your voice that is hard to ignore. You convey a sense of leadership that others feel confident relying and acting on, because what you say is both logical and future oriented. You have the natural gifts of a director, guiding groups, projects, or organized activities and leading people who are swayed by what you say. You can consequently influence and encourage others to achieve personal or universal goals.

Gate 31 brings an assurance that points out what lies ahead in the future, and most of what you say is intended to direct others in what you perceive is a beneficial direction. You express yourself as someone who understands exactly what should happen next, and everyone falls in around you. People will no doubt have remarked how influential you seem or what an impact you've had on them.

You are most effective when you speak your turn, follow your cue, and don't force the issue. Be clear that it is up to others if they want to do anything on the back of what you've expressed. It is also important that you speak from your own independent vision of reality and be wary of not talking your way into trouble by convincing yourself that you must do what you've just heard yourself saying.

Gate 33
The Gate of Retreat

"Once upon a time, there was a person with gate 33 in their Human Design…"

Welcome to one of two natural storytelling gates that reside in the Throat. Your stories, unlike those told in gate 56, are reflective, sober, and not highly embellished. Your succinct storytelling smacks of authentic life experience and can be woven into a magical moral from an old fable.

The truths of your accounts stem from the stories that the Universe makes you sample. Indeed, the experiences and challenges come so thick and fast that you *must* retreat from time to time and take a complete break from everything. Retreat brings you strength — and clarity about any wisdom garnered during your experiences.

In retreat, you mull over your experiences and then present your conclusions. Essentially, gate 33 sends you into the thick of action in order to subsequently guide others by using your storehouse of accumulated experiences.

Your memory capacity is also sharp, meaning there is a database inside you that would overwhelm any publisher or moviemaker with an embarrassment of creative riches. More can happen to you in a day than can happen to most people in a week!

Your difficulty is knowing when to retreat from the front line. If you don't get it right, you can face chronic fatigue and near collapse. Remember, the wise man knows when to retreat for his own health. Seek solace in spas, silent retreats, the countryside, meditation, or gentle pastimes. Refreshment and recharging are essential if you are to cope with the pace of your life.

One thing I would point out is a proclivity to be secretive. You like telling stories for the enjoyment and insight of everyone else, but matters learned in confidence can remain locked away. Until, that is, your design comes into contact with someone with gate 13. Then, beware, because their attentive listening abilities will be mining all that you know to the point where their energy literally draws all secrets and deep confidences from you!

Gate 35
The Gate of Progress

You just don't believe it's possible to progress in life without squeezing every drop out of every possible opportunity. As a result, you can have a highly charged, tempestuous, sometimes volatile nature, fueled by gate 35's impatience to get on with life and dive into the unknown. "It's time for change!" or "It's time to try something new!" your voice is inclined to say, and you can become irritable if you don't feel life is progressing in tune with your desire for expansion and new horizons. You have a low boredom threshold and seek experiences at any cost, keen to learn and fearful of regretting the things you *didn't* do in life. This encourages the personal nourishment you need in order to grow.

Gate 35 is restless by nature and impels your glass to be full, as opposed to half empty. Should an experience ever start involving goals, you might well find this irksome and frustrating. Over time, you will find that you become expert in discerning the difference between natural experiences that make the soul soar and the ego-driven pursuits that leave you materially catered to but asking the question "Great, but what did it all *mean?*"

The name of your game is what an experience teaches you. Many people with gate 35 will enter retirement feeling drained and spent but having seen it all, and with the awareness to steer others toward experiences that they will find rewarding.

Gate 45
The Gate of Gathering Together

I often tease people with this gate by calling them "Your Majesty!" That's because you can sit on your throne in this material world, looking regal, with an astute perspective that distinguishes between wealth and riches. You are someone who is here to oversee the wealth and well-being of your household or community. You strike the balance between what commands the best investments and what can be ignored. Group enterprises can thrive or collapse, depending on your financial wisdom, education, and administration. Like any king or queen, you have the capability to amass great wealth and then sit back on it. Gate 45's characteristic of "gathering together" means you can be a shrewd saver and great administrator of money. It is no surprise that Bill Gates has this gate activated in his life chart.

Your voice will often express itself with phrases such as "I have..." or "I don't have..." Your nature feels impoverished if you ever become a have-not.

One of your abilities is bringing others up to speed in terms of *their* material well-being by providing sound financial education. Your test is this: can you offer your unique services without becoming part of everyone else's money and material dramas? This is why your nature asks you to remain regal. Don't ruffle your feathers. The best rulers usually give the best advice from the high seat, leading to a harvest of great wealth for all their subjects.

Gate 56
The Gate of the Wanderer

I have yet to meet anyone with gate 56 who doesn't like traveling, broadening their horizons, and wandering to pastures new to discover fresh things in life. Consequently, home is wherever you lay your hat. I suspect you don't like sticking around one place or project too long — until you reach the time to put down roots. In the meantime, your thirst for traveling is not about attaining goals but about enjoying the experience.

This is one of two storytelling gates, both residing in the Throat, and this one expresses itself in a voice that says: "It happened like this..." I wouldn't even put it past you to start tales about great adventures with the phrase "You'll *never* believe this, but..." Your stories come hard and fast, on the bounce. You collect experiences and weave them into fascinating stories, probably because storytelling allows you to make sense of an experience. You also tend to arouse feedback from your audiences to challenge your own beliefs. Why would you do that? Basically, because you sometimes feel lost in your own life and seek reassurance, like any true wanderer.

You can even provide dramatic embellishment to add to the purpose — which is to stimulate and provoke others into discovering something more about life through what you experience. Just like movies, some of your stories might as well carry the "Based on a true story" qualifier. And yet, ironically, because of your ability to thread a good yarn together, you have an eye for the stories of others that don't add up or are weak in presentation.

As far as you are concerned, life is about finding constant stimulation. You are hungry for new experiences that add to the story of your life.

Gate 62
The Gate of Expressed Details

You are highly conscientious and your expression for detail fosters a broad understanding of potentially complicated concepts and stories. While others may well be getting entangled in the morass of information, you will find clarity with a voice from the Throat that says something like "I think you'll find that..." and, all of a sudden, the fog clears and everyone gets it.

Indeed, it's hard for you to be misunderstood. Gate 62 doesn't miss a trick and you will provide a supply of factual, logical, thorough information, whether it is what you say, the notes you leave, the instructions you provide, or the plans you make. Honoring detail supports your performance in every regard.

When you speak, you are authoritative and compelling. Consequently, your audience is assured by the authenticity of what it hears, knowing the "devil is in the detail." Your natural ability to express both general and little-known information can sound so convincing that you could almost turn fiction into fact or persuade someone black is white. Remember, your provision of detail doesn't mean you have to get involved in the follow-through. An observance of detail tends to come about with a sense of detachment or objectivity.

Extra Dimension

With no gates on, the Throat is open as well as undefined, meaning you have almost unlimited ways of expressing yourself by utilizing the gates of this center in the designs of those people around you. Therefore, you are always able to become the medium in terms of what gets said and done.

There is one important thing to appreciate: you will forever be getting caught up in the expressions and manifestations of others, and people will hear from you exactly what they want to hear, because you are always reflecting something of themselves back to them. In this respect, be aware that what you say may or may not bring agreement or appreciation — it's up to your audience.

GATES WITHIN THE SELF

Gate 1
The Gate of Creativity

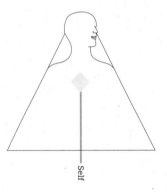

Self

Gate 1 implies you are highly creative, and there is something relevant about the number 1, because you often prefer to work alone and be left to your own devices. You have a strength of purpose that drives you on and an innate creative flair that can reap a rewarding dividend when applied in the realms of the family, career, dreams, art, music, or sport.

Certainly, getting paid for your creative acts is gratifying, but using your creativity solely for financial return will often jar your inner sensibilities. What matters about your creativity is not necessarily the reward or acclaim, but the act itself.

You're not afraid of pushing the envelope and finding fresh forms of expression that explore new avenues and break new ground. Yours is a creativity that goes beyond the tried and the true. Self-creative, self-motivated, there is something of the mover and shaker about you.

You know that your best work often takes place when you get out of your own way and allow your natural flair to express itself through your abilities. Never underestimate the creative input you can bring to any project or endeavor.

Gate 2
The Gate of Receptivity

You know your true direction in life. Getting there is the issue. But, as they say, don't waste time worrying about the "how"; just focus on the vision and allow a resolute purpose to guide you. For you, the diamond shape of the Self center might as well be a direction sign saying "This Way." You know where you're headed, whatever obstacles you might face. Your sense of direction is as reliable as a GPS system, whether you are literally lost or others are seeking guidance from you. A core strength means you are receptive and adaptable to what life offers and always seem to know the paths to follow.

Once you have found a direction in life, you can become devoted and determined in your pursuit of it. This is unusual in the sense that you often attune to directions that defy normal expectation or explanation, seeing footprints in the sand that are invisible to others. Indeed, you can be expert in showing others the way, too, and they can return months or years down the line to thank you, long after you've forgotten what you told them.

The strength of this Receptivity really does depend on two factors. If the Self center is defined, your strong sense of purpose will be consistent and lead to much fulfillment. But if the center is undefined, you may well find that your guidance is more reliable for others than for you. Or it might just take you longer to reach your destination. Just scrunch up the map and throw it away, along with the compass, and trust your inner guidance.

Gate 7
The Gate of Uniformity

You are a natural authority and leader, directing everyone to the same page to work toward a common understanding and purpose. You are unlikely to be the ruler of your world, more the efficient general or manager who shoulders responsibility for how things are organized.

Disciplined and regimental within yourself, you know that goals can be attained if your followers, or those who look to you for guidance, fall in with your ways of doing things. You stand for the way forward and hope others see what you see.

With this certainty, it is likely that people will look to you for advice and instruction. It's as if you have the map and the compass and people know to follow. You can be firm but fair, yet can only move forward on the basis of a shared consensus. Without inner discipline, though, you can get swept away by trends, opinion polls, mob mentality, and the apparent likes and dislikes of those around you. This does not mean that you have to be rigid in your views, but it does mean that it's important to recognize and stand by your own truth. If that means going against the crowd or even giving away your leadership role, that is exactly what is needed, provided your stance aligns with your own truth at that moment in time.

However you play it, remember that success doesn't have to come by force but can come from capturing the hearts, minds, and enthusiasm of those people who look up to you.

Gate 10
The Gate of Behavior

You tend to have a unique, individual expression of behavior, stemming from a self-respect that is unafraid of what anyone else thinks. Gate 10 represents a love for the journey of life and behaves in a way that is good for you — and you alone.

How you behave, especially under pressure, is dependent on a sliding scale of self-worth, but you would hate to know your actions had done you an injustice or let others down. Indeed, you like to think your unique expression and approach can positively influence how others behave around you.

One thing that underpins all your deeds, manners, and actions is an inherent love of life. So as long as your demeanor matches this joie de vivre, you're on the right track! This is one of four "love gates," and the Universe's intention is for you to bask in self-love and love life itself.

In a sense, having this gate allows you to withstand all the bumps along your way, accepting any indignities heaped on you and staying true to your own vision and trust in life — and yourself. Of course, real life, hard knocks, and the conditioning of others may well have tainted this natural trust. But gate 10 wants you to be comfortable in your own skin and expression, without trying, without fitting in. Individual expression, aligned with what you know to be right and true, brings integrity. There is a need for freshness and you can be versatile and adapt your approach to whatever challenges, troubles, or new directions show up. But happiness only exists when you are following your path, in line with your authority, whether it suits anyone else or not.

Gate 13
The Gate of the Listener

Now, are you sitting comfortably and are you listening? It's a stupid question, really, because *of course* you're listening. It's in your nature — you are a born Listener.

You could absorb the stories of the world, your shoulder could be drenched by a torrent of tears, and your very being could be mistaken for a listening post where strangers could unburden themselves and divulge all their deepest, darkest secrets. There is something about your depth that mines stories from everyone around you. "I've no idea why I'm telling you this! I hardly know you..." is something you've no doubt heard many times.

You might well intend to mind your own business when you enter into social or business environments, but don't kid yourself. I'm not saying you are nosy. Far from it. You can become fatigued by hearing the life stories of others, but you happen to be a magnet for them. The Universe programmed you that way!

The key to honoring your nature is to move from a position of sympathy to a place of empathy where you can attune deeply to what people are experiencing instead of simply feeling sorry for them. Empathy will lead you to compassion.

You are helping people to find their purpose and direction in life by acknowledging them, and their efforts and challenges, in the stories they bring to you. Many healers and therapists have this gate.

Gate 15
The Gate of Humanity

Your modest, unassuming, nonjudgmental nature views humanity as one big family, all interconnected. You are the archetypal humanitarian, committed to improving the lives of others.

This is one of four "love gates" and your love of humanity encourages a unified welfare. You are someone who easily wins the respect, support, and admiration of others with your all-embracing approach to life and your kindness. Equality and fairness are key elements to this gate. Of course, this doesn't preclude the possibility that bitter experiences may have dampened your enthusiasm for being a true humanitarian, but never lose sight of this natural inclination within you.

Your love for interactions with others means you're likely to have many friends in all situations and strata of society, from beggars to princes. You will often find yourself the linchpin in social circles, bringing everyone together. But you will feel uncomfortable in any situation where others have control over you, because you are a free spirit who likes to be in the flow of life, unrestricted. Just be prepared for your doorstep to be the first that people arrive on when life gets tough, because they are drawn naturally to the respectful humanitarian that you are.

Gate 25
The Gate of Innocence

There is a gentle, childlike innocence about you that belies a life that is often complicated and demanding. You almost have a secret smile for adversity, because you have a deep trust that the Universe will look after you and love will conquer all. You can therefore embrace the unexpected, knowing you will come through.

This is one of four "love gates," and you attune to a universal, unconditional form of love that stands in the face of unexpected chaos and drama and keeps on growing wise. You interact with the world with honesty, truthfulness, and sincerity. How you express yourself is rarely premeditated and often comes with the innocence of a child, regardless of repercussions and sometimes leaving your loving nature vulnerable to being taken advantage of by others. Your good virtue can forgive transgressions but doesn't forget them. You are a tender being who is susceptible to rude and obnoxious people, so avoid them if you can. Your innocence — which can be misinterpreted as reckless naïveté — can't quite grasp why certain people have such a problem with life when love is all around. "What is their problem?" is something you might often catch yourself saying. For those who wish to offer a reply, they must be ready for your stock response: "I hear you, but just trust in life."

You might attempt healing in the world through your unwavering love and trust, but never underestimate your own need for recuperation when a challenge has been overcome.

Gate 46
The Gate of Serendipity

You have a knack of being in the right place at the right time, living the very definition of the word *serendipity* — accidentally discovering something beneficial or fortunate, even when looking for something or someone else.

They say that at least half of success in life is down to simply showing up. However, luck is not only about being in the right place at the right time but is also reliant on your attitude while there! For you, fortune smiles when you are available and trusting. Watch the personal advancement that can happen when you fall back on an inner confidence that is ready for anything that life serves up. This gate naturally tunes in to the Universe's need for your presence and gives you experiences that may bring recognition or essential lessons. You need to let go of expectation and be open to all experiences offered.

Gate 46 is another of the "love gates," and its essence is all about the love of the body. So keeping trim and healthy and looking after the physical form helps foster your serendipitous nature. Keeping fit is an essential part of your life. Or maybe you have a strong inclination to keep going to the gym or spa, but a conditioning influence holds you back. Your true nature appreciates nothing more than your body being honed and pampered, and you need to take responsibility for your body; otherwise, you will feel down and frustrated. So book that massage, take a run with the dog, schedule those manicures and pedicures, reserve that spa day, and implement a good diet. When your body is purring, you are ready for anything!

Extra Dimension

With no gates on, the Self is open as well as undefined, meaning you can be a mystery even to yourself! "Who am I?" and "What is my direction in this life?" may well be ongoing mantras for you, because there are no distinguishing features within your inner compass. Basically, where and who you are in life are heavily influenced and directed by the company you keep. Where you are is who you are, so choose your company according to what your authority tells you.

This affords you great freedom if you can recognize the gift and not feel unduly lost, because this is your nature. You might well feel without objective or purpose from time to time, but you can benefit enormously by embracing periods of being alone, which will release you from the influences others unknowingly assert over you.

GATES WITHIN THE HEART

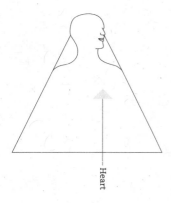

Heart

Gate 21
The Gate of Control

I'll refrain from calling you a control freak. That would be unfair. Possibly. But life brings all sorts of challenges and demands, and you're someone who thrives when in a position of control, seizing the reins and taking decisive action over money, property, business, or relationship matters.

There is something of the hunter/huntress in this gate, and the skillful hunter knows how to hide and wait for his opportunity, to let the "game" come to him. You decide what game you are hunting and mark out the territory accordingly. Then you will feel balanced. At the very least, be in charge of your wardrobe, what you eat, and where you live.

In all aspects of life, you want to be the go-getting, front-running, dominant force — the big boss, the managing director, the one in charge. Partners and colleagues require great understanding to appreciate this. If your partner happens to share this gate, then welcome to a tug-of-war. It really will require great understanding of each other's respective authorities to know when to allow and concede if this power struggle is to be tolerated long term.

When you are permitted the driving seat, no one could be more dependable. Indeed, you'll feel completely out of control should anyone else take the reins, and this frustrating prospect is more likely when your Heart Center is undefined. In that case, see that your wisdom extends to recognizing exactly who else merits control and can handle it well.

Difficulty arises when you use Control to arrange situations that are not yours to direct. You will find that these kinds of situations only happen when you are pushing with your ego and not paying attention to your true and wiser wishes, or not following your Human Design authority.

Gate 26
The Gate of Accumulation

Maximum results at all times — that's what you wish to squeeze out of life. The Accumulation of material wealth and prestige is possible, as you vigorously and cleverly chase — or dream about — positions of great power or status. You don't beat about the bush or waste time haggling if something doesn't have value for you. But if it does, the rewards must compensate your efforts.

The Heart is always striving to strike a balance between fulfilling wholesome wishes and ego power trips, and you often find it a challenge to find that equilibrium. There can be something of the egotistical salesperson about your attitude, something power hungry, but you will also know the value of your contribution to others in pointing out to them what they really want to have in their lives. You're not interfering, just trying to better what you see by recommending enhancements, improvements, or renewal in all aspects of life, be they new art, architecture, diets, fashions, vacations, philosophies, music, or travel.

You might tend to exaggerate your abilities, exuding an air of "I'm the greatest" or "I'm the best," whether you say it out loud or state it silently to your reflection in the mirror. But stature is important in your life.

Pitching to people and being persuasive come naturally, but these skills bring with them a responsibility to acknowledge when something is of genuine service to others and not just your own reward.

Gate 40
The Gate of Deliverance

I suspect you are in great demand. This is because you are capable of always delivering the goods, whatever is asked of you. You engage the Heart's willpower to work hard and efficiently, in the interests of everyone. You might even announce to the world, hands on hips, "I don't need your help, thank you very much!" but take care that you do not isolate yourself unnecessarily.

Once you have accomplished what you set out to do, you will know the satisfaction of a job well done but also know that need for peace and quiet afterward. Then your nature craves alone time. People can tend to overlook this, so you need to explain to them your need for uninterrupted replenishment. You enjoy supporting many kinds of people — in fact, you don't take friendship lightly — but you have to be firm in honoring your alone time, too.

A big question is also asked by this gate: "Can you forgive yourself and others for the wrongs you have committed?" You see, some of the abilities of Deliverance involve being able to untangle and resolve life's complications, ultimately within yourself. If you learn to find forgiveness in your heart and genuinely let the past go, it can feel like an enormous release and clear the complications that may block progress or cooperation in the present. Matters of the ego may well challenge this natural inclination, but once you discover the power of true forgiveness, it brings tremendous relief. Forgiveness is part of your nature, whether you realize it or not.

Gate 51
The Gate of Arousing

Physically, this gate relates to the gallbladder, that part of our makeup that has a reputation for being shocking or full of gall, meaning that if you have this gate turned on you have a level of audacity that goes beyond plain cheekiness as you spur people into action.

Life brings its challenges and we tend to get caught up in mundane and material issues. Gate 51, however, is ready for something more brash, competitive, and unpredictable. You therefore have a great knack for creating — as well as handling — surprise. You know how to push all sorts of people's buttons, using shock tactics to elicit and inspire positive reactions, and also become adept at handling shocking situations in your own life. Gate 51 can light the fuse under people, shocking them into a reality that gets things moving in *their* world. You are that great clap of thunder that acts as an alarm call to make everyone sit up, take note, and get moving!

This can come across as a devil-may-care attitude, so be aware of this and understand that your words and actions can stun people like a lightning bolt. Nothing is quite the same afterward.

This is your nature, so celebrate it, but perhaps learn to temper it — and choose your moments. That way, you can arouse astonishment instead of shock! And know that in the moment in which people's jaws drop, they are open to receiving all sorts of fresh insights.

Extra Dimension

With no gates on, the Heart is open as well as undefined, meaning you are generous to a fault. You can find it difficult to place a value on anything in life, including your own self-worth. This openness makes you naturally openhearted and modest and constantly perplexed by those who proclaim how great they are. You'll avoid such egotists wherever possible, preferring more intelligent folks.

Whenever you seek to place a value on a service, or something you are offering or considering purchasing, it's probably wise to seek a friend's, colleague's, or consultant's advice to ensure your values are appropriate and respected, especially when negotiating deals or contracts.

GATES WITHIN THE SPLEEN

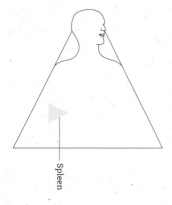

Spleen

Gate 18
The Gate of Improving

There is a Chinese saying that states, "Work on what has been spoiled," and the essence of the message is that we can undo damaging patterns from childhood and become whole again. With this gate, there is an inclination, even a yearning, to undertake inner work that heals the scars left by parents, relatives, teachers, or society.

Something can be "spoiled" by accepting somebody else's way of doing things as being cast in stone, and that can be personally disempowering. This can relate to patterns from your childhood in the way you've been raised, or fossilized traditions with no relevance to your present-day life. Gate 18's goal is to review the old ways and traditions to bring about improvement for yourself and society.

The Improving gate senses when you are being overly hard on yourself and perhaps blaming yourself for episodes from the past. It therefore nudges you into addressing matters that, once healed, will make your nature sing with a newfound freedom. It provides an inner prod to be aware of certain attributes that might have been "borrowed" or "imprinted" through conditioning and have nothing to do with your nature. Noticing the difference between learned behavior and your true nature is key to your happiness. Gate 18 is essential to uplifting and updating society's ways, balancing patriarchal and matriarchal patterns. Are the old traditions relevant?

With this gate, there is a tendency to blame yourself for everything that appears to go wrong in your life. It is a form of guilt complex that can lead to personal decay. So learn to be softer and kinder to yourself and recognize that your path to relieve yourself and others from conditioning only requires your presence, determination, and alertness.

Accepting your weaknesses instead of blaming yourself for them requires an inner strength — and you can fall back on gate 18 to provide it.

Gate 28
The Gate of the Game Player

A subtle undercurrent of the fear of death pulls on gate 28, potentially turning you into a great risk taker who enjoys excess in the "game of life," seeking to cram everything into whatever lifetime you've been allotted.

Certain cultures insist that life is a play, that humanity produces the characters and that destiny will ultimately be reached. With that awareness, you are here to maximize your role, pushing onward and upward and living a life that is alive and kicking. This can lead to extraordinary moments of sublime courage — or foolhardiness. But you will remain undaunted because the spontaneity of the Spleen means you are always up for a challenge and your nature feels better nourished when you live life on the edge.

Of course, some people with this gate can fall prey to the fear of death, and that can become paralyzing and the cause of much inner resistance. Also, there is a risk you could turn into a doormat who has almost given up on life because the concept of death is so restricting. But your nature finds fulfillment when watered with the very juice of life.

Living life to the full requires great courage and total commitment, and that is a part of the territory that comes with the Game Player. Can you look life in the eye even when you are beset by chaos and trials? If you can, the game of life is yours for the taking...

Gate 32
The Gate of Duration

Just as farmers, deep-sea fishermen, and sailors can detect the slightest shift in weather, so you can sense shifting circumstances in your world. Gate 32 "smells" when something threatens to bring instability or unrest. It could concern a relationship, a venture, the economy, or the community, but you'll sniff it out and become twitchy when change is coming. That's because your nature seeks a path that is sure but steady. Enduring relationships and careers, shored up with commitment, are what your life is all about and your goals are long term.

"Going the distance" should be the motto of this gate because you'd be quite happy if life found a plateau, just as long as that plateau promised continuity and long-term success. The longevity, consistency, and sustainability of things matter, so whatever change you engage with must smell right first. People, places, and projects are forever coming under such houndlike scrutiny. As you pivot on the spot, there is an unshakable sense that, whatever you face, your resolve will sail through any storm or challenge. You will do all you can to avoid failure, because that is the biggest fear within you. This fear will be more prevalent if your Spleen is undefined. When fear starts chipping away at your endurance, remember to trust your authority.

Gate 44
The Gate of Patterns

You have a nose for spotting potential and emerging patterns and trends. Whether this is an instinctive gift employed in the fields of business, finance, creativity, fashion, technology, or any other sphere of life, you utilize a deep cellular memory of the past to sense what is going on in any moment. In this regard, your senses keep you in touch with the present and potential trends for the future. You could be the agent with an instinctive feeling about an emerging talent, a fashion designer who gets a hunch about what the next designs should be, or the economist who can sense trouble brewing in the markets. You can have a nose for news or be able to smell a rat.

This ability can also be applied in your personal life, where your instinctive memory can help you detect certain behavioral and repetitive patterns that may be forming in others and could happily be avoided.

Ironically, gate 44 has a fear of the past. It's as though you are always looking over your shoulder to see if you are clear of whatever happened before. But you can be so busy looking backward that you trip over the present. This is especially the case if you have the Spleen undefined. Not everyone understands your instinctive gift for sensing emerging patterns. Also be aware that the Spleen does not have unlimited supplies of energy — it is more an internal alarm system — so your knack is best applied as a guiding influence rather than a call to personally get involved in everything you sense.

Gate 48
The Gate of the Well

There is potentially great depth to you, and I'm not even sure you've plumbed the Well to find out how deep you go! Some people may even scoff at you for being "too deep" sometimes, but gate 48 explores such depths to find personal well-being and keep things fresh. It affords you great awareness and perspective and makes you highly resourceful.

The founding feature of any civilization is a good supply of water — a well that is kept fresh to ensure health and security. People keep going to the well to sustain themselves. So it is with gate 48. People come to you to draw from your knowledge of life and tap into your resourcefulness. I suspect that's probably why you are someone who fiercely guards the Well within. The quality of your existence, what you share with others, and who you allow to explore these depths with you are directly proportional to the depth at which you're prepared to live your life. You may well wish to live on the surface and keep all relations at that level. If you do, just ensure you keep everything fresh. But the deeper you choose to go, the closer you get to your source of fulfillment.

Whatever you engage with, refreshing your interest and knowledge will bring continued expansion. For example, knowing how to play the piano is not enough — you have to keep practicing to expand your repertoire.

Bear in mind that it's also in the depths that fear can arise, the fear of being caught out of your depth because you don't know your subject well enough, and this can play out as paralysis or stage fright at the key moment. This is the time to trust your authority. If people and projects seem "tasteful" to you, allowing them to share your depths will be as refreshing as splashing yourself with cold water from your Well.

Gate 50
The Gate of the Values

This is sometimes called the Cauldron, because this is where values in life cook and simmer. Nothing matters more to this gate than that these values that preserve and support family, workplace, or community are espoused and honored.

Values are something that often get handed down from generation to generation or are acquired in the home, church, or school. But with this gate on, you are naturally attuned to what is appropriate or not, fair or unjust, in any situation in any moment. Gate 50 enables you to identify and honor all values and correct actions that, in your book, lead to sustainable and effective living. Some values endure, some need replacing, and your gate 50 will constantly be called on to tune in to the needs of the situation.

Your big questions are "What *are* the values that are going to best serve society?" and "Can everyone be encouraged to be personally responsible?" These questions tie in with an inherent fear of taking responsibility. Standing up for right and appropriate values brings the pressure to be an example in society, and you sense that responsibility acutely. This is a heightened fear if your Spleen center is undefined, so fall back on your authority for reassurance and guidance. But no one will be more vociferous than you if you sense that moral decay is jeopardizing the common good or a secure future for the community.

Gate 57
The Gate of the Gentle

You are like a gentle but chilly wind that cuts to the bone, penetrating other people's auras and the environment around you, detecting harmony or disharmony. Your sharp intuition is constantly updating what is going on around you to safeguard your well-being.

People with whom you engage in social interaction could be forgiven for thinking you're not listening or paying attention, but your gentle senses will already have read them perfectly; or your gentle persuasion will have seeped in and turned them around. Your inner intuition latches onto the sound of what you're hearing to decide its merit or interest, tuning in to the tone and inflection in someone's voice and the general sounds around you. Anything abrupt or harsh can trip the intuition of your highly sensitive nature. We live in a world of mayhem and chatter and yet you walk through it oh so gently, guided by what appeals to you and administering slow and gentle change. There is a subtle "gently does it" approach to your life and the influence you wield.

Your nature is acoustically sensitive and music needs to be in harmony for you. Plain noise can easily bother you, and you will often tune out from people with discordant, whining voices, especially if you sense underlying agendas and potential complications.

Your senses are heightened by an inherent attention to the future and even fear of it. If these "what if" fears take hold, you can be like a deer in headlights and this can destabilize you, especially if your Spleen center is undefined. This is the time to trust your authority. Don't be put off by the ways in which you are confronted in life. Trust your intuition and move gently toward challenges — that is your nature.

Extra Dimension

With no gates on, the Spleen is open as well as undefined, meaning you can read your immediate environment better than most because you tend to be devoid of inherent fears and therefore see the situation clearly. However, one conditioning potential to be watchful of is that if surrounded by people who are constantly fretting or fearful about certain aspects of life, you can get sucked into that process. What you need to do then is step aside and acknowledge that these are merely adopted fears, not fears inherent within you. People with an open Spleen can also find themselves tuning in on psychic levels.

GATES WITHIN THE SACRAL

Gate 3
The Gate of Beginning

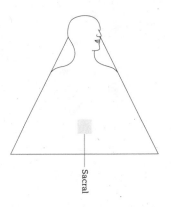

Sacral

Embracing all the trials involved with new beginnings and fresh starts is the hallmark of gate 3. You plant seeds to foster new beginnings but require patience for your plans to grow and blossom. Whenever something new is introduced, it can meet resistance and difficulty. Your challenge is to find the means to bring about change in ways that are accepted and assimilated by yourself and others.

A foundational imperative, therefore, is to wipe the slate clean, become organized, draw up fresh plans, prepare the infrastructure, and ensure everything is geared for the transition you seek to push forward. Something can only truly grow from solid foundations, be it a personal or professional matter, so your preparation is almost as important as your execution. Then, with everything ready, you must await the green light... from your authority.

One thing you must learn to appreciate is that endeavors originating from Beginning will evolve spontaneously and in their own time, so it is pointless to apply pressure and to wear a hole in the carpet as you pace the floor waiting for things to happen.

Also be aware that fresh beginnings can only prosper once old disappointments, failures, and resentments have been honestly cast aside. Once you've respected all the requirements of this natural process, you'll be amazed at the fulfillment you can experience. Projects can be kick-started with fresh invigoration, and relationships can feel brand-new.

Gate 5
The Gate of Waiting

You are someone whose nature has the knack of right timing — if you exercise patience. Gate 5 asks you to be comfortable with biding your time, waiting for opportune moments. When you learn to trust your authority, you'll align yourself with universal timing and know the right moment to act.

That need to wait can generate a restlessness that craves action or worries that something may or may not happen. You can feel the potential of what can be done and just can't wait for the starting gun to sound. "I can't stand all this waiting around! Shouldn't I be doing something?!" can be a common voice of frustration. But waiting is a part of your nature, so honor it and relax.

Gate 5 also has its finger on the natural pulse of timing for the seasons and you might well have green fingers that are adept at gardening. You may also notice that you can adopt certain routines in life. If you are someone who needs to have a cup of tea first thing in the morning, that is what needs to happen before you can do anything else. A routine leads you to keep in step with the natural rhythms that maintain your momentum.

Like you, the Universe has its routines, and I'm reminded of a Japanese haiku that you can assimilate while you wait:

> *Sitting silently*
> *doing nothing*
> *spring comes*
> *and the grass grows — by itself.*

So just wait, trust your innate sense of timing, set your intentions and long-term goals, and fall back on the reassuring confidence that matters will proceed in their own time.

Gate 9
The Gate of Applied Details

You are born with an eye for detail. I could throw you the most befuddling and technical thousand-word document and you could locate the one essential detail that needs conveying in a clear and concise manner. You notice all sorts of tiny details in many aspects of life.

There is a distinction between gate 9 and gate 62 (Expressed Details). The 9 must, right at the outset of all it does, have all the little details in place and everything set up, otherwise it can be tripped up by the one detail it missed, whereas gate 62 is more about the expression and conveying of detail to others.

With gate 9 turned on, you can be attentive to things that others only see long after you have already noticed and perhaps discounted them. Or you can be questioning others about minutiae concerning matters that really don't interest them at all.

You are constantly checking to see what is relevant to you at any moment. When every little detail is in place, you can start applying your Sacral energy to your endeavors. Progress and accomplishment come bit by bit as you tackle the small details that build toward big success. You have great staying power for the most complex, detailed tasks, applying focus that is both conscientious and efficient. No stone is left unturned or unexamined.

Gate 14
The Gate of Prosperity

This is one of the most potentially fortuitous gates in Human Design. If you have it, you are capable of harvesting great wealth. It all depends on whether your considerable capabilities are applied in the direction of passions that mean something to you and further the good of everyone else. Please note this gate's motto: "Passion projects with the universal good in mind can lead to prosperity."

Prosperity can mean you accumulate great wealth or find yourself managing everyone else's. Somewhere in your being there is a knack for handling resources, be that currency, property, or fields of corn. Either way, this gate represents possessions on a grand scale and the potential for expansive success.

It is in fact a mix of fate and good fortune. Fate is said to give wealth to whomever she wishes and, while everyone is given the choice to feel wealthy regardless of their access to resources, this gate senses that it is all a matter of perspective. You have, without doubt, the ability and commitment to drive projects through to a successful end, and your drive can generate great financial reward when it is applied in the right direction. What you will come to realize is that being comfortable and confident around finances and assets is something that can come naturally to you, and any responsibility that comes with prosperity needn't faze you.

Gate 27
The Gate of Nourishing

Just as a plant needs soil, water, and light to grow, so humans need the nourishment of food, shelter, and caring. You would gladly provide such necessities to anyone. Your caring arm would stretch around the community, while the other hand offered help elsewhere. You think nothing of giving with both hands to help and care for others, but this can lead to neglecting your own nourishment. So the foundational need of gate 27 is to take care of number one first! You need to balance the caring of others with the need to ensure you, too, are sufficiently nourished with a sound diet, the support of good people, and healthy finances. There is a tendency to become lost in caring for others and addressing their nourishment. The old saying "Physician, heal thyself" could not be more relevant.

Be clear that when you do this you are always entering into a win-win situation: as you care, so others care for you. When your body and spirit are amply provided for, you are at your strongest and most effective. And an eager compassion means you are here to preserve, protect, and nurture.

Gate 29
The Gate of Commitment

In 2008 a Jim Carrey movie called *Yes Man* was released, in which a man challenged himself to say "yes" to everything life offered him over the course of a year. It could have been made with gate 29 in mind! Certainly "yes" can open the doorway to all sorts of amazing things for you, but unlike in Hollywood, a wholesale "yes" can find you overloaded, taken for granted, and thoroughly depleted without feeling fulfilled.

My experience of people with this attribute is that you can struggle to contain an indiscriminate "yes" to anything and everything, regardless of troublesome outcomes. "Can I borrow some money?" "Yes!" "Will you come over and mow my lawn while I watch TV?" "Yes!" "And while you're at it, will you let me spoil your day?" "Yes! Yes! Yes! No problem!"

This arises from a predisposition to commit without any awareness of the commitment in hand. I know people with this gate who forever overextend themselves, getting caught up in every flight of fancy that goes past them and ending up burned out and frustrated. And this well-intentioned but frustrating pattern is in danger of being repeated over and over almost mechanically.

Commitment becomes a gift when you say "yes" to the right things, but a potential curse when engaged without clarity. Remember, you are searching for a "yes" that is in genuine alignment with your nature.

Gate 34
The Gate of Power

You are someone who is given power in this lifetime, and you need to get used to it! This is the only one of the Sacral's nine gates that is asexual, because it is purely about empowering the individual. It's about achieving on your own, without the support of anyone. In fact, you have no natural compulsion to engage directly with the lives of others. You are naturally independent and can happily go it alone much of the time in your pursuit of great accomplishments and self-empowerment. You are individual and, at times, can come across as unreasonable and detached, but your power to achieve is impressive. It's almost as though you were born with blinkers to keep your eyes solely on your goals and achievements. When you walk into a room or add your input to a project, the level of energy will go up a notch or three because you are an energetic shot in the arm.

What you will come to know is that you need to monitor and balance the use of power according to the people and situations that confront you. There is no point in cracking a nut with a sledgehammer, but also no point in trying to open a nut with a pair of tweezers! You might well be a potential powerhouse who can easily drag anyone or anything toward the finishing line, but there's no point applying this resource to worthless and unrewarding pursuits. And yet this is the Achilles' heel for you go-getters. So be aware and practice discernment.

Gate 42
The Gate of Increase

The ethic within gate 42 wants to realize potential everywhere, and its energy is such that what you receive matches what you give. This give-and-take dynamic models the truth of "what goes around, comes around" and this is a truth that finds alignment with your nature.

When you undertake to help others and strive toward the common good, rewards flow back to you. If you become self-serving, then Increase becomes blocked. You don't find fulfillment when you become the sole beneficiary of your actions. This gate expands rich experiences that can be shared generously with everyone. It is not confined to personal benefits. It recognizes that the Universe is so generous that there is more than enough to go around. You have the capacity to tap into this natural surfeit, harnessing your abilities to further other people in their efforts to become successful. You might well wonder why you should do all the hard work for them, but your flair and sustainable energy will make things happen for you, too, as a consequence of your actions. It's a natural law. Just as a gardener tends his or her own garden and watches numerous plants prosper, so it is with Increase.

If you sense that you could gain greater personal prosperity through your efforts, be watchful that you do only one thing at a time, in accord with your authority, and avoid spreading yourself too thin. This gate encourages you to realize that giving is more important than receiving — and the sure path to increase and reward.

Gate 59
The Gate of Intimacy

Gate 59 could be your own radar beacon, slowly revolving in its environment, emitting strong signals of intimacy to see what and whom it attracts into your life. It seeks bonds with sexual partners for procreation and means you are highly fertile by nature — so you have been warned!

You will maintain an inclination to open all sorts of doors to share intimacies of varying intensity in many arenas, often expressing an eagerness to "give birth" to creative projects. You are dispersing your natural life-force energy throughout your world, throwing out signals and sowing seeds, both personally and professionally.

People approach interactions in many different ways, from bold contact to shyness, promiscuity, friendliness, dominance, and outright aloofness. To derive fulfillment, be clear about engagements and stay aligned with your authority.

There is also a biological imperative about gate 59 to procreate, and this leads to a buildup of sexual energy looking for an outlet, so I often urge caution when it comes to the sexual act because of the latent fertility within you. This can be a highly charged gate of sexual prowess that is fueled by a genetic imperative to mate, but Sacral activity can easily become sacred activity with a shift in your consciousness. Ultimately, the right people and right projects will arrive if you practice discernment.

Extra Dimension

With no gates on, the Sacral is open as well as undefined, meaning you can easily ride the energies of people around you. In this regard, you need to be extremely watchful about committing to people or projects that require your sustainable energy, because it matters what team is around you. People with open Sacrals need to learn to delegate more, simply because they do not have high levels of sustaining energy!

Sex is always going to be something of a mystery as well, because you are a blank slate where sex is concerned — leaving you open to all forms of expression if and when you engage with it. Indeed, sex can become a constant exploration, meaning you will be either adventurous or left daunted. Accepting this will allow you to invite your partner to lead you by the hand...

GATES WITHIN THE EMOTIONS

Gate 6
The Gate of Conflict Resolution

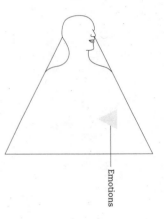

Emotions

You stand as a giant set of scales, balancing high emotions in one hand and clear resolution in the other. Your presence in any situation can either inflame circumstances or calm them. It all depends on the clarity you bring with you as the chief diplomat who weighs each situation on its merits. You accept that for some creative processes and alliances to grow, there has to be a certain amount of friction. At other times, you need to be the peacemaker.

Many things in life are emotionally driven and not rational. Gate 6 has the responsibility of bringing clarity to these situations. You can find it hard, sometimes, to remain on the tightrope with the scales in hand, lurching from the extremes of "Get me out of here!" to "Now *listen to me*, it's like *this*!" But you seek resolution by meeting people halfway, seeking compromise and settling matters creatively, equitably, and with a sense of justice. You can be the arbiter at work or in relationships.

Gate 6 is built on a furrowed field where seeds for emotional growth can sprout and flourish. There is a maturity to this emotional gate.

Physically, Conflict Resolution regulates the pH in our body's chemistry, representing that fine balance between acid and alkaline that counts for so much of our well-being. If you overindulge in any areas of your life, you can lose that balance. Overindulgence comes in many forms, from greed to anger to addiction, from overeating to being oversexed. Conflict Resolution fosters an internal balance, an emotional awareness, and the responsibility to bring an equilibrium into life. This is a powerful emotional gate, meaning your emotions rule the environment you're in. How you feel dictates how everyone else is going to feel. Clear feelings — clear environment; unclear feelings — trouble!

Gate 22
The Gate of Grace

Grace can either be a divine benevolence that shapes our lives or relate to beauty and elegance. Either way, it can be an enabling gift for expansion and enhancement in all aspects of life. Whatever you do, you deliver it with grace.

It will be evident to people around you, if not to yourself, that you are attractive in your own individual way in how you conduct your life. Your Grace can show itself in many ways: through your graceful movements, the stylish clothes you wear, or the refined ways you treat others. The chances are that God's grace often smiles down on you and that you've lived a charmed existence, pulling through even the most distressing moments. Gate 22 means grace shines out of you.

This doesn't mean your life is a bed of roses. Light is followed by darkness, and so your Grace can be followed by Three Ugly Sisters and all their troubles, just as Cinderella was. So you have to be prepared for such challenges. At these times, be watchful of your emotions because there is a tendency to turn grace into disgrace when tested.

You also have a romantic view of the world, like the charmer you are. Even animals can't get enough of you and will come as close as they possibly can, regardless of any allergies you might have! They seem to recognize in you something that is mysterious but magnetic.

It is said that the greatest kings and queens gain their reputation not necessarily through their wisdom and conquests but through the grace they represent — and so it is for you.

Gate 30
The Gate of Desires

Sometimes called The Clinging Fire, this gate relates to the desires burning within you, the longing to engage with life and experience all its offerings.

One lesson with this gate is for you to let go of any expectations before entering into a relationship, pursuit, or experience, because attachment to an outcome leads to disappointment, whereas being receptive and open to what you feel and what an experience teaches you leads to fulfillment.

As you go through life, your desire to try new things will expose you to pleasures and pains and their associated rewards and penalties. You will ultimately learn to restrain a wanton, and sometimes random, penchant for trying anything and everything. Tending the inner fires in an appropriate manner is what matters, drawing wisdom as you proceed.

Too often we are persuaded that life is a school of hard knocks where we come to learn our lessons before going to a better place. We forget that the Earth can be a paradise and that we also come here to have fun while enjoying illuminating experiences. You will know that life can be lived out in two ways: one, where you get the sense that something might be worth doing but are not sure if it is "allowed," so you tiptoe into it and get trapped in never really having the experience; or, two, where you find your clarity, follow your feelings, and dive deeply into the totality of an experience, coming out of the other side with a "Wow! That was impressive!"

I often say this is the gate of sex, drugs, and rock 'n' roll, to illustrate the sense of outrageous desires burning inside you. The challenge is to determine which ones — if any — fit with your nature, and which are desires for desire's sake. It's all about clearly feeling which ones to embrace.

Gate 36
The Gate of Crisis Resolution

Emotionally speaking, it may well feel as though you're forever teetering on the brink of catastrophe. As the gate's name implies, you have a tendency to attract emotional crises, which can feel highly destabilizing. Yet your crises seek resolution in the same way that darkness calls for light. So when you don't have them, some might say you even invent them. This challenges you, but then I can hear you retort: "I don't *need* to invent them — they always find me!"

The source of any anxiety stems from a feeling that each new experience represents the unknown, as if you're stepping into the pitch dark. What you'll find is that taking the first step with clarity can immediately dispel your anxiety. What you've got to do is learn to let go of anxiety and embrace the experience of all manner of tumultuous human emotions. Then you'll always come through.

Your true nature will feel its harmony, and increased balance, once you can accept the inevitability that you, more than most, are going to be presented with all kinds of situations that test your resolve. What you perhaps don't realize is the strength of this resolve. If you remember your inner brilliance and outer gentility, you can become better and better at anticipating and handling trouble by allowing a little objectivity into the emotional ride. Once you've braced yourself and taken a deep breath, apply your authority. Profound emotional experiences can become your teacher, not your enemy, and a source of great wisdom.

Gate 37
The Gate of the Family

There is a strong sense of the family about you. Sitting around a table breaking bread with those you love can make up some of your favorite moments — and also explains your fondness for food!

Family is everything to you, the solid foundation of your life. You are someone who has an intrinsic sense of responsibility toward the family and community you serve. You thrive in tight-knit communities and feel good when a family or household comes together. You'll be the proud head of the household or the key family member, teaching cooperation and mutual respect and bringing guidance and good communication. Domestic matters are important in your world and there is something traditional about your views in regard to the roles within a home.

People may well observe a degree of familiarity about you. Perhaps you are tactile, sometimes overly so, but you have a natural inclination to make people feel welcome and part of your circle through a sense of touch — whether that's via warm handshakes, embracing hugs, or reassuring touches on the shoulder. This is important to your bonding and trusting process. Woe betide anyone, therefore, who reneges on a handshake or double-crosses you. If that happens, their seat will be removed from around the table and the family door shut in their face.

Gate 49
The Gate of Revolution

You are someone who *feels* when it is time for change, renewal, or revolt, driven by a need to "get life right." The inclination is to move with the times, breaking free from old established ways to revolutionize life, sometimes abruptly. Transformation happens when you reach a breaking point and your emotions rise up and say: "I've had it — I'm moving on!" You *feel* your way through life and feel when something is no longer working.

If the tendency of gate 29 is to always say "yes," the tendency of gate 49 is to say "no." It can come about in many situations. "No, that suggestion doesn't feel right to me" or "No, you can't behave in that way" or "No, you can't just ride roughshod over how I feel!"

Revolution can be most effective when it addresses communal discontent, opening ways for practical improvements. The French Revolution took off because most of the population was starving. Likewise, you'll feel it when areas of your life are depleted, starved, or neglected and will look to amend things with a swift, down-to-earth approach.

Often, you can find yourself coming to a fork in the road where you part company with those who have been companions or allies. In this way you bring about emotional revolution. You can be particular about the people you allow into your life and the attitudes they hold. Whether you are aware of it or not, you have a breeder's eye that can discern strong bloodlines and lineage.

You must learn to go beyond being concerned about getting everything right and move into and through the transformations that are a natural part of your life. It might well take courage at times, but the rewards are worth it.

Gate 55
The Gate of Abundance

You can feel abundance with five bucks in your pocket — or five million. It's not the currency that counts; it's more the emotions and moods it brings. What matters in your life revolves around a sense of spirit — be that the spirit of higher aspirations or the spirited nature in which you live day to day. When your spirits are high, you can be outrageously silly and effusive, skipping down the street or whooping with joy, embracing the abundance of life itself. But should those spirits drop, you can still be found beating your chest, being unreasonably emotional and demonstrative.

Abundance has you brimming with all sorts of emotions that can spill over the top — and gate 55 struggles to contain them, or keep them private. You would rather just let it all out and I would dare to suggest that some may have described you as a bit of a drama queen at times! Your overexpressive demonstrative nature means that you can be selective in the company you choose. It matters that you find like-minded, like-spirited people; just never expect anyone to be able to extricate you from a dark mood. Only your favorite music and sounds can soothe you then. Be left alone.

This gate carries an urgency for you to honor emotions. It also asks you to recognize that it is in your darkest hours that you can find the greatest creativity. Your moods are your gateway to great things. "Gather ye rosebuds while ye may." "Make hay while the sun shines." "Strike while the iron is hot." Pin these sayings to your wall — and live by them.

Extra Dimension

With no gates on, the Emotions are open as well as undefined, making you amazed at the dramas and fuss that other people allow in their lives. You are the detached, fascinated observer in regard to the emotions of others. This can make you appear a little cool and uninvolved but also means you can ride the emotions of people around you. It is no surprise that some great performers and Hollywood stars have open Emotions, allowing them to ride the required emotions of writers, directors, or co-stars.

Open Emotions does not mean you don't have feelings — it's just that they are not at the forefront of your expression in life and you'd prefer, if possible, to keep them private.

GATES WITHIN THE ROOT

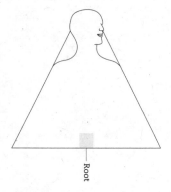

Root

Gate 19
The Gate of Approach

Gate 19 carries a want to be wanted and a need to be needed. These two factors combine to determine a joint Approach to life that's continually seeking and promoting an interconnection with others. Togetherness, companionship, and cooperation breed a platform for success in your world. This doesn't necessarily make you a needy individual, but it does require your needs — in terms of emotions, sex, and appreciation — to be met if you're to find alignment with your nature. Consequently, there is a flirtatious element to this gate until a successful interaction or partnership is established, one that ticks the required boxes.

The Root pressure here makes you reach out, wanting to be included in a family, group, or community. Any sense of separation or duality disturbs you; you have a yearning to end division and restore a sense of wholeness. You will do almost anything to bring people together and to be part of that grouping. Being the outsider or alone runs contrary to your nature.

Your need for belonging is no bad thing, because it helps foster cooperation and enables you to sense everyone else's needs and wishes long before they've realized them themselves. I would go so far as to say that you can often find you know someone better than they know themselves. It's as if this gate gives you the ability to look inside them and see what they require for their own improvement.

Your difficulty can be in distinguishing between *your* needs and those of others. Your danger is personal sacrifice. Your gift is showing other people the way to find greater alignment in both their worldly and spiritual lives.

Gate 38
The Gate of Opposition

You are someone who could, quite easily, take on the world, grinding your teeth with a steely determination and not inconsiderable truculence. You have a particular penchant for challenging authority. The pressure of the Root drives you to challenge for the common good and this can turn you into a defiant soul who will take on all comers and rule systems, meaning you feel challenged by, as opposed to connected to, any particular setup. You can be argumentative, antagonistic, and controversial. Sometimes this can lead to your becoming overly contentious and always up for a fight or debate, which some people find off-putting. Whereas most people seek to avoid confrontation, you stalk the places that require you to shake things up a little.

Gate 38 isn't deaf but only hears what it wants to hear. And yet it is really worth your while to listen for allies who will be attuned to the same challenges.

Your biggest challenge is finding out whether your struggles have any personal merit; otherwise, you will find yourself challenging life for no real reason. If your struggles *are* personal, however, you will most likely have causes worth fighting for. In the end, you will find that Opposition's efforts are played out in gaining an appreciation for your stance for truth in the world.

Gate 39
The Gate of Provocation

Provocation cuts both ways. You will either stoke the fires around you or find yourself easily riled. There is a pressure from within the Root to poke and tease life, provoking reactions that can be troublesome, mischievous, fun, or sexual. Your nature likes prodding the sleeping lion within other people to see if any spirit can be aroused. But you can even provoke somebody by standing in a doorway at a party, scanning the room, and missing them with your glance, inadvertently making them feel ignored. That's because you literally bring a provocative energy wherever you go.

Gate 39 is naturally flirtatious and can tease and tempt within social circles, a bit like casting fishing lures into the water and then waiting to see if the fish will rise to the bait. With this gate, your behavior is rooted in an attention-seeking drive toward being recognized and appreciated. You might well experience melancholy as you go through life, falling in and out of love in all kinds of instances, but if your provocation doesn't receive the attention you're looking for, you'll quickly look for other people and pots to stir.

Just be aware that all your attention-seeking provocation means that people can literally lose it in your company if you push and prod too much. In such a situation, my suggestion is to watch what is going on as objectively as possible, take a deep breath, and, if necessary, walk away. In effect, you are triggering someone else's emotional upsets and it may not be your responsibility to fix them at all. Strangely, some people enjoy having their emotional problems, so attempting to resolve them is going to make them even crazier! Many people have forgotten they can be such spirited beings, but coming into contact with you can revive that dramatic feeling. In this way, you're capable of providing spiritual CPR!

Gate 41
The Gate of Imagination

You have the keys to a rich imagination that can lead to all sorts of amazing experiences, just as long as you know the difference between realism and fantasy. Your dreams are so vivid that they can empower others to believe in them. The pressure from the Root brings a need to make your fantasies happen — whether they're realistic or not. You are a moviemaker within your own life, scripting fantastic plots in which you star. You are the one who can see and smell the blooms on a pruned rosebush.

Gate 41 is at the starting line of all life's experiences. It acts a bit like the mind's eye, looking into every conceivable possibility from every angle to find that missing experience that will bring about a sense of completion and wholeness. The danger is that this inclination can lead you into the realms of fantasyland and get you lost there. It pictures campaigns that can save the world, knights in shining armor, and imaginary conversations with icons. It may be best to focus your imagination on more attainable goals.

Essentially, Imagination represents finding an inner balance between giving and receiving. Even if you can imagine every conceivable notion of what you might desire, you'll also appreciate that the saying "Sometimes less is more" is quite true for you. Appreciate what you have and see that lightening your load can give you an enormous sense of freedom.

Gate 52
The Gate of the Mountain

When you stand and observe Mount Kilimanjaro, Everest, or K2, the first thing you'll notice in your awe is the stillness that defies time. No matter what thunderclouds envelop them, blue skies surround them, or people climb all over them, they are immovable. With gate 52, you are a mountain, containing the same core strength and carrying a silent stillness that others admire. Whenever there is a situation that calls for your attention or a drama that brings pressure for you to get involved, remember that from the Mountain you have an unparalleled view of things and can bring an unrivaled perspective.

This also means you can sometimes be immovable and obstinate, but your clarity is what counts. There is always something considered and sure about your input. You know when it is time for action and when it is time to keep still and reflect.

For you, the Root's built-in pressure to expand and evolve means allowing that pressure to build and build until you are launched into activity. From your vantage point, you know where the better future lies and the improvements your input can make. As the world goes crazy around you, you can be still and remind everyone that "This too will pass!"

Gate 53
The Gate of New Beginnings

Every story requires a beginning, middle, and end. Except, that is, the story of gate 53. You are a "serial starter," always chasing new beginnings but rarely sustaining yourself to reach the middle or end.

New Beginnings has an inherent openness to new experiences. It senses an almost unbearable possibility of boredom that prods it to pick up or try something — anything! — different. A little like scratching an itch, you are compelled to try all kinds of new endeavors. You may often find yourself entering into partnerships, projects, and activities that even at the outset you know might not work out or reach completion. I also find that people with this gate have a dozen books open and unfinished at page 28, garden projects that hang in permanent suspension, or a list of chores that somehow never get past the initial planning stage. Such is your way and there is no fault in it; you are a natural starter of things, an effective launchpad. As such, you often find that getting other people launched into new endeavors is really easy, and people seek you out for your gift of getting things under way.

In life, there are natural starts, like waking after sleep. With New Beginnings, you have an opportunity, as you wake, to get in tune with exactly what your life is calling for there and then. You might sense that getting up and having tea would be good, or going for a walk, or emailing someone. When you allow yourself to ease into starting what is natural to you, you will find that your life moves toward days filled with successful and pleasing actions.

Gate 54
The Gate of Ambition

This is a gate of blind ambition that can leave you head down, running for some unseen and distant goal. You want to clamber up a greasy pole in your career, climb the social ladder, and become top dog — all at the same time!

Ambition brings a drive to go beyond all limits to succeed socially, materially, and spiritually. It is a pressure that pushes you to forge contacts and alliances at every opportunity. You might well recognize a tendency to sometimes ride forces bigger than yourself or take on more than you can chew. It's as though you are kicking your feet frantically to push yourself up toward the ocean's surface after finding yourself deep underwater, desperate to breathe. Once you take in a lungful of intoxicating air, your hunger for more will send you swimming furiously to shore, at the same time hailing any available boat that can take you there faster. You will grab onto anyone and anything that propels you forward. It almost doesn't matter where you are headed; you just want to get there. Blind ambition just sets you in motion. Nothing will stand in your way, and you will do everything in your power to get where you need to be to find your freedom.

With this gate, you are capable of defying the odds. Be attentive to the drive that is your prime motivation and then fulfillment will become an attainable target.

Gate 58
The Gate of Joyous Vitality

We've all seen a newborn baby kick out eagerly or start giggling at the mere sight of an adult face. In the early days of life, we embrace the pure and natural vitality we are given by the Universe because we don't know any different, but for a lot of people it is a sensation that is soon lost. Not if you have gate 58, though. Then your cup runneth over with pure vitality, and the more you share, the more comes to you.

You trust in life and this becomes contagious, a natural spark capable of igniting everyone around you. You make a difference to the world with a natural exuberance that trusts in the challenges and windfalls that come your way. You seem to have an insatiable appetite to have it all — and savor it all. You run in the rain as much as you bask in the sun. But this can lead to you getting swept away by exuberance. So your lesson is to continue to see the joy in everything but to commit to that which resonates. This exuberance can be experienced as an internal pressure compelling you to hurl yourself into life, but the task is to become wise and engage with experiences that bring joy on your terms. For example, being a party animal doesn't mean having to attend every single party unless it really appeals to you.

There is always an essential balance in your life between the gifts that come to you and what it is you offer and give to others. As a natural celebrant of life, enjoy the dance!

Gate 60
The Gate of Limitation

You live within limitations, working with what cards life has dealt. You make the best of what you can. Hand you a bowl of lemons and you'll make lemonade. Ground rules are your stable platform. No one will take into account the realism of limiting factors more than you do. But you also know the difference between insurmountable handicaps and realistic opportunities that allow you to seize the moment, make your stand, and power through.

Limitation plays itself out in all its restrictive shapes and sizes when applied to your health, ambitions, finances, relationships, and family endeavors. The lesson here is not to become fixated on what you cannot achieve and what lies in the distance, beyond your parameters.

For each gate in the Root, there is an inbuilt pressure to expand and evolve, and gate 60 pushes you to move on with life by *accepting* your limitations. Stop fighting for things beyond reach and start looking under your nose. Then that framework becomes a springboard because you're no longer trying to flatten the boundaries that surround you. The moment you move into serenity and accept the qualities you have, you discover the freedom to evolve.

Extra Dimension

With no gates on, the Root is open as well as undefined, meaning your nature is not great at handling stress, especially the stressing out of others. You can become overwhelmed by imposed deadlines or goals, so be watchful about not being pressured into accomplishing or deciding anything without first falling back on your authority. Your challenge is not to cave in to outside pressure. The benefit of an open Root means that you can bring a sense of grounded calm into the stressed-out lives of others because you are adopting a detached view.

Between the Lines

That concludes the exploration of the sixty-four gates. Or does it? Because there's always more than meets the eye, more than merely the face-value meaning. Indeed, each gate carries six different nuances or flavors that enhance its influence. And that requires a certain amount of reading between the lines ...

Each of the gates in Human Design also has an invisible multifaceted structure containing extra elements to your true nature. As you now know, each gate corresponds to a hexagram in the *I Ching*. Anyone who is familiar with this ancient wisdom knows that a hexagram is composed of short, horizontal solid or broken lines stacked one above the other, six high. Consequently, there are six separate levels to each gate's structure. In Human Design, these are known as "the six lines."

Each line adds a subtle nuance to a gate's meaning. A gate with a first line, for example, is very different from the same gate with a sixth line.

Examples of Gates and Lines
from Prince Harry's Chart

Unconscious	Conscious
16. Jun 1984	15. Sep 1984
00:02:41	18:20:00
GMT (0.00hE)	WET/S (1.00hE)

12th Gate, 3rd Line = 12^3 ☉ 6^1 = 6th Gate, 1st Line

11^3 ⊕ 36^1

61^4 ☾ 23^4

16^1 ☊ 8^6 = 8th Gate, 6th Line

9^1 ☋ 14^6

35^6 ☿ 59^6

12th Gate, 3rd Line = 12^3 ♀ 57^3

44th Gate, 5th Line = 44^5 ♂ 26^1

38^1 ♃ 10^6

44th Gate, 3rd Line = 44^3 ♄ 44^6 = 44th Gate, 6th Line

9^6 ♅ 9^5

10^3 ♆ 10^1

50^4 ♇ 50^5

You will see from the illustration that the top left-hand corner of your life chart indicates a matrix of gate numbers that are either conscious (black, the right-hand column) or unconscious (pink, the left-hand column).

Attached to those gates, like identity tags, are the smaller numbers. These are the lines that denote the flavors to that gate, 1 to 6.

In the illustration, for example, taken from Prince Harry's chart, you will note that he has the 12^3 — gate 12 with the third line. Then 6^1 — gate 6 with the first line. And so on and so forth, as the illustration makes clear. These lines add an extra dash of flavor to Prince Harry's character.

The minutiae of these nuances, gate by gate, line by line, are another book for another time. There are, after all, 384 different permutations created by 64 gates × 6 lines, and limitless interpretations. I don't wish to take you to that level just yet, but here we'll explore the *general* meaning of each line, because there is a theme that binds all first lines together, all second lines, all third lines, all fourth lines, all fifth lines, and all sixth lines.

Something you might like to do at this point — and this is something I do when reading a life chart — is to add up the 1s, 2s, 3s, 4s, 5s, and 6s attached to your particular gates and see which line predominantly features in the top left-hand columns, both conscious and unconscious. If you have a majority of sixth lines, for example, this means that your nature is flavored by sixth-line qualities, so read the sixth-line section to glean its emphasis in order to better understand your true self, while appreciating the meaning of the other lines relevant to your chart.

First Lines

All first lines bring a foundational quality to a gate. With these lines, you seek sturdy foundations to work from. You need to understand and feel secure. You require something to be definitive, not uncertain. Without such knowledge and sure foundations, deep insecurity can set in. First lines need underpinning with trust; otherwise, insecurity can stifle a certain quality or potential.

In this respect, it is no surprise that first lines represent the subterranean level of a gate. They are hidden away, unsure whether to let something emerge into daylight. Yet they can bring an inherent discipline to embrace an aspect of life completely. They can make certain traits also appear hard and assertive, with a deep introspection attached. There is a slightly selfish "it's all about me" element here, a need to work alone or go it alone.

First lines can also induce physical reactions when it comes to inter-actions with other people or new projects, and this is manifested as awk-wardness, nervousness, edginess, sweats, or internal shakes. So note any physical reactions you have in both your personal and professional fields. Essentially, first lines bring a need to get to the bottom of a situa-tion or a particular trait.

Second Lines

All second lines bring a natural effortless and carefree quality to a gate. There is little self-awareness and much self-consciousness here, so with these lines you will seek reflections to gauge whether your input or con-tribution is recognized and appreciated. Whatever is expressed by a sec-ond line requires the feedback and assurance of another, which is why this line's theme is "you and me" and one-on-one interaction. It emits a projection field to glean feedback. In that feedback, it draws a sense of identity. It also brings gentleness, cooperation, and partnership but can sometimes lean toward submissiveness.

Paradoxically, a second line can render a particular trait more de-tached, unavailable, and withdrawn, almost as if it doesn't wish to be interrupted from whatever it's concentrating on. And if you *are* inter-rupted or distracted, be aware that there is an explosive, reactive element to second-line traits, so you will let others know about it! Here shyness often belies a fierce passion, but when that passion is harnessed and recognized, second lines add a dash of innovation and an easygoing attitude.

Third Lines

All third lines bring a touch of innovation and flair to a gate, but there is something noncommittal, evasive, indecisive, and quite impersonal about the third-line influence. Third lines bring movement, mutation, and some unpredictability. There is a versatile, adaptable element to them that adds an uncertainty to any expression.

Whenever a third line appears, know that there is the propensity to push the envelope and break new ground, regardless of the conse-quences. As a result, all third lines come armed with a certificate stating

"Qualifying from the School of Hard Knocks." With third lines, you will know all about making mistakes and picking yourself up again. Innovation and hardship walk hand in hand with this cutting-edge line that is undaunted by experiments and change. Failures become lessons, successes enable growth. That's why there is something of the "try it and see" attitude about all third lines. They bring an element of spice, danger, risk, excitement — and haphazardness — to all relationships, situations, and projects.

Fourth Lines

Fourth lines bring a heartfelt, selfless, all-inclusive element to a gate, carried by an "all for one and one for all" attitude. Their honorable expression is all about "we" and "us," belonging and being charitable. Yet there is a hidden fragility here as well, a wariness of rejection and not being acknowledged or appreciated.

Fourth lines foster friendly networking that attracts opportunities. But there is something quite rigid about this approach that can easily bring the single-minded belief that this way is the *only* way. Fourth lines like to direct the way ahead — in the interests of everyone, but they still like to do it their way. Consequently, that inflexibility runs the risk of being challenged, slapped down, or denied. This is what fuels the fear of rejection.

Once a fourth line feels challenged or unappreciated, it retreats. When in rejected mode, it breathes ice and its open arms become folded across the heart. It is self-protection coming across as hardness and meanness.

Fifth Lines

A fifth line brings the influence of a teacher or guide, instilling leadership and management qualities. It adds an educational, inspirational, and warriorlike flavor to any gate. This can make people with fifth-line traits seductive, mesmerizing, convincing, and artful.

Yet all is not necessarily as it seems. The performance might impress, but behind the convincing facade there is often questionable substance to whatever is playing out. I say this because fifth lines can float in a bubble removed from the real world. These lines are all about staking reputations and making big promises. Success beats its chest in grand, undefeatable glory. Failure hits hard, inducing self-pity. In reality, a fifth-line trait prefers to project outward rather than inward, avoiding its own frailties, issues, and complexities. So if you have many of them, you may struggle with an honest acceptance of the real world and how lost you feel within it.

Sixth Lines

A sixth line adds a compassionate, humanitarian element to a gate. It represents the uppermost level of a gate. If first lines are all about operating from sturdy foundations, sixth lines use their commanding view to oversee everything and capture the bigger picture. That's why most sixth-line traits tend to bring an authoritative flair to proceedings.

Having sixth lines induces an air of detached authority and objectivity, complete with an all-seeing wisdom. The difficulty here is maintaining interest because, due to your lofty position, your head can be in the clouds. You are looking over everything and so there is a low boredom threshold.

Sixth lines also tend to bring high ideals to a gate. You will seek to convey what the future holds and want everyone to believe in your vision. You may wear rose-tinted glasses and appear dreamy and unrealistic.

And yet a sixth line can bring the power to make dreams happen. With it, you can grasp situations with expert hands and take charge. Unlike the third line, the sixth line brings a wholehearted commitment that can lift and carry everything and everyone.

7

Design Profiling

The Twelve Profiles

Human Design has brought me great clarity and inner peace. It's as though I can exhale now after holding my breath for a very long time.

KS, Texas

As we enter the final stage of this journey, it is time to pull over, take stock, breathe, and take in the scenery. Take a good look around and become a conscious observer. You are witnessing life through your senses, no one else's, respecting your perspective, no one else's.

We've been looking at your unique contribution to the world, how you fit into the beautiful scheme of things. And there is no clearer illustration than the one provided by your Human Design "profile."

This profile is almost a portrait of your primary way of being and orientation in life. It is the third key to unlocking a fundamental part of your inner nature, following the other two important keys to remember: type and authority. Your profile completes the picture. It is the icing on the cake. It depicts how you interact with life and other people. If someone were to ask for a description of you, I would argue that your profile would provide the most compelling and insightful snapshot.

These days, profiling is a widely used evaluation tool indicating a person's typical behavior, temperament, communication style, and attitude. That's why sales teams use profiling to target potential customers, why companies are profiling employees to maximize performance and contribution, why psychological profiling brings a better understanding of clients, and why criminal profiling helps narrow down suspects. There is nothing more enlightening than the reality check of an accurate profile, an inescapable reminder of the person at the center of all curiosity.

Human Design profiling is slightly different in that it reveals not just the person, but their interactions. The profile, together with type and authority, says so much about someone, which is why, in the fields of

Human Design, you often hear a person introducing him- or herself as a "Manifesting Generator with a 3/5 profile and Emotional Authority" or perhaps a "5/1 Projector with Spleen Authority." However expressed, it provides an immediately insightful introduction. Which is why I say, "Forget your sign; what's your design?"

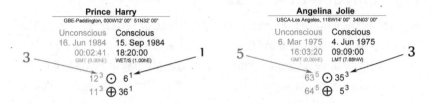

Your profile is a specific combination of the six lines, paired to create one of twelve profiles. How and why these twelve profiles come to be part of the system is something for more advanced teaching. For now, all you need to know is what your profile is and what that means for you.

Your profile is instantly recognizable in the life chart, jumping out from those columns of numbers in the top left-hand corner. *Quite simply, your profile is determined from the top two numbers on either side of the encircled dot that is the symbol for the Sun.*

In your life chart, you'll note the two larger fonts of the gate numbers, but *the profile is determined by noting the two line numbers*, the smaller numbers. It is these lines, when paired, that form your profile. In Human Design, we always place the black line number first, followed by the pink, because the black represents what is conscious, followed by the pink, representing the undercurrents of the unconscious. For example, in the illustrations provided, Prince Harry has a 1/3 profile and Angelina Jolie a 3/5 profile.

Due to the correlation with the *I Ching*, different dynamics are played out when different lines are matched in any one profile. It is here that we discover common ground with one another and potential compatibilities for friendships and working and loving relationships. Just as certain sun signs in astrology dovetail harmoniously together, so, too, do certain Human Design profiles. It is the principle of the yin and the yang. Some profiles find synergy and harmony together and some don't.

In my life, I know exactly which people I will and won't get on with based on profile information alone. I can instantly tell where the common ground is and if an association is going to be easy and instantly harmonious or need extra consideration.

Harmony and Resonance

As already indicated, the sixty-four gates in the life chart correspond to the sixty-four hexagrams in the I Ching. There are six lines in each hexagram, thus six levels to each gate's structure. All first lines have a common accord or harmony with all other first lines, all second lines harmonize with all other second lines, and so on. Also, a resonance or common frequency, like symphonic notes in a musical scale, exists between all first lines and all fourth lines, all second and fifth lines, and all third and sixth lines. The first line is like a personalized, foundational frequency of the more outgoing and heartfelt fourth line frequency; the second line is a more introverted or natural frequency of the more complex and expounding fifth line; and the third line is a less experienced frequency or more risk-taking version of the administrative and naturally authoritative sixth line. In the twelve profiles, half the profiles are made up of harmonizing lines, like the 1/4 or 6/3 profiles, indicating that they have a very particular, self-inclusive way of interacting in the world.

So, as you play with this information, take into account the compatibility notes at the foot of each description that follows. However, please don't take these suggested profile compatibilities literally, or as hard-and-fast rules for choosing a romantic partner or determining whether an existing relationship is truly viable. After all, there are many other factors at play within your Human Design to be considered before determining true compatibility... and that's an entirely different book!

So have some fun and treat the information as guidance within one area of your design, specific to profiles only.

In my life, I know exactly which people I will and won't get on with based on profile information alone. I can instantly tell where the common ground is and if an association is going to be easy and instantly complementary or require some extra considerations to work out.

THE TWELVE PROFILES

The 1/3 Profile

You are a restless soul, so I will endeavor to make this engaging enough to retain your interest; otherwise, you'll be off in pursuit of the next stimulation, in an endless search for stability and steady ground in a changeable world.

Despite an introspective side, you are an engaging and down-to-earth person with a profound and personal connection to the world, unconsciously thirsty for the juice of life, eager to learn and seeking the "latest, greatest, and newest." As such, you have a tendency to enter into projects or relationships with an open yet inquisitive nature, forever trying to determine their quality and value before committing 100 percent. Herein lies a first-line deep insecurity: the fear that the rug could be pulled from under your feet at any moment. When coupled with the unconscious noncommittal nature of the third line, this keeps you hopping, a cat on a hot tin roof. Yet you are privately crying out for rock-solid foundations and something to hold on to.

If something or someone doesn't feel secure, you will find fault, express boredom, or provide any excuse to disengage and retreat, sometimes abruptly. You don't like feeling hemmed in and you have an innate sense of what is and isn't working, be that a relationship or a project.

If we were engaged in conversation, I would notice a directness in your communication and an eagerness to get the point of the subject matter.

It is typical of your nature: getting to the bottom of things, absorbing, learning, taking away... and moving on.

Walk into any gathering and the first line in your profile will make direct contact, determining the foundations as the third line begins its engaging-disengaging exploration, hungry to meet new people, hungry for experience. One minute, you'll be the social bee, the next minute, outta there! Your eagerness for new things and people means you are liable to jump into projects and relationships and think later. This is symptomatic of a slightly self-absorbed, head-down, driving-forward approach that is oblivious to its impact on anyone else. In this respect, you need to be watchful of cutting people dead just because your interest levels have waned.

You are a competent individual, but there can be a bit of the hit-or-miss about your approach because of the "try it and see" side of the third line. You experiment on the job. When things go well, you can be jettisoned into exciting and successful orbits, leaving you in a state of awe and joy, embodying and *being* the experience. Until, that is, the restless moment comes to move on yet again! But you keep building through life, layer upon sturdy layer, seeking to improve yourself and your future.

In the end, you come to realize something repetitious about the way you live. OK, so you might have made all the right moves and lived life to the fullest, but there will be no real sense of breakthrough or lasting success.

Ultimately, you will reach a point where nonconfronted insecurities cannot be avoided and the need for stability will have to be addressed. Your bottom line — the bedrock of who you are — is the need to find secure and trusting foundations. When a project or person feels so important that you don't wish to lose it, you will, finally, put your stake in the ground, claim the land, and start to build home, business, and family in the interests of longevity. When you find that place, your commitment is total. In the unusual surroundings of self-assurance and steadfast support, you find fulfillment, meaning, and much sought-after acceptance of who you are.

Relationships with a 1/3

Your 1/3 partner has a secretive, introspective side, often talking quietly to him- or herself and asking: "What am I getting out of this?" and "Is there enough value to sustain a secure future?" Notice there is no regard for what *you* are getting out of this. 1/3 profiles need to receive, receive, receive before they learn to trust and give, give, give. Appreciating this self-indulgence is to understand that, deep down, it is nothing but well-hidden insecurity.

Trust is imperative if they are to wholly commit, so be watchful for the prodding, probing, and provocative questions of an investigator, trying to determine their safety in your arms. Until they are sure, they can adopt an almost evasive, slippery attitude. This can make them appear detached and impersonal. Indeed, there is always the risk that they will suddenly be out the door, leaving not a single clue as to the reason for their abrupt exit. This, inevitably, can be both distressing and confusing for those left behind. But this is the nature of the 1/3 profile.

I often find that it is the partner of the 1/3 who has to be the anchor, providing the reassurance. But when assured of love and security, the noncommittal 1/3 profile is the most solid and faithful partner to have at your side.

FAMOUS 1/3 PEOPLE
William Blake, Jon Bon Jovi, Michael Caine, Charlie Chaplin, Eric Clapton, Hillary Clinton, Princess Diana of Wales, Sally Field, Jesse Jackson, Michelle Pfeiffer, Pablo Picasso, Leann Rimes, and Nicolas Sarkozy

Compatibility

Your ideal profile matches are other 1/3s and 4/6 profiles. Away from such synergy, you would also find easy company with 3/5, 3/6, 5/1, and 6/3 profiles.

The 1/4 Profile

In the movie *One Hour Photo*, Robin Williams plays a photo-lab technician who says: "The things which we fear most in life have already happened to us." I suspect it's a quote that may resonate with many 1/4 profiles, whose hearts are vast but cagey and whose nature treads carefully in the pursuit of opportunity.

You are an opportunist but have a disciplined, cautious approach, because the foundations and security of a situation have to be right. This represents a certain push-pull contradiction because of the perpetual balance between the more outgoing yet selective first line and the socially capable but wary fourth line. You will always need to establish the whole picture and comprehend every aspect of a personal or professional opportunity because your feet need sure ground and your heart needs protecting.

Essentially, you are an openhearted person with a great desire to embrace whatever life throws your way, but you need to feel secure first. The insecurity of the first line and the rejection fears of the fourth line can foster an overbearing need to retain control of many situations, especially personal ones. In your Utopian vision, everyone walks around open armed, exuding warmth and hugging strangers. A good heart provides sturdy foundations for success and growth in your book. No wonder like-minded souls become the target of your pursuit for security in life. In general, you are selective about forging close relationships. I wouldn't dismiss the theory that the most secure relationship you know is with your own heart. I say this because your insecurities tilt you into internalizing, turning the focus on your own needs, sometimes to the cost, in neglect, of those around you. When in doubt or crisis, your world stops to find stability. At such times, you can be consumed by a sense of dread, retreat, and become unreachable.

However, there is a flip side. Such an intense self-focus makes you a passionate, direct opportunist with an entrepreneurial flair who can attack projects and endeavors with determined gusto. You will throw your heart into achieving success and don't shirk risks in the workplace, eager to impress bosses and peers alike. When you are passionate about what you do, there is no one better to have on a team. You can be a real trailblazer, bringing innovation and opportunity that have far-reaching effects, and nothing makes your nature swell more than the recognition and acknowledgment of your unstinting efforts. In fact, your skills, warmth, compassion, and kindness are already likely to have drawn a long list of admirers, probably more than you realize.

If we were in conversation, it would become apparent that you were sensitive, honorable, and frank and spoke from the heart, exuding capability and strength. Your warmth is capable of melting people. But fragility lies beneath the surface. If people prod and poke too deeply or recklessly, you tend to back away until you are certain of them. When hurt, the open arms are folded and the barriers erected.

Walk into any gathering and the first-line element makes direct contact, determining the foundations of the situation as the fourth-line element scans the room, wondering who shows promise and who appears genuine. Authenticity is everything to you.

I tell 1/4 profiles to be discerning in who and what they embrace because within your makeup there exists the possibility of a breakdown if pushed too far. What you are seeking are projects or pursuits that stabilize you and reward your efforts. In both personal and professional arenas, ensure there is a healthy balance between what you give and what you receive. All relationships need to be reciprocal if your open-hearted nature is to shine. When you find that trusting foundation, you can brilliantly express who you are.

> **FAMOUS 1/4 PEOPLE**
>
> Muhammad Ali, Fidel Castro, Albert Einstein, Dwight Eisenhower, Ewan McGregor, Sid Vicious, and Willie Shoemaker

Relationships with a 1/4

Your 1/4 partner has a compassionate heart, but the first-line element makes him or her wary about opening up. The result can be an extremely sensitive and closed-off partner. These people are aching for a warm embrace but are extremely difficult to get close to, so you will require patience and strength, at times, to pry their folded arms apart and bring them out of introspective retreat.

So much goes on inside their heads that they can be very hard to read or understand. What they require is gentle coaxing, reassurance, and a sense of being valued and appreciated. They need you to be tactile, so throw your arms around them and hold their hand. Physical reassurance is important. If you pull away an inch, they can retreat a mile. When they hear the words "We are in this together" or "It's all about you and me, no one else," it underpins the world in which they stand, trust builds, the emotional walls come down — and you can become the main beneficiary of an immensely loving, loyal, and warm individual.

Compatibility

Your ideal match is with other 1/4 profiles because no other match carries the same level of resonance. Away from such synergy, you find easy relations with 2/4, 4/1, and 4/6 profiles.

The 2/4 Profile

I shall tread softly, trying not to distract you too much. I have already noted the "Do Not Disturb" sign on the door and appreciate you are someone who likes your own sanctuary and hates being interrupted while focusing on something — even your favorite television show! But there is a mystery to crack here — and that mystery is you.

I suspect you can come across as something of an enigma, even to yourself. A 2/4 profile neither sees itself clearly nor projects itself easily. You are extremely shy and retiring one minute then bold and outspoken the next, interacting with the world in a bright and breezy manner, then disappearing behind a closed door into a self-made "cave."

It is hard to pin down your moods from one moment to the next. Observers tend to see in you more than you see in yourself, which probably explains why you seek your reflection in them, gleaning feedback. Without such feedback, you really can be oblivious to who you are. It's as if you need others around you to find essential support, strength, and purpose. In turn, this creates a propensity to give too much, as someone who is naturally submissive and cooperative.

If we were in conversation, I'd detect a natural, easygoing warmth and a big heart. You would listen intently to my responses, not because you'd be interested in me but because you'd want to learn something about *yourself* from my observations. Life is your eternal university, and all interactions form the basis of your teachings, inspiration, and guidance. You tend to derive identity from others. If someone you admire does something that enhances their life, you'll mimic it. If you witness inspiring advice on television, you'll adopt it. *Anything* that helps you discover who you are is explored. This is who you are, so don't allow the mystery to get you down.

The one thing you might recognize (or not, because it's unconscious) is a certain vulnerability and fear of rejection. You are naturally heartfelt, with an abundance of love and giving, but this coexists with a wariness of exposing yourself too much, just in case you are misinterpreted and then cast aside. This probably explains why you prefer one-on-one interactions as opposed to great crowds of people. Walk into a room and the first thing you'll do is stand to one side, waiting to be approached. You are a social fisherman, throwing out an invisible line, throwing certain looks or odd remarks to lure people into a one-on-one interaction.

When riled or upset, you can display an unintended and reactive meanness. There is a latent irritability, and flashes of anger can erupt. In some cases, this anger can be explosive. An amenable nature can be pushed into an impressive fury, especially when you are distracted from focusing on something that is mentally engaging.

One thing you certainly won't appreciate is that there is something of the genius about you, a special quality that people can't quite put their finger on. You also happen to be a highly creative being. When you are engaged in a pursuit or profession that comes naturally, you can excel and your creativity will shine when you throw your heart into it. You can pursue objectives with vigor and focused determination if they grab your interest. And the more success you embrace, the more you thrive.

Ultimately, your aim in life is to embrace your naturalness. When you are functioning naturally, without the complication of a preponderance of thought, you can soar. Being natural and honoring what comes naturally, be it an expression or deed, are important to your ability to shine. The more natural you are, the less fearful you become. Overexposure may well feel daunting, but left to your own devices you run the risk of being left to your own devices forever! So learn to trust life — and yourself — more.

When you begin to feel more comfortable with the advice and knowledge you can impart, you can become one of life's great parents, wise sages, teachers, and instructors. So never limit yourself from the exposure to every experience life can offer — your heart and naturalness are a breath of fresh air in the modern-day world.

Relationships with a 2/4

You cannot help but love your 2/4 partner because he or she can be the sweetest, most gentle of individuals, with the biggest heart and a vulnerability that is irresistible. One thing you mustn't take advantage of is their natural tendency to give, give, give without honoring their need to receive. So however cooperative, submissive, or even malleable a 2/4 profile may seem, don't take them for granted — they have needs, too. And when they are pushed to the breaking point, their peace can turn to anger! The fragility of the unconscious fourth line requires them to be valued, and they'll quietly resent one-way traffic . . . until they blow. So it's important to strike a balance that appreciates their wants and needs.

They can be maddening to be around: carefree, oblivious, and bright one moment, sulking and brooding the next. There is also a propensity to share a conversation in which you are convinced they are listening, but then, the next morning, they cannot recall its detail. 2/4 profiles soon discard information that they regard as trivial.

One thing to recognize is your partner's need to have solitude and space to retreat. And don't interrupt 2/4s; these are solitary people who decide when *they* are in the mood to engage. Don't ask me why — that's part of the curious enigma.

One thing I would say about 2/4 partners — especially if you are in the infancy of dating — is that their shyness means they take some time to warm up and be coaxed into a natural state of all-embracing intimacy. The good thing for partners of these people is that 2/4 profiles can be absolutely devoted when they find someone who answers all their questions about themselves and life and provides security. A relationship can soar when you reflect back to them a sense of worth and appreciation and put their needs on an equal footing with yours.

Compatibility

2/4 profiles find an ideal match with other 2/4s and 5/1 profiles. Away from that ideal matching, they relate easily with 2/5, 4/6, 5/2, and 6/2 profiles.

The 2/5 Profile

I feel like giving you a compass to find your way home, because you are someone who can be caught in the uncertain middle ground between the solitariness of the second line and the distant fantasies of an unconscious fifth. This creates a strange yet fascinating profile of a capable leader who is almost reticent to lead, unsure whether to engage or not. But when you do engage, you are a naturally imaginative, charismatic leader.

Your sense of detachment can leave you feeling lost in space, observing the dramas on Earth. This is caused by the curious combination of the feedback-seeking projections of the second line and the illusory projection field of the fifth, leaving you bouncing between the suppositions of others and the illusions you create. No wonder you harbor an underlying uncertainty about whether you ever will meet *anyone* who will understand and complete you. Will you *ever* feel a connection to anyone and anything around you?

This is probably why you tend to indulge in surface interactions, wary about letting anyone in. You yearn for that special relationship, great job, or purpose where you hear the click of perfect synergy, but such a yearning can be rooted in a dreamy perfection. In personal matters, this makes you picky and over-fussy. In professional terms, there is a tendency to move around, not wishing to feel exposed in one position for too long. In the workplace, you think outside the box and dream up innovative, off-the-wall ideas. Your clever input arrives from nowhere, surprising many — including yourself! But you won't bask in self-praise. Such a thing doesn't exist. You will engage peers or colleagues in conversation to receive praise that makes you feel good, recognized, and appreciated. There is something of the natural genius about you, and I suspect you underestimate how truly wise and brilliant you can be.

Keeping up appearances matters greatly to you. Indeed, maintaining your reputation and "act" is essential for your own sense of status. The cloak of a great actor is only removed when alone. You are content to live in a hermitage yet are fascinated by people around you, a spectator who doesn't want to be in the spotlight. Indeed, you can find yourself caught in a web of others' problems and dramas because a sense of detachment allows you the perspective to become the great rescuer, confidante, and crisis manager, the person everyone turns to and seeks out. So you can be viewed as a savior and a seductive knight in shining armor — and, consequently, the second-line element sees itself in such feedback and the danger is that you live up to a false image of everyone's suppositions, praise, and compliments. This provides the beneficial side-effect of getting to play out many amazing parts in a life rich with experiences *made by other people*. Yet there will always be the niggling uneasiness that you are only appreciated for what you *appear* to be, not for who you truly are.

If I were in conversation with you, I would sense a reluctant leader, yet hear a convincing voice carried by a charismatic punch. There may be a risk of shyness but this will soon be concealed. I'd no doubt detect something shifty and not quite straightforward, and could have a conversation with you a million times without really learning anything new about you as an individual. I would go so far as to say that you will probably only ever have one or two *meaningful* relationships in your lifetime.

Ultimately, you will come to recognize that your skills and potential leadership provide a true nature that is far braver and more capable than you give it credit for. For 2/5 profiles, life is a potential playground. If only you could unbind yourself! You need to come down from the top tier of the stands, join in, and start living — because that's where true fulfillment is found. Once you stop giving importance to the approval of others, remove the straitjacket, and let yourself go a bit, you'll start to feel the buzz of authentic interactions and the genuine praise of people who see you for all that you have to offer.

Relationships with a 2/5

Your 2/5 partner will forever scrutinize your authenticity and whether you can be trusted. 2/5s cannot abide artificialness or insincerity, so when you tell them something meaningful, *mean* it. These people need someone who honors, appreciates, and recognizes them. Until that bond is created, there is a danger they will act out a relationship role from behind a convincing smoke screen.

They are capable, resolute towers of strength. But one frustration likely to emerge from you is the cry, "Why won't you let me in?" It is notoriously hard to get close to anyone with a fifth-line element, especially when coupled with the self-consciousness and self-denial of the second line. Yet you will mean much more to 2/5s than they will openly concede. Believe me when I say that you are their ballast, sounding board, and source of courage and reassurance.

What you need to do, over time, is ground 2/5 partners, hold them by the hand, and lead them into life's raw experiences. "Keeping it real" will help coax their true natures out and free them from illusions and false realities. When this happens, the joy they can bring will be rewarding to both of you.

Compatibility

You find an ideal match with fellow 2/5s, but away from that synergy, you also find easy relations with the 5/2, 2/4, and 5/1 profiles.

**FAMOUS
2/5 PEOPLE**

Coco Chanel, Kevin Costner, Richard Gere, Gladys Knight, Shirley Temple-Black, Mark Twain, Prince William of Wales, and Robin Williams

The 3/5 Profile

You are the last person who needs reminding that life is a school of hard knocks, filled with the exhilarating chaos on which your nature thrives, aided by a potentially wicked sense of humor and a polished, charismatic air. I can almost see you adopting a James Bond air, blowing those cheeks, wiping that brow, and saying, "Tell me about it...but I live to fight another day!"

Pain and pleasure are the twinned realities of life, though I suspect you've known more pain due to living life on the edge, leaping in with both feet, and learning as you go. Of all profiles, you are the most likely to stick your fingers into an electric socket just to find out what goes on in there! You are your own worst enemy, such is your insatiable inquisitiveness and curiosity. You like to leave no stone unturned in your pursuit of reward and joy, and there is an indefatigable spirit to the way you embrace life, come what may.

3/5 profiles are here for a fast-track lifetime. In failure, trauma, and survival, you glean wisdom. Life will bounce you into dead ends, heartbreak, crushing disappointment, and wrong situations while asking you to take the blessings in disguise. It's almost as if your role is to witness, endure, or lead from the front in order to educate and guide others.

You are a capable and adaptable leader in a crisis, with a wisdom that shapes a visionary element, and there is something of the rebel in you, wanting to challenge authority and point out what is and isn't working.

You want to be a force for change in all areas of life. Your adaptability makes you expert in a storm of crisis, because you've been there, done that, and know how the drama ends! Your understanding of life also arms you with a natural forgiveness.

The fascinating mix of this profile is the third-line element, which needs the juice of life, together with the illusory yet hypnotic nature of the fifth line. This turns you into a charismatic, persuasive seducer, subtly reeling others into relationships, projects, or pursuits. But it is a profile that is noncommittal by nature and doesn't wish to hang around if there is not a sustainable engagement with its interest. Nevertheless, you are always strategizing, seeing how it can all work in your best interests, toying with experimental and grand ideas.

If I were in conversation with you, there would be an outgoing, engaging eagerness about your communication style and obvious zest for life. I daresay you could come across as a bit of a dreamer, but doubtless there would be a multitude of crazy anecdotes, all carried off with a self-deprecating humor concealing the pain of the time. When you fall back on your sharp wit, you are one of the funniest people around. Humor is both your medicine and your master deflector.

But not all 3/5s can look on the bright side. Life can become too much and leave you defeated. You can get to the point where all you crave is a settled life. You are done with the trials, tribulations, and tests and want to throw in the towel. When 3/5 profiles feel beaten, despite their best efforts, they surrender. But their nature will not rest and will always seek to propel them into a fresh adventure. So surrendering will only exacerbate any inner frustrations. The third line will never stop catapulting the 3/5 into all sorts of relationships, projects, travels, travails, purchases, and lifestyles. The unconscious fifth line sometimes paddles hard to make real life match the fantasies.

Ultimately, you are seeking the reward for your hardship. You are always seeking that special someone who can bring inner peace amid the chaos. When that person is found, commitment is total. In accepting chaos, you accept yourself. Life will never be a destination but is an eternal journey. Embrace it, find medicine in laughter, and absorb all the consequential wisdoms that make people admire you so much. And at the end of your days, I guarantee you will have traveled, loved and lost, succeeded and failed, and amassed a veritable library of personal experiences to recall and ponder.

Relationships with a 3/5

It is quite possible that 3/5 partners have no real idea of how restless they are, particularly in a relationship. Of course, they will have the gift of gab and say all the right things, but as they're stroking your face and whispering sweet nothings, keep an eye out for the feet inching toward the exit door. An escape clause should be written into any love contract with a third-line element, especially when coupled with the dreamy nature of the fifth line, which brings a strong degree of romanticism and big promises.

The 3/5 profile is forever in search of the perfect relationship and will not compromise its ideals. Did I say "perfect"? What I meant to say was "purrr-fect." These people need to be met, and understood, on every possible level before they give 100 percent commitment. These are highly selective individuals when searching for a life mate.

One thing you need to appreciate is the essential ingredient to throw into the mix with a 3/5 partner — laughter. Let life bring the dark side; let you be the source of light. They can be deeply emotional partners, but the tears of laughter need to balance the tears of pain. Grant them this much and you will come to know and admire a true ally and arbiter and the bridge builder of an unpredictable but exciting future. When 3/5s feel they have met their match, they bring the greatest level of commitment and stability to a relationship that is possible. Just be prepared to be dragged off in pursuit of big dreams!

Compatibility

Your ideal matches are with other 3/5s and 6/2 profiles, but away from that synergy you also find common ground with 3/6, 5/1, 5/2, and 6/3 profiles.

> **FAMOUS 3/5 PEOPLE**
>
> Jane Austen, Beethoven, Tony Blair, Gisele Bündchen, Winston Churchill, Jodie Foster, Ernest Hemingway, Angelina Jolie, JFK, J. Z. Knight, Rupert Murdoch, Ralph Nader, Dolly Parton, Diana Ross, William Shatner, and Meryl Streep

The 3/6 Profile

Your life has two speeds: one for the fast lane, one for the slow; sometimes you will be engaged in the breakneck speed of raw experience, sometimes retreating to higher, wiser ground. Indeed, you are a mix of the exhilarating chaos of the third line and the overseeing governance of the sixth, a fusion of hungry daredevil and detached wise owl.

As such, you will no doubt be aware of having a different style of living than most. You wrestle with an internal dilemma over whether you should actually get involved in the action of life or rise above it all. But experience and astute perception combine to create a deeply wise person, transforming crash-and-learn experiments into profound insights, which turns you into something of a role model and expert on life.

What tends to happen is that the daredevil tires to the point of withdrawal, then retreats to a position of wisdom on the hilltop. The action man becomes the commander in chief; the factory-floor worker, the manager; the actor, the director. 3/6 profiles command respect because they arrive with a "been there, done that, listen to me" attitude. For them, life is a graduation from eager student and accomplished "doer" to wise administrator or guide. Whatever chaos and "try it and see" experimentation the third line takes on, the sixth line is expert at pulling them through.

Unlike a 3/5 profile, the 3/6 profile *can* look forward to an end to the limited chaos. Indeed, most 3/6 profiles mature through three stages in life: at the ages of eighteen, thirty, and fifty. You might well have been a daredevil teenager, ripping through adolescence, but then the threshold of adulthood led you to adopt higher responsibilities. If not, the transition would have been likely at thirty, after cramming in life, and earning the scars, in your twenties. Whatever the route, a 3/6 profile matures into a role model.

Come fifty years old, having risen above the chaos you now observe, you will count yourself as one of the most proven and knowledgeable humans alive. You are someone whose input can really make a difference. Your sixth line has flashes of insight and sees the bigger picture that other third lines fail to see because they're too busy crashing through life. There is therefore a substance to you that few profiles can match.

If I were having a conversation with you, there would be something resolute and authentic about your communication style, softened by the humor of the third line. You engage people to the point of fascination, leaving a lasting impression with your wisdom and take on life. I would probably advise others to talk to you, nudging them with words like "That 3/6 profile is really worth listening to!"

Of course, there is no escaping the noncommittal nature of the third-line element. Indeed, the need to know the whereabouts of the exit door can be exacerbated by the sure knowledge that you can escape to higher ground. But then the sixth line ultimately tempers this restlessness, foreseeing the consequences of cutting and running from projects, pursuits, or people who no longer hold your interest.

The 3/6 profile conducts an internal balance, especially when it has matured. So it really matters to your sense of fulfillment that you only engage in situations that resonate. The crash-and-learn days need to evolve into true discernment. A sense of being trapped will tell you when you've come down from the hill to engage with inappropriate pursuits and people.

You 3/6 profiles are on a journey to a destination of great wisdom, but you do experience a hard time getting there. However, you are led by a higher calling and find fulfillment in taking responsibility and providing direction. Ultimately, people will come to you to seek emotional, spiritual, and life advice, and I can almost see your wry, wise smile as you tell them, with the good soul of a wise old sage, "My dear child, where shall I begin . . . ?"

Relationships with a 3/6

3/6 partners will soon learn that they are capable of attracting anyone and anything, and discernment is their key to fulfillment. These are people who appear wise beyond their years and yet have been fighting an inner tumult to rush into the chaos of life. However learned, however wise, however certain they may sound, never lose sight of the fact that they will always need their own space and room to breathe. Don't be fooled into thinking that the hilltop of the wise sage provides freedom per se; a 3/6 profile can still feel caged within itself. They are free spirits and independent souls who need to be understood and embraced on that level. Asking them to change or trying to control them will send them running to the hills in fear of a life spent in a straitjacket. So I'll say it again, just so we are clear: they need an *awful* lot of space.

When that freedom is honored, your commitment to them is reciprocated and they are steadfast partners. There will be no obstacle you cannot overcome together. In time, they come to learn that their mission in life is to understand that they are here not to get lost in their dreams but to make them happen. A strong union or ally makes that mission possible. So, harness your partner's self-belief, enjoy the ride, enjoy the view — and take on the world!

Compatibility

Your ideal match is with like-minded 3/6 and 6/3 profiles, but you also find easy relations with 1/3 and 3/5 profiles.

The 4/6 Profile

I'm not sure whether I should first ask you to come down from the hilltop where you've been contemplating inspired thoughts or tell you to stop sitting on the fence with your internal dilemmas. As an astute observer of life, you are someone who spends too much time either in the head or in the heart, not knowing where is best! But when you do arrive at a point of conclusion or conviction, the combined wisdom of the head and heart knows which direction to go in and can be of enormous help to you and influence on others. When opportunity knocks and you grab its coattails, you can be a true trailblazer, directing yourself and others toward exciting horizons.

The "head versus heart" dilemma is a potential theme for your life, played out whenever there is an invitation to join a project or make a personal commitment. This leads to internalizing, which works something like this: from the hilltop there seems to be a grand overview, clarity, inspiration, and a degree of rationale, but then a wary heart kicks in and something contracts at the faintest prospect of disappointment, hurt, or failure.

What the conscious fourth line needs to rely on more and more is something it doesn't automatically know — the wisdom of the unconscious sixth. If 4/6 profiles can learn to fall back on that wisdom, a liberating trust can be embraced. Of course, that's a big ask when the more conscious fears of rejection are fueled by the fourth line. This leads to a tendency to reject before being rejected and to withdraw rashly from projects. Yet each time this happens, you ignore a higher wisdom and forget the extent of your valuable contribution and the love you are capable of bringing into the world.

Maybe this explains why friendship first forms the platform to everything you engage in: getting to know someone first enables you to gauge who and what is reliable and genuine. All you want to do is be accepted by a well-knit group of people or a community in which your abilities and gifts can work toward the common good. This can, on occasions, lead to a tendency to try too hard to be liked.

If we were engaged in conversation, your transcendent aura would be the first thing I'd notice, emanating from the glow of a warm heart and wise soul and granting you exceptional social skills. You can radiate in any environment and if an audience is accepting and receptive, you come into your own, holding court and bringing great entertainment and wisdom through which others feel educated. When this happens, you are like the wise sage on the hill with people gathered around, listening intently.

What matters is that your surrounding family and social community prosper and grow. You want others to succeed as much as you want it for yourself. You are a compassionate humanitarian with an open heart whose nature finds affinity in united and harmonious relations. *Teamwork* and *togetherness* are your watchwords. Yet within that cohesive desire, there is alertness over how much you *personally* wade in and commit. This gives voice to your preference for being the overseeing director, organizer, or authority figure, the compassionate leader who brings wisdom, optimism, and hope to many situations as you grasp the bigger picture from your place on the hill. You make a great ally, sponsor, or consultant.

There is almost a regal sense to your aura. The irony is that despite your inherent fears you are at your best when embracing responsibility, applying sound knowledge. You wish to convey and bring higher ideals into the world. Indeed, the lofty dreams of the sixth line combine with the opportunism of the fourth line to create a potent dynamic that can make great things happen for you and everyone around you.

However, failure or rejection can easily wound a sensitive heart and then your warmth turns cold. The arms that were once open wide are folded across the heart, like armor plating across the chest. Self-protection kicks in and you retreat, the fears of the fourth line and the escapism of the sixth line combining to hastily construct an ice palace beyond the reach of interaction. If I were sent in as the negotiator to coax you out, I'd merely remind you that you had jumped impulsively into a wrong situation. I'd remind you that your demonstrative love was a pure gift; that you could turn hatred and misgivings into love in the blink of an eye; that you could lock onto an inspiring vision when everyone else seemed stuck and standing still. I would tell you that you were a force for great love and great change. So what a waste, therefore, to be cut off and isolated. How would you feel then?

When you recognize and start to honor an innate wisdom, you can dovetail it with your heart's desires. That way, the head and the heart can stop fighting and walk hand in hand through life. Use the head to educate the heart and you can find a lasting fulfillment.

Relationships with a 4/6

Your 4/6 partner is a potentially complex soul: oh so wise and sure on one hand, oh so afraid and vulnerable on the other. Great hearts and wise souls need to be treated with kid gloves in the modern-day world. So don't be fooled by the "everything is just fine" mantra of someone whose appearance of success and steely strength can be deceptive. These people need buckets of love and appreciation. Otherwise, you'll be forever coaxing them out of an ice palace.

You need to be aware that 4/6s can sometimes jab so hard that you've no idea where it came from or why it happened. When something wounds their heart, it brings out the mean streak of the fourth line and the aloof withdrawal of the sixth. You must realize that this is not personal, but a trigger reaction that requires understanding and patience to assuage. Also know that they regard themselves as being right about most things and need to be acknowledged accordingly.

4/6 profiles make easy friendships but commit rarely. Indeed, such is their selectivity that they are more likely to make special friends than great intimates. But should you be the fortunate one blessed with custody of one of these warmest of hearts, then take a leaf out of the book of that great romantic singer-songwriter Michael Bolton and practice "time, love, and tenderness," day in, day out. Let down or betray 4/6s and they will retreat into a faraway place, brooding and miserable, pretending to be brave but lashing back with meanness and cruel words. But the tenderness of unconditional love, hugs, and honest emotions warm their hearts, and when you've encouraged them to feel comfortable and secure with their heartfelt expressions, you can enjoy a mutually beneficial, giving relationship. When they open their hearts, you will find the warmest and wisest of lovers.

> **FAMOUS 4/6 PEOPLE**
>
> Julie Andrews, Drew Barrymore, David Beckham, Chuck Berry, Prince Charles, Julie Christie, the Dalai Lama, Bob Dylan, Bill Gates, Camilla Parker Bowles, Brad Pitt, Vanessa Redgrave, and Condoleezza Rice

Compatibility

Your ideal match is with fellow 4/6 profiles and 1/3s. Away from that synergy, you also find easy relations with 1/4, 2/4, 4/1, and 6/2 profiles.

The 4/1 Profile

I have only one clear thing to say to you: "Stick to your path. Follow your heart."

You are a rare individual, being the only fixed profile among the twelve. This means you have one theme in life and an extremely precise and particular way of living — and it's all about a heart's desire guiding you toward your destiny. This is because you have what is called a "fixed-fate vibration": one path, one purpose, one perspective, meaning that your true nature must stick to a rigid course, as plotted by the Universe, without deviating and without exception.

In some ways, this is a loner's profile, mainly because your immovable and inflexible nature makes you hard to understand. Your foundations are built by one determining factor — the fate you have been handed in life. And whatever that might be, you'll throw your heart into pursuing it.

Just as there are sixty-four genetic codons to the human makeup, there are sixty-four gates in the Human Design system. Your "fixed fate" is determined by just *one* of them. This one aspect presets the tone and context of all your interactions. You hold true to a particular and vital aspect of the human psyche and that's it. For example, I knew a male pensioner with the 4/1 profile. His one fixed fate from the sixty-four gates was Stimulation. As such, stimulation became the fixed theme to his life. He drove the most impressive car, owned properties around the world but was too busy to visit them, had endured several medical surgeries, had just been bankrupted after one business turned sour, and yet gambled and drank with the best of them, regaling everyone with outrageous stories of adventure. No one and nothing could stop his endless search for stimulation. He was true to his profile.

So how do you determine *your* fixed fate? Look at the conscious-unconscious column of information in your life chart, and find the top number in black (where the conscious fourth line is attached). That is the gate number relating to your fixed fate. Turn back to chapter 6 and read its meaning. This is your immovable theme in life.

You can expound genius in your particular expression but can suffer when you're not appreciated by a world with a short attention span. Yet it is so important that you are not deflected from your course in life. I cannot overstate the importance of this truth, because if a rule system, job requirement, or family pressure diverts you from a heart-felt purpose, your life will fall to pieces as you lose connection with any sense of purpose. The first-line foundations will fall away and the fourth-line heart will break. You are not here to live in the styles that everyone else takes for granted; your agenda is unique and you need to be aware of those who support you to live that truth, and those who, for one reason or another, are intimidated by your steadfast pursuit and do not understand its importance to your sense of balance and well-being.

I admire anyone with a 4/1 profile because you have a tough agenda that is challenging at every turn. You see everyone else being flexible and possibly random, and when you try to follow suit, you feel derailed.

So, please, I implore you to remain true to your nature. Thank the naysayers for sharing their opinion, but live your life from your heart. Put on the blinkers, become focused, and stick to your particular path. When you do, you become a pillar of strength and conviction. You are all heart, mean well, and will forever give 100 percent. Ultimately, once you stop struggling against your nature's restrictions and accept your fragility, you will find success and fulfillment by following your heart — and finding your destiny.

> **FAMOUS 4/1 PEOPLE**
> Fabio Capello, Mary, Queen of Scots, Bette Midler, Peter Sellers, Gianni Versace, and Stevie Wonder

Relationships with a 4/1

You will soon discover that your 4/1 partner can be a little fixated in one direction. If 4/1s' nature is embraced, and respected, they won't wish to try anything new and won't thank you for trying to expand their horizons. You just have to let them be if you truly have their interests in mind.

Acceptance means the world to 4/1s because they are so rarely understood or appreciated for their sometimes rigid approach. They feel as though they are constantly trying to protect their heart, when all they want to do is sing its song. They will feel a lot of pressure to change and will need you to embrace them for who they are.

Once 4/1s feel free to be themselves, they can make an amazing heartfelt connection that brings about a sense of security. Acknowledgment, appreciation, and unconditional acceptance are expressions of love in themselves. It might not be an easy relationship, because anything that is immovable can lead to friction, but your 4/1 partner has a big heart, and if you can cut your cloth accordingly, a warm and unique relationship can soar in a freedom the 4/1 rarely feels.

Compatibility

Because of your particularly unique profile, the most important thing is to honor yourself and life process first and foremost. You'll find a certain degree of synergy among other 4/1s and 1/4s and will also get along with 4/6s.

The 5/1 Profile

Here come the natural leaders, guides, and teachers in life. You are bright, clever, and expert at problem solving and lead with great vision and an imaginative approach to resolving issues and overcoming all manner of obstacles. You cope. You solve. You advise. Your research and homework are meticulous; you are determined to get to the bottom of things. No one could seem more thorough or dependable than you. Indeed, there is a discipline to your leadership. But you are the swan whose appearance impresses everyone. What they don't see is the furious paddling beneath the surface and the concealed insecurities that you would hate anyone to discover.

I suspect that if I asked you to describe who you actually were, that would constitute the one conundrum you couldn't solve. Indeed, I can almost see you shifting to the back foot, ready to deflect such a searching probe, which is typical of 5/1s: great at looking outward, but not so keen on looking inward. You are highly capable performers, but you're prone to building a world of barriers and deflectors. No wonder there is something unrecognizable about you. I'd even argue that some of the closest people in your life don't really know who you are, yet remain captivated by the great dreams you paint onto a projection screen, portraying the person you want them to believe you are — or sometimes the person *you* believe you are!

You tend to project an image and live by it, reluctant to show too much of your real self. This has the effect of creating an image that fits the observer's perception — an image you're happy to bask in because you put yourself out there as the one with the know-how.

Those who are charmed by you can place you in positions of great trust, responsibility, or influence, but you need to be clear that who you lead and what you teach are in accord with what resonates in *you*, not them. Otherwise, it is easy for you to assume roles that don't serve your interests.

The truth is that you derive self-worth from work, and work alone. That provides you with a sure foundation in life. Outside this, personal interactions can feel vague, uncertain, and perhaps even awkward. And so the same old pattern emerges: you conjure an image that deflects and projects. Some people could accuse you of being a subtle manipulator; I would argue it's more the concealment of something vulnerable, because your manipulation is all about self-preservation. 5/1s tend to be accomplished, wise, and effective people in many ways but live with a nagging insecurity that the foundations to their world are never quite strong enough. Most 5/1s would deny such insecurity exists, but that's because it's an unconscious element they'd rather not explore.

I suspect only one or two people will ever get to see the real you — and only after you have spent hours internalizing about whether they are substantial enough to be "let in."

If we were in conversation, you would come across as interesting, sharp, intelligent, and incisive. I'm sure you'd talk a lot about work and impart knowledge you'd hope would impress me. Yet I'd be deciphering the shifting stance, fidgeting hands, and uncertain stare. Later, I'd find you edging around the room, working out whom it was best to interact with and then soaking up their problems and solving them. There is something of the rescuer about you. I've often observed 5/1s holding a captive audience in the palm of their hand, providing a vision of how life should be.

What if the world were ever to see through your defensive projection field? That is your greatest fear, but ultimately it would be no bad thing — it would free you to be yourself. If you had lived in integrity, your reputation would withstand the exposure. If you had merely found shaky ground in the projections of others, you would feel rudderless. Either way, you would come to realize that reaching out, being authentic, and setting boundaries were your only liberation and path to fulfillment.

Relationships with a 5/1

As with all fifth-line profiles, it is hard to get really close to a 5/1 once you are past the alluring image. But 5/1s can be the most supportive of individuals as long as things are going their way. They are great problem solvers in relationships, albeit on a practical rather than emotional level. They can easily slip into the role of teacher, counselor, or rescuer, which may induce a level of co-dependency. You'll most likely hear them telling

**FAMOUS
5/1 PEOPLE**

Jennifer Aniston,
Richard Branson,
George W. Bush, Cher,
Queen Elizabeth II,
Hugh Hefner, Paris
Hilton, Katie Holmes,
Madonna, Liza Minnelli,
Arnold Schwarzenegger,
Britney Spears, and
Margaret Thatcher

you how dependable they are and how much you need them in your life. The truth is that *they* need *you* just as much.

5/1s are tremendously effective when guiding or teaching their followers in a professional sense but have a tendency to be wary within one-on-one and more intimate interactions. Partners note this more than it is readily admitted!

Should you ever become needy or insecure, be prepared for big promises and great romantic visions. Hollywood movies have been based on fifth-line portrayals of how relationships should be. 5/1s will also have the expectation that you will fall in and follow their lead.

Your challenge is to discern the relationship's substance, because a 5/1 never will! Once terms of engagement are agreed, be wary of making projections onto 5/1s, feeding their illusions. Keep them grounded, keep popping their balloons, and keep the reality checks coming. If you don't engage on a deep level, you can both end up bouncing around a supportive but false relationship. But when something feels real, it can be the most enduring and fulfilling union.

Compatibility

Your ideal match is with other 5/1s and 2/4 profiles. Away from that synergy, you also find easy relations with 1/3, 2/5, and 3/5 profiles.

The 5/2 Profile

You can be a curious mix of projections, denial, and self-illusion. But far from seducing others into your world, you almost need to seduce *yourself* into emerging into the outside world. The solitary person of the second line collides with the outgoing fantasies of the fifth. Here, you are led by the hand of the more conscious fifth-line element, putting yourself and projections out there, providing leadership, teaching, and fascinating imagery. Then, come the end of the day, your reclusive side pulls you into social retreat. In your professional life, you'll propose great schemes or projects, and even embark on them, but solitude will make you question your progress or involvement.

Your naturalness can have some difficulty with your illusory, somewhat make-believe tendency, meaning you're not quite sure where you stand — somewhere between natural and fake. Consequently, whereas 5/1s thrive on the projections of others, you become wary of how you are perceived and become concerned about how naturally you may or may not come across. This can lead to a tiptoeing around the edges of social interaction. Only when it feels conducive, and when you feel relaxed enough to engage, will the projected grandeur of the fifth line show its face and start spinning its stories and weaving its mystery. Inwardly, though, there is the underlying fear that the bubble you live in could pop at any moment.

I would release your concerns about others' opinions of you because no one is truly going to get you on the intrinsic level you desire. The feedback-seeking projections of the second line and the outward projections of the fifth make that highly improbable. What this means is that you walk through life being almost anything and anyone in any scenario, as long as you don't swallow the make-believe yourself. The opinions of others do not and cannot form a reliable barometer for you.

If we were in conversation, there would be an enchanting presence and a truth seeking to come out from behind the projections. You would be the consummate actor, sparkling with your communication style. And then I'd momentarily turn around, then look back to ask you something else, and you'd be gone. The gold dust would have left to spread its mark elsewhere, while wondering about the impression it had left with me. Illusive and elusive by nature!

You can pull a rabbit out of a hat without thinking and put in an impressive performance that is capable of stopping people in their tracks. You can hold the stage, captivate an audience, and leave your mark on all that you do but also be the performer who retreats from the stage having left everyone applauding. Accept the adulation, but don't believe that your act is who you really are.

It is an impossible dilemma for a 5/2 profile, because you need life to be truthful, so no wonder there is so much angst within. This truth requires you to acknowledge your brilliance and objectivity, but also your need for relaxation and fun. You are someone who needs to be exposed to every nuance of life. And when you feel in touch with others' lives, you are able to universalize concepts and issues that have relevance and practicality.

We all make mistakes, and for you there is always an inner discussion going on between guilt and forgiveness — mainly forgiving yourself for your perceived shortcomings. Self-forgiveness will provide a healing release when genuinely embraced, so bring forgiveness, bring your teachings, and make an impact on the world around you.

Relationships with a 5/2

5/2 profiles can provide the perfect partners, playing whatever role you want them to be. A delicate mix between extrovert and introvert, they'll take you to the sparkling parties but find a balance with cosy nights at home.

In many respects it is like living with a performer who forgets to leave a particular role at the door. The 5/2 will lead and orchestrate many things central to the relationship and be a great problem solver and confidante. One-on-one relations need to be tight and mutually appreciative for 5/2s but, as with all fifth-line profiles, it is notoriously hard to get really close to them.

Still, there are great prospects for a happy-ever-after of sweet nothings. If you allow them to lead you by the hand and you respect their need for solitude, you can enjoy an enlivening, versatile relationship and a jolly good ride through life. So embrace their uncertain nature and keep providing the reassurance that everything is on the right track, and a keep-you-on-your-toes, unpredictable, but fun relationship will provide you with much fulfillment.

Compatibility

Your ideal match is with other 5/2s and 2/5s, but away from that synergy you find easy relations with 2/4 and 3/5 profiles.

The 6/2 Profile

You have probably always felt like an authority in life, from the moment you were born. I suspect you even lay in your cot, looking up at those looking down and wondering to yourself, "Do you *really* appreciate what you are dealing with here?!" From cradle to grave, you are, quite literally, a natural-born role model whose wisdom, perception, and vision can be both a gift and a stabilizing force in your world.

You are just one of those people who can see what needs to happen and how to bring all the missing pieces together to form a bigger, more coherent picture. It is a natural gift. You are here to be a role model and are known as someone with high ideals, high standards, and high goals. This, in turn, leads to a tendency to take charge *always*, because very few people can do anything as well as you, leading to the sometimes frustrated cry of "Do I have to do *everything* around here?" You are liable to micromanage every little detail, and the prospect of delegation only happens once you have established that the people around you are both willing and capable.

Throughout life, you're constantly absorbing information on an insatiable quest for knowledge and new interests. I'm sure you are regarded as either a master of general knowledge, a fount of all wisdom, or a great visionary of your time, finding balance between spiritual and earthly connections. It can sometimes frustrate you that no one sees the same bigger picture as you. Understand that no one is being shortsighted or dumb; it's just that the majority of people you come across will not get it in the same way you do and might not share the same zeal to grab life by the scruff of the neck and make a difference. Few people ever find themselves on the same page as a worldly and wise 6/2 profile. You simply have a view of life that is often beyond the scope of most people's comprehension, save for 6/2 and 6/3 profiles.

If we were in conversation, I would immediately detect your grasp of the world and a joie de vivre that comes with eternal optimism. There would be something assured, clear, well-rounded, and precise about your manner. You have the social and professional ability to stand above irrelevant dramas and see things for how they *truly* are or what they *really* mean. I suspect you grew up hearing the words "Wise beyond your years."

What you might not readily appreciate is an unconscious reticence to use your abilities to the fullest. Indeed, there is the possibility of your appearing standoffish at times, wondering whether you can be bothered. This is the more subtle undercurrent of the second line at play. You personally prize your precious time and energy, so a commitment really has to be worth your while if it is to be fulfilling. It's almost as if there is an air of "Well, make me a good offer and I'll think about it" about you. If you're not conscious of this aspect, there is a danger that you'll spend life avoiding your true calling and true potential, forever backing away, making excuses, and bowing to the second line pulling you into the shadows. Just remember that your wisdom and inspiration need air and appreciation, which require you to put them out there.

When you are engaged with a person or project, there can be a tendency to juggle too many plates or try to conquer the world. You are the manager, conductor, and forward planner. But take on too much weight of responsibility and you get bogged down and bored with life. Suddenly, the joie de vivre evaporates and the great overseer prefers being an efficient functionary or assistant, letting everyone else do a far less competent job.

As with all second-line profiles, you need a place of solitude in which to recharge and take stock. 6/2 profiles have no problem in their own company. These are women quite happy to shop for an entire weekend by themselves or men content to be wrapped up in a solo project or pursuit.

As with all sixth lines, there are three potential turning points in your life: the ages of eighteen, thirty, and fifty. Most 6/2s feel like applying some form of authority or adopting some responsibility from the threshold of adulthood, getting involved in community groups, social clubs, movements, or rock bands! Come thirty, you will have related to, interacted with, and tasted most things in life, and your boundless enthusiasm will calm down, probably because it has dawned on you that not everyone in life can meet you on your level. And so you can take a backseat or transfer from the front line to the office, where your sixth-line overview can be best utilized in the interests of everyone. Expect your arrival at age fifty to summon you to serve your fullest purpose. Life now recognizes the role model you are and can place you in positions of great power and influence. With your deep love of fun, you have the potential to bring great light to the world and to perk up the lives of everyone around you, as the role model you always knew you'd be!

Relationships with a 6/2

There is something reassuring and solid about being with a 6/2 partner, because it feels as though, together, you can take on all comers and tackle any problems. 6/2s have probably already earned *your* admiration, but believe me when I say that you, too, will be regarded as the special one. That's because 6/2s worry that they might never find the soul mate who truly sparks with them and understands them on a higher level. If you are their chosen one, feel very special and appreciated indeed!

Be aware that all 6/2s are looking to keep a relationship fresh and compelling. There can be a low boredom threshold, so keep things interesting. What 6/2s really seek, whether expressed or not, is someone who can climb mountains with them and keep expanding mutual horizons. Show 6/2s a new place, or surprise them with something novel, and their natures will coo.

Acknowledge the wisdom of your partner and enjoy the uplifting journey he or she will take you on. Once 6/2s have found what their perfectionist streak is looking for, they will have found their best friend and soul mate and can relax into an incredibly fulfilling relationship.

Compatibility

Your perfect match is with fellow 6/2s and 3/5s. Away from that synergy, you also find easy relations with 2/4, 4/6, and 6/3 profiles.

The 6/3 Profile

The fact that the sixth-line wisdom represents this profile's conscious side makes you the supreme, unrivaled role model, someone few people can keep up with in terms of knowledge, experience, and activity. You, more than anyone, know what life is all about. You say: "Been there, done that, and you know what else? I can see the way ahead, too!"

It is because of your eminent wisdom, I suspect, you find it difficult to find lasting relationships or associations in which you are fully understood and appreciated. This is because 6/3s only really like being engaged with extremely highbrow, bright, and challenging situations and people. It's as if you wish to relate on a higher level than most. It wouldn't surprise me if you preferred being in your own company most of the time.

I am confident that if you have embraced the 6/3 profile as intended, there will have been nothing mundane about your life. Your wisdom thrives on being fueled by the risks and challenges you take as someone intent on pushing the envelope and boundaries in life, driven by ambition and seeking the fast track to advancement and higher planes. I could argue that you are a rebel without a cause, but that wouldn't be entirely accurate, because you *do* have a cause: to shake life up and live it on the edge. I daresay you'd strap yourself to a rocket and be quite content to be fired into another orbit if possible. That way, at least you'd feel the out-of-this-world excitement you always crave.

You are a curious mix of great authority and wisdom and the recklessness of an adrenaline junkie with a devil-may-care attitude. Maybe you adopt a position of seniority at work and then hurl yourself into wild abandon on weekends; responsible one minute, thrill seeking the next. Either way, I'm sure you are becoming used to the emerging pattern of a powerful life that is forever sending you through the rough and tumble of experience and taking you to new heights of awareness.

If you have a 6/3 profile you'll harbor the private thought that you've hardly ever met anyone quite like yourself. From the day you were born, you have been devoted to expanding your life and pushing yourself forward, wanting to embrace the bigger picture that enthralls you, seeking bigger and better experiences all the time. You have a built-in means of challenging anything and everything that comes before you, testing its authenticity. You tend to see through the veils of mystery in a life that confounds everyone else, and yet the third line's thirst for adventure means you are as susceptible as anyone else to being tripped up and making mistakes. Thankfully, you have the wisdom of the sixth line to provide better steerage than most by applying a degree of foresight.

As with all sixth-line profiles, there are three built-in turning points in life for a 6/3 — the ages of eighteen, thirty, and fifty — and you could find the brakes being applied to the third line's thirst for life at any one of those junctures. Your nature has to reach the point of handing over the baton and going to sit in the tree or high office, armed with innate wisdom bolstered by rich and educational life experience.

You hunger to have a greater impact and make a meaningful contribution from higher ground. Responsibility doesn't daunt you. You thrive on taking charge and administering your view of the way things should be done. Most 6/3s have been crying out to be an authority figure from an early age and seek professional advancement by climbing the greasy pole toward management, business ownership, board level or some other senior position.

If we were in conversation, I'd instantly detect that I was engaging with someone who had an enormous amount of knowledge about the world and the spiritual realm. I'd hear firsthand experience of life, enhanced by an impressive and inspiring wisdom. You tend to see the beginning, middle, and end of most stories — before they have ended! The stories you recount would speak of someone who had been around the block and returned with bundles of wisdom, lessons, and life scars. There would also be a provocative sense of humor that sought to make light of all life's dramas because, quite frankly, you can't take everyday life too seriously when you've such a clear view of a bigger picture. You're always putting things into a sobering perspective, uninterested in unnecessary drama and yet imparting a wisdom that might well steer others in a true direction. But nothing bores you more than having to deal with repetitious problems; you have no time for people who can't help themselves.

Life can start to become boring for you at around the age of eighteen, but if you still have the zest for it, you will go on challenging the world and trying everything that confronts you, at least until the age of thirty. Your gifts of authority and the benefit of the experiences you accumulate at speed in your life are much-needed qualities in the world, and you are someone with a highly distinctive presence.

Relationships with a 6/3

If your partner is a 6/3, be aware that his or her nature contracts at the thought of any commitment that feels restrictive. Partners need to appreciate not only their gifts but also their great need for openness and freedom. These are the quintessential free spirits, in which a sense of being alive walks hand in hand with a wisdom that can sometimes regard "ordinary" relationships as beneath them.

6/3 profiles are forever growing and mutating, and if you don't move with them, there's the risk that you could grow apart. There really is a propensity within most 6/3s to believe that there is something better out there, be that in terms of experience, inspiration, or partner. Sometimes they can appear distant and detached, not fully engaging. This is not necessarily because they are not interested, more because they are preoccupied with searching for something inspiring or the next first-hand experience. Engage with this thirst for life and join in with their thinking outside the box and you then engage with them. They are always seeking to up their game and keep climbing to higher ground, so 6/3 partners require loose reins, much trust, and a steadying hand from someone who appreciates and meets them on a spiritual level.

It is a challenge to keep 6/3 profiles fully satisfied all of the time, but when you honor these basic ground rules, they can be the most attentive, fun-loving, and wise partners. When they do engage and come close, the relationship can be satisfyingly intense, as if they are penetrating you on a deep level.

When 6/3 profiles come to a place of calm and quiet within themselves, the internal itches tend to settle down. I suspect there will always be an uncertain edge with them — they will never be quite sure if they can maintain a state of stability — but, believe me, the relationship will never be dull and you'll always be kept on your toes!

Compatibility

Your ideal match is with other 6/3s and 3/6s. Away from that synergy, you will also find easy relations with 1/3, 3/5, and 6/2 profiles.

That last profile wraps up all the major components of Human Design, completing the exploration of the nine centers, the thirty-six channels, the sixty-four gates, and their six lines. These nuggets of insight dovetail with the three essential keys of type, authority, and profile to form an overall picture of what it means to be you.

What matters now is building on that understanding and fitting the jigsaw together, because it's one thing learning about your Human Design; now it's time to live it.

> **FAMOUS 6/3 PEOPLE**
>
> Warren Beatty, Humphrey Bogart, Matt Damon, and Harrison Ford

8

Living Your Design

Bringing It All Together

Human Design has restored integrity to my life. Thank you!

DB, Wyoming

Ultimately, our life's quest is to be the person we were born to be. Living true to our Human Design makes such a mission easily attainable for all of us. But such self-realization first requires *acceptance, allowing, awakening, and authenticity*:

- Accepting the realities of your true nature, overcoming conditioning, and releasing limitations
- Allowing yourself to fall back with confidence on the potential within, revealing your true expression
- Awakening to an inner direction and discovering the freedom and fulfillment it brings
- Exercising authenticity in your way of being, neither being afraid of the judgments of others nor seeking their approval

Accepting leads to allowing, which catalyzes awakening, resulting in authenticity.

Once we all reacquaint ourselves with the person we were born to be, we are empowered by a connection to our higher truth, our authentic being. This might not be an overnight process and you'll discover that it requires patience and practice and, in some cases, courage, but the more you integrate these truths into your life — your conscious choices, your way of being, and daily interactions — the more you'll sense an inner stability and an attunement to harmonious, effective living.

Walking through our respective journeys to the tune of someone else's interpretations and expectations of life seems such a ridiculous waste. Discovering our unique being is the only way of reaching fulfillment. To do this, we must be ourselves. We must live our Human Design.

Bringing It All Together

By now, you will have learned all the components of your distinctive blueprint. Inevitably, you'll need to knit everything together, but how do you actually go about living as your authentic self?

I know people who, ten years after their first Human Design reading, keep close at hand the life chart and notes they have made, continually checking in with the wisdom in their possession. But I also know people who have so fully integrated their design that they simply live it. So I will share with you what I have shared with them — a practical way of applying all the learned information to your life.

First, be conscious of the messages contained within your centers. These represent an essential starting point and form the foundation to your nature.

The most telling insights and understandings stem from knowing your type, supported by adopting the correct strategy of your authority.

And then your profile provides the framework to your place in and interactions with the world.

So, view type, authority, and profile as the three keys that unlock the secrets within. When I interpret a life chart, it's these three components that inform me right away of the most salient features about a person. When you're interpreting your own chart, therefore, apply your main focus to these chief areas, because they show how best to utilize your design.

Once you've established that platform, you can then explore the deeper layers and finer points of character contained in the centers, channels, and gates. But it's when you thread together type, authority, and profile that you are, in effect, discovering the essence of your Human Design. You are creating the acronym TAP — type, authority, profile — tapping into the most immediately informative insights.

For instance, you may find you're a Generator, meaning you've an enormous wellspring of life-force energy, but do you also have Emotional authority? If so, you'll need to wait to reach an internal truth with clarity, to get a green light before acting.

Maybe you've a 6/2 profile, with an authoritative overview that will help others come up to speed, or you've a 2/4 profile and will startle everyone with your guileless and heartfelt input.

Then, from that TAP platform, explore the facets to your character by reading the channels and gates. You'll discover that all these pieces combine to form a fascinating picture, your complete inside story.

As you're piecing together your design, you may find, as sometimes happens, that one channel or gate's meaning appears to contradict another. If this is true for you, all you're seeing is different facets coming into play according to the needs of the moment. Your authority will inform you which influence takes precedence at any given moment. If one gate, for example, suggests going it alone but the rest of your chart shows a requirement to belong in a community, you'll know what message takes precedence once you've consulted your authority in context with your circumstances. Your overall Human Design is more than the sum of its parts.

It's not just about living your design, of course — it's about trusting it. When David Beckham positions the ball before a five-man wall, he has confidence that he can bend it into the top right-hand corner of the net. When Tiger Woods lines up a thirty-foot putt on the eighteenth, he has confidence that he can read the green and sink the putt. When Angelina Jolie steps onto a movie set and into a role, she has confidence that she will *become* that character. When people with a skill, talent, or art approach their moment of truth, they don't rely on anything tangible; they rely on something within. Likewise, when you know your Human Design, you know the truths you can rely on with confidence. You, too, have only to learn to trust what's consistent and forever available to you.

Such awareness isn't magic, and there will always be the risk of being sucked into the wrong project, wrong direction, or wrong relationship. The temptations of fear and ego will always hover nearby, but it's at such times that you must stand still and step into your awareness, consult the counsel of your design, and be the master of your own game.

When you accept your design this way, the age-old question "What am I doing here?" dissolves into simple acceptance of how you are. This amazing device allows us to see ourselves as part of a greater whole in which we each have our own precious role to honor, our own place in the cosmic scheme of events.

On a personal level, I have watched clients' lives become more and more meaningful and relaxed as they are drawn deep into a respect for, appreciation of, and love of who they are. Communications with friends and family have dramatically improved in countless cases, and situations that in the past would have caused tension and friction have been resolved because of a new level of understanding. The unconditional truth of people living their design is something that leaves me in awe and wonder.

Predestined?

We live in an age that promotes the belief that you can be anything you wish to be. However, your Human Design is who you were *designed* to be. This, of course, re-energizes the age-old debate of free will versus pre-determination.

"Are you seriously telling me that I'm saddled with this design and there is nothing I can do about it?" asked one female client, sensing some kind of restriction being applied and wondering whether it was all predestined. Many people ask similar questions and my answer is always the same: "Each design is a blessing that, when honored, brings about fulfillment and satisfaction." The focus is not on restriction but on the freedom that comes with the ability to be your true self.

If anything, therefore, Human Design is the promoter and cultivator of personal freedom, because there is nothing more freeing than being allowed to be yourself. This system does not remove or tamper with your freedom of choice, nor does it predetermine your life, or fate. It *does* pre-determine your makeup and true nature, but within that predetermination lie your freedom, truth, happiness, and integrity. *A predestined design brings freedom when honored.*

Working with Your Design

Imagine life as a journey that has to be made across water. Your design is a sailboat and you are the sailor. Any experienced seaman knows the design and capability of his boat and uses the elements to make the journey. It won't matter that differently designed boats may be able to chart a more direct or quicker course; he works with what he's got, trims the sails, and steers the most expeditious course in alignment with his design and the prevailing wind and weather. Because it is a journey, not a race. Like life.

You, too, must understand the strengths, weaknesses, and capabilities of your design in order to enjoy the most effective journey, without comparing yours to anyone else's route, strategy, or tactics. Being well acquainted and comfortable with your own vessel is a strength in itself and allows you to set a true course. If you attempt to copy the sailing styles of other boats, your boat can get into difficulty.

Any sailor appreciates that you sometimes have to tack and zigzag, depending on the tides, winds, and waves, and so you also need to harness your design's particular capabilities in alignment with your true nature.

Ultimately, everyone's destination remains the same — a place called personal fulfillment.

Learning and Laughing

Finally, I like to remember one thing: life is not at all serious when you stand back and breathe.

We only have to look at a dog wagging its tail, a bird chirping on a wall, a tree dancing in the breeze, or the moon beaming its reflection onto the ocean to realize both the beauty and the simplicity of a life at its most natural. You, too, can dance to your own tune, and be simplicity itself.

I appreciate that the demands of the modern world can be overwhelming and make everything appear a pressured blur, with little time to appreciate the present because we are so bound by our yesterdays and daunted by the tomorrows. If only we could accept that life is intended to be a mystery to be lived, not a problem to be solved. If only we could step back and see that to nurture our nature leads, with practice, to a self-acceptance that transmutes into a self-love that dances into the challenges of life.

This book has been all about embracing a unique and personal design, but the one trait we were all designed to share is the ability to come to our senses and ultimately laugh at the ways of our world. We can laugh at ourselves, at others, at rule systems, and at the sometimes ridiculous jokes that fate seems to be playing.

If I've learned anything from giving Human Design readings, it is that so many people are needlessly wrapped up in unnecessary dramas, angst, confusion, and chaos that are nine times out of ten generated by too much thinking, or the fact that their happiness is being denied, by themselves or others.

We are now entering an era when we can no longer deny our truth or sell ourselves short in this way. It is essential that we honor and trust ourselves if we are to interact honestly with our world and move forward together.

Human Design doesn't ask you to be anybody new. It simply invites you to be the person you *always* have been, deep down. It cannot provide a quick fix. It cannot guarantee fulfillment. It cannot do anything other than guide you to the truths within. And ask you to keep smiling.

In the teachings of Osho, the enlightened mystic, laughter is the one device that returns us from darkness to light. As the great man said: "In life, there is no place to be serious. Everybody is slipping on banana peels — you just need the insight to see ... I do not ask you to pray; I ask you to find moments and situations in which you can laugh wholeheartedly. Your laughter will open a thousand and one roses within you."

So I encourage you to play and laugh with Human Design and swap and share your discoveries with family, friends, and partners to create hours of endless fun!

Believe me, in spite of the treasure trove of insights this book has provided, we have only scratched the surface. There are many more dimensions to your Human Design, but they really do require the experienced interpretation of an expert. I hope to have laid the foundations to a basic understanding of your design for life, but I would absolutely recommend a personal reading with someone experienced in interpreting the hidden story contained within a life chart.

Further education in this amazing system is available through our websites:

www.earthstarconsulting.com
www.humandesignforusall.com

For more Human Design software, I also heartily recommend:

www.newsunware.com

In the meantime, you now have the opportunity to keep consulting your own design and settle with assurance into everything you came into this life to experience. It is said that a journey of a thousand miles starts with a single step. You have taken that first step with this book.

When you truly understand and accept yourself, you can create the world you have always dreamed about.

You can just be yourself.

Appendix

Designs of Famous People

In an attempt to train the eye as to how to thread it all to-gether, in this appendix we're going to take a look at the Human Designs of some well-known individuals.* Even behind the mask of fame, there is a real person to be discovered!

*These designs are based not on personal readings I have conducted for these people but on the time, date, and place of their birth.

DIANA,
PRINCESS OF WALES

Type: Projector
Authority: Emotions
Profile: 1/3

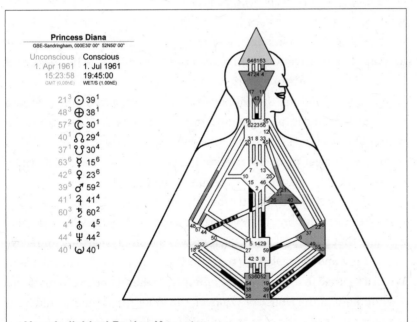

Princess Diana

GBE-Sandringham, 000E30' 00" 52N50' 00"

Unconscious	Conscious
1. Apr 1961	1. Jul 1961
15:23:58	19:45:00
GMT (0,00hE)	WET/S (1.00hE)

21^3	☉	39^1	
48^3	⊕	38^1	
57^2	☾	30^1	
40^1	☊	29^4	
37^1	☋	30^4	
63^6	☿	15^6	
42^6	♀	23^6	
39^5	♂	59^2	
41^1	♃	41^4	
60^3	♄	60^2	
4^4	⚷	4^5	
44^4	♆	44^2	
40^1	☍	40^1	

Your Individual Design Keynotes

TYPE: Projector (Chapter 3)

AUTHORITY: Emotional, Feeling Clarity, Patience (Chapter 4)

DEFINED CHANNELS: (Chapter 5)

    1. 63 / 4   Logical Mind. Critical perceptions

    2. 40 / 37   Community. Seeking one's larger Family

    30 / 41   Recognition. Focusing Imagination

PROFILE: 1 / 3 (Chapter 7)

On August 31, 1997, the world mourned the tragic loss of Diana, Princess of Wales, killed in a car accident in Paris on the eve of returning home to London. There have been numerous commentaries on her life and character in the intervening years, but the truth about Diana is contained within her Human Design . . . and the person she was designed to be.

This iconic Projector had five centers defined — the Crown, Mind, Heart, Emotions, and Root — and these consistent energies provided her constant bearings. My snapshot view is: Her head was always spinning, entertaining inspirations and grand schemes (Crown) and preoccupied with thought, unable to shut down at night (Mind). She had constant access to willpower (Heart) to strive for what she wanted. She was someone who, quite literally, set her heart on achieving goals or winning over certain people. She probably placed herself under a lot of pressure but was also grounded and capable of dealing with chaos and stress (Root). But the major part of her design stemmed from the Emotions. Here was an emotionally driven woman whose feelings could rule her head and lead her into all sorts of situations — and dramas!

When you combine the willpower of the Heart, adrenaline pressure from the Root, and intense feelings from the Emotions, you see someone who felt internal pressure to get ahead in life. Diana was never designed to be a wallflower princess, meekly following in the shadow of Prince Charles. Indeed, I suspect many people didn't appreciate how bright she was. I dare say even she didn't! After all, emotions ruled her life chart. She was led by her emotions, however erratic a course they set. When you also consider that she was a Projector, here was a woman yearning for recognition, to be invited to play her part and appreciated for her contribution. When it seemed that wasn't forthcoming from the austere, nonemotional environment of the House of Windsor, the inner frustration would have felt unbearable and the emotions would have been unleashed.

In the lull between emotions, she would have been forever thinking and weighing up all situations. The 63-4 channel indicates a logical mental process that sifts doubts to find practical solutions but also creates a great worrier! In the privacy of her own mind, Diana was always working out ways to create a better tomorrow, yet was fearful about what the future held. But this deep worrier was a lot smarter, cannier, and more considered than most people gave her credit for; she was also someone who, on an unconscious level, liked having control (gate 21), and this would explain why she sometimes rebelled against the controlling forces of the royal family and wanted such a hands-on role with the charities and causes that were close to her heart.

A notable feature of her design is that the Sacral, Self, Spleen, and Throat centers are all undefined. As with all Projectors, there was no Sacral energy to depend on. However, because her presence and input were often requested for projects and charity work, the Projector's need to be recognized and invited was often honored and brought her much fulfillment in public. But in her marriage, by her own admission, she rarely felt recognized, and that would have led to a deep sense of upset and feeling misunderstood, as with any Projector.

Diana's lack of connection to the Throat meant that when she was in the company of people with a defined Throat, she was desperate to talk, talk, talk, and release pent-up conversation and thoughts. No wonder she indulged in three- to four-hour phone calls! It's also interesting that she received voice-coaching lessons to improve her public speaking, reflecting a lack of confidence that can affect people with an undefined Throat. But when in the company of defined Throats, she would have been competent at expressing and helping resolve *their* problems from an objective viewpoint. Her difficulty would always have been expressing *herself* personally. When Diana spoke, she spoke for the benefit of the audience, not herself.

Diana's Self center was also turned off, meaning she struggled with a sense of identity and self-worth. Gate 48, from the Spleen, made her an intensely deep person who questioned whether she was good enough or could relate her understanding of life well enough. Privately, as evidenced in her butler Paul Burrell's book, *A Royal Duty*, she struggled to work out who she was when stripped of the royal persona and couldn't quite understand her public adoration. The only path she felt absolutely certain of was the one that led to humanitarian projects. As she told the BBC in 1997: "I'm a humanitarian — always have been, always will be." And the one gate Diana had on in the Self center was gate 15 — the gate of the humanitarian.

The 37-40 channel from Emotions to Heart meant she was extremely tactile and could determine through a handshake or a hug where someone stood with her. Diana was known for reaching out to the world, being the first royal to hold the hand of an AIDs patient, to remove stigmas and break down barriers. That was the 37-40 in motion, because the Channel of Community seeks to embrace all people. People who met Diana said she broke the ice and made them feel like a friend. The skeptical media often observed that this was mere PR, but the truth is that people were actually feeling the qualities of someone with this channel. She was heartfelt by nature and had one of the 37-40's main attributes: a winning smile that instantly wooed everyone and bound strangers to her.

The 41-30 channel between the Root and Emotions meant there was a perpetual internal struggle to determine whether her glass was half full or half empty. This would have led to a sequence of changing moods that others may have found hard to judge. But this Channel of Recognition also meant she was a great visionary, someone ahead of her time. She would often have applied tremendous focus to a project or cause and refused to be sidetracked. Her dedication to the anti–land mine campaign remains a vivid case in point. Newspaper archives are full of references to "a royal princess ahead of her time," typifying this channel's attributes.

An in-depth reading would inevitably take into account many other factors in Diana's Human Design, but that is the general, snapshot view, illustrating an emotionally led, deep-thinking princess who was both heartfelt and vulnerable, full of self-doubt and yet determined to pursue her humanitarian causes. And someone who, regardless of the trappings of royalty, simply wanted to be recognized for the work she did.

DAVID BECKHAM

Type: Manifesting Generator
Authority: Emotions
Profile: 4/6

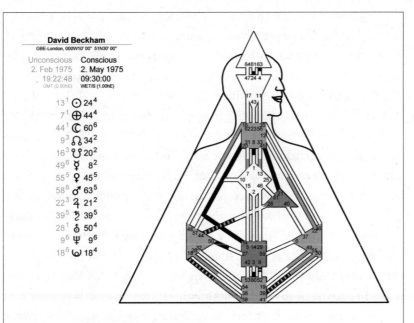

David Beckham
GBE-London, 000W10' 00" 51N30' 00"

Unconscious	Conscious
2. Feb 1975	2. May 1975
19:22:48	09:30:00
GMT (0.00hE)	WET/S (1.00hE)

13¹ ☉ 24⁴
7¹ ⊕ 44⁴
44¹ ☾ 60⁶
9³ ☊ 34²
16³ ☋ 20²
49⁶ ☿ 8²
55⁵ ♀ 45⁵
58⁶ ♂ 63⁵
22³ ♃ 21²
39⁵ ♄ 39⁵
28¹ ♅ 50⁴
9⁶ ♆ 9⁶
18⁶ ♇ 18⁴

Your Individual Design Keynotes

TYPE: Manifesting Generator (Chapter 3)

AUTHORITY: Emotional, Feeling Clarity, Patience (Chapter 4)

DEFINED CHANNELS: (Chapter 5)

    1. 18 / 58 Judgment. Reaching towards Perfection

        55 / 39 Emoting. The Full Emotional Spectrum

    2. 21 / 45 Money Channel. The Material World

        20 / 34 Charisma. The Drive to be Active

PROFILE: 4 / 1 (Chapter 7)

The sporting legend that is David Beckham is renowned throughout the world for both his soccer skills and, together with his wife, Victoria, "Brand Beckham." From Manchester United to Real Madrid, from LA Galaxy to AC Milan, the England midfielder has a massive public profile but a private personal life. So his Human Design promises to be an enlightening story about the inner being behind the famous persona.

I can instantly tell that David Beckham is a highly motivated individual who finds it hard to sit still and do nothing, as evidenced by all four motor centers being defined — Sacral, Root, Emotions, and Heart — together with the Spleen and Throat. These six defined centers provide consistent energies that provide his bearings in life. With so much color in his chart, he can be perceived as someone who is quite rigid and fixed. As well as being driven with masses of staying power (Sacral) and applying an iron will (Heart), he is also highly emotional (Emotions and 39-55 channel) and extremely sensitive (19-49 channel).

The 39-55 Channel of Emoting means he is passionate about everything he does and yet deeply melancholic when he turns in a bad performance or the press is on his back. Here is a sportsman whose adrenaline pressure from the Root stirs his emotions. So he may well brood at home or in the dressing room but will come tearing onto the pitch to prove a point. I suspect some of his best performances have stemmed from his darkest, meanest moods. His family would probably support the Human Design truth that he is hypersensitive to criticism and has needed to grow a thick skin (19-49 Channel of Sensitivity), but this also means he is attuned to the needs and wants of others. I would even speculate that with this channel he is Victoria Beckham's *emotional* tower of strength, not vice versa, able to balance his own emotional needs with those of his wife.

People feel safe within his company and recognize his sensitive soul. This makes him tactile by nature and keen to hold face-to-face business meetings, preferably over dinner or lunch. His sensitive side will also make him responsive to the needs of deprived children, or even struggling teammates. David is someone who wants to be there and include everyone, and this would have been a forte that he no doubt utilized as captain of England, as a role model both on and off the pitch.

When you add into the mix the charisma of the 34-20 Channel of Keeping Busy, you start to see the seductive picture emerge of a motivated man, passionate about what he does, sensitive and emotional, with the kind of charisma that turns heads. David Beckham doesn't simply smolder on the covers of magazines — the smoke rises for the ladies from his life chart, too!

Gate 16 denotes his limitless enthusiasm, and gate 22 denotes his grace. Combine those attributes and his evident passion, and you soon see a graceful football player whose enthusiasm has got him where he is today and whose grace has led to his living a charmed life. Few would argue with that!

Also note that, quite appropriately, he has the 21-45 Channel of Money. He is a man who has an immense capability to make money and feels at home in the material world, as befits Britain's highest-paid sportsman of all time. He is someone who generates money for himself or for the clubs he plays for and he'll also be adept at handling his resources.

The defined Throat center means he has the ability to manifest and make things happen by harnessing his skill. Gate 33 in the Throat means that he can be secretive, but that his life story is one great adventure that sends him here, there, and everywhere . . . and then he must retreat to recharge.

One thing you'll see about David Beckham is that he has an undefined Self with not a single gate turned on, meaning this center is open. This means he doesn't have a particularly strong sense of self-guidance so can be all things to all people, depending on the situation he finds himself in. I'm sure, therefore, that he has come to rely on the guidance of his managers, agents, and wife to point him in the right direction. Once that compass has been set by others, his Sacral energy will build and power him toward success.

I'm sure his teammates and family would agree that he is a perfectionist who can be extremely hard on himself, as seen in the 18-58 Channel of Judgment; he is someone who weighs up situations quickly and jumps to judgment. His Sacral-Throat connection, via the 34-20 channel, makes him a Manifesting Generator. But, being an MG type with defined

Emotions, he needs to await his gut response and exercise patience to ensure he finds emotional clarity and *feels* sure before committing to anything or anyone.

All gates emerging from his Emotions center are pink, meaning that a lot of his emotional reactions and feelings are unconscious. This can be confusing at times until one starts to recognize what is happening. He often needs his emotions reflected back to him to make sense of them. I suspect, then, that he needs Victoria Beckham close to him all the time because she can clue him in to the feelings she'll recognize better than anyone. It is "Posh" who puts him on the emotional map and, with his undefined Self, provides essential guidance, too. Away from her, he'll be unsure of himself and his feelings, and gate 63 makes him doubt and gate 24 leads to a tendency to overthink and overanalyze. He likes to work things out for himself, no doubt with Victoria's guidance, and mull matters over in his own mind. With these mental gates, he'll love getting out onto the soccer pitch just to escape all that thinking!

An in-depth reading would take into account many other factors in David Beckham's Human Design, but this snapshot view illustrates a highly motivated talent who strives for perfection, harnesses an enthusiasm and natural energy to give 100 percent to all that he does, and, in the process, generates wealth. But behind the cool exterior is a hugely emotional being, hypersensitive to criticism, who can be hard on himself. I suspect that's why "Brand Beckham" has been such a success both on and off the pitch.

JENNIFER ANISTON

Type: Manifestor
Authority: Spleen
Profile: 5/1

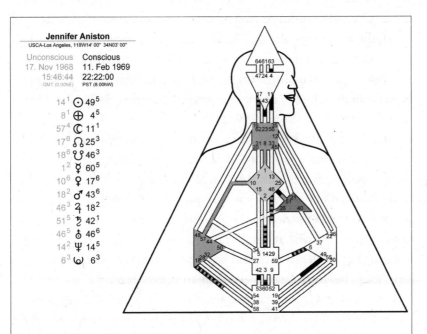

Jennifer Aniston
USCA-Los Angeles, 118W14' 00" 34N03' 00"

Unconscious	Conscious
17. Nov 1968	11. Feb 1969
15:46:44	22:22:00
GMT (0.00hE)	PST (8.00hW)

14^1 ☉ 49^5
8^1 ⊕ 4^5
57^4 ☾ 11^1
17^6 ☊ 25^3
18^6 ☋ 46^3
1^2 ☿ 60^5
10^6 ♀ 17^6
18^2 ♂ 43^6
46^3 ♃ 18^2
51^5 ♄ 42^1
46^5 ⚷ 46^6
14^2 ♆ 14^5
6^3 ☋ 6^3

Your Individual Design Keynotes

TYPE: Manifestor (Chapter 3)

AUTHORITY: Spontaneous Manifesting (Chapter 4)

DEFINED CHANNELS: (Chapter 5)

1. 10 / 57 Survival. Intuitive Interaction with Life

    8 / 1 Inspiration. The Creative Role Model

    25 / 51 Initiation. Questing for Unity

PROFILE: 5 / 1 (Chapter 7)

The career, loves, and life of actress Jennifer Aniston have long taken over the front pages of glossy magazines and newspapers and the annals of Hollywood gossip columns. It's hard to find the truth of the woman in such surface portrayals, but her Human Design reveals the character of a true survivor…

On first impression, I'm sure, Jennifer Aniston could come across as meek and mild, almost laissez-faire, but the snapshot view of her Human Design is that she is a pure go-getting Manifestor who can move mountains in all that she does. She is determined to achieve her heart's desire, commanding attention en route, with the roar of a lioness if you stand in her way. I suspect few people emerge from interactions with her unscathed or unimpressed because, with her power, tenacity, and heart, she will always leave a forceful impression by her presence alone.

She has four defined centers — Spleen, Self, Heart, and Throat — and the 25-51 Channel of Initiation makes her an indomitable force, a powerhouse determined to break new ground, bringing tremendous focus to bear on everyone she works with to draw out their authenticity. It also means she adopts a spiritual, unconditional view of love. Her heart requires something profound if she is to be met on the same level. Indeed, people with this channel can appear cool and distant until they find a match that fits. When you throw into the mix that she's a 5/1 profile, which tends to adopt an arm's-length strategy even within relationships, it means that Jennifer Aniston is extremely selective about lowering her barriers and the caliber of person she lets in. Her 5/1 profile also cloaks her in an air of ever-modulating mystery.

With a defined Spleen, she will walk into any room and light the place up with her feel-good nature, but her big concern is ensuring she commits to the right people and projects. Spontaneous instincts and intuitions are Jennifer's reliable guide and authority, and she intuits instantly when something clicks for her. She need not get caught up in thinking or feeling — she is someone who *senses* when a situation is right. A Manifestor with a defined Heart and Spleen — here is someone who instantly knows what she wants, and acts on it. She seeks instant gratification in this regard, going after something in a heartbeat. At least, that's her nature. This might also mean that her attention span is best suited to ever-changing environments and projects.

One most insightful aspect of her design is the 57-10 Channel of Survival, meaning there is something of the risk taker within and yet, despite all the pitfalls of Hollywood and the trials and tribulations she may face, she always finds a way through. She always survives. If you've ever wondered how she pulled through the whole Angelina and Brad episode, here's the answer: a born survivor.

Any active channel stemming from gate 10 also indicates someone with a strong sense of identity, and she is also a creative role model, as evidenced by the 1-8 Channel of Inspiration, taking charge of situations and leading by example. "Trust me, and here we go!" is what she's about. When combined with her defined Heart, this indicates someone with immense courage, striding forward into new territories and taking on all the challenges that life can throw at her. Jennifer Aniston is someone who is empowering to be around and she will always seek to make a valuable and inspired contribution to whatever project she's involved in.

With no gates turned on in the Crown, this center is open, indicating that she loves being around inspiring people and situations, and gate 4 in the Mind will be forever seeking to repair things or find solutions to everyone's problems. Her mind receives insights (gate 43), dreams up ideas that foster social harmony (gate 11), and isn't afraid of forming strong opinions (gate 17). But, with no activation from the Mind to the Throat, she probably struggles to express what her mind is truly conjuring until she recognizes that these gifts are best offered to other people's life situations.

With an undefined Sacral, Jennifer will find she has the willpower of the Heart but does not have sustainable energy so, after giving all she's got on a movie set, she'll always need to rest and recoup. But that's not a handicap to a Manifestor, because these types achieve in five minutes what it can take someone else an hour to accomplish.

The undefined Root means that this is an actress whose system probably doesn't handle everyday stress induced by others well. The Emotions are also undefined, but with two gates turned on, including gate 6, which rules any emotional environment, so she can boss or calm others with her ability to forge friendships. But the risk taker in her may entertain risky partnerships in love, with an experimental approach. She can jump into matters of the heart and learn from the experience, to her joy or cost. Gate 49 means she is someone who doesn't mind sparking mini-revolutions in her world. She feels when something isn't working and can turn her world upside down to instigate change and freshness. I suspect there is a strong flirtatious side to her character, with gate 6 entertaining slightly risqué interactions before gate 49 rejects with a swift "no." Indeed, this could be the theme of her entire design: someone forever balancing the people and projects who can meet her high standards.

In an interview with *Vogue* magazine for its December 2008 edition, Jennifer's friend and business partner Kristin Hahn said: "One of the things that people don't realize about Jennifer is that she's a brilliant businesswoman. In our group of girlfriends, we always joke that she can cut hair better than anyone; she can mix a drink better than any bartender. I think producing and directing for her is going to be the same. Wherever she points her wand, flowers grow."

I read that interview and thought: "That'll be the Manifestor!"

An in-depth reading would take into account many factors of Jennifer Aniston's Human Design, but the snapshot view illustrates a high achiever who is not afraid of taking risks, in career or love, because she always seems to come through. She probably struggles to find a perfect balance in relationships, but the drive of a pure Manifestor is the hallmark of this life chart.

MADONNA

Type: Generator
Authority: Sacral
Profile: 5/1

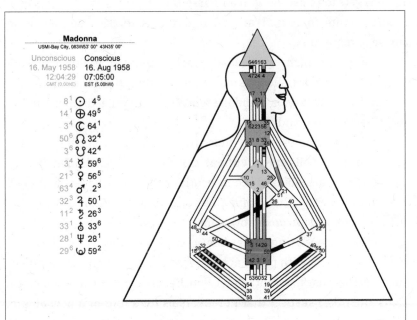

Madonna
USMI-Bay City, 083W53' 00" 43N35' 00"

Unconscious	Conscious
16. May 1958	16. Aug 1958
12:04:29	07:05:00
GMT (0.00hE)	EST (5.00hW)

8¹	☉	4⁵
14¹	⊕	49⁵
3⁴	☽	64¹
50⁶	☊	32⁴
3⁶	☋	42⁴
3⁴	☿	59⁶
21³	♀	56⁵
63⁴	♂	2³
32³	♃	50¹
11²	♄	26³
33¹	☊	33⁶
28¹	♆	28¹
29⁶	☋	59²

Your Individual Design Keynotes

TYPE: Generator (Chapter 3)

AUTHORITY: Follow your gut (Chapter 4)

DEFINED CHANNELS: (Chapter 5)

    1. 63 / 4   Logical Mind. Critical perceptions

        11 / 56   Curiosity. Seeking and Searching

    2. 2 / 14   The Beat. "Alchemy". Turning base metal into gold

PROFILE: 5 / 1 (Chapter 7)

Madonna has carved out a hugely successful career in the music industry, with an image that has endured for the past two decades, but a snapshot view of her Human Design depicts a very different woman from the steely and sexual persona she projects.

Of course, projecting a convincing image is how she naturally interacts with the world, and this is evident with her 5/1 profile — foreshadowing people's expectations with a particular image or message that both impresses observers and protects her soft center. Consequently, she is a capable leader and someone others look up to — just as long as nobody gets too close. As with all 5/1s, either in professional or personal environments, there is an arm's-length proximity because there is an image to maintain.

In her music, if she ever gets the feeling that her audience doesn't appreciate her work, she'll be relentless in attempting to win back fans and self-respect. She is someone who constantly needs to prove her worth — to herself and others.

In relationships, especially those that break down, she'll be forever projecting the "I will survive without you" message, even though the rupture will have destabilized the insecurities that are inherent within all first-line elements of her profile. She's also an archetypal rescuer, showing everyone what to do or how something should be.

Madonna's enduring career has *everything* to do with the fact that she's a Generator with pure Sacral energy, providing constant momentum. And because music is her passion, her energy is correctly engaged. Consequently, I suspect that in rehearsals for a tour or a new album, observers describe her as a tireless workhorse with boundless energy. She lives true to the Generator motto: "Only engage with people and activities that resonate." I'm sure she could testify to situations or people that didn't and yet she found herself committed anyway. Herein lies the classic pitfall for Generators: if the gut response isn't honored, the momentum of your energy will be a propelling force, regardless. Once in motion, Generators are compelled to keep going. Trying to stop Madonna in full flight would take enormous effort — and cause her great annoyance!

She has a Sacral authority, meaning she must rely solely on that gut response. Undefined Spleen and Emotions means there is nothing else to take into account, so her true responses emanate from the gut. People or opportunities receive either a "yes" or a "no." There's no room for quibbling and no gray areas. People around her must learn to ask questions that elicit a "yes" or a "no" answer — a gut response.

She has five centers defined: the Crown, Mind, Throat, Self, and the Generator's engine, the Sacral. With no channel activation between the Throat and Self, she may well struggle to truly express herself — until she gets in front of a big audience with her Generator engine fully wound up. It is the audience's presence that makes that connection between the Self and Throat, allowing her to be totally expressive. Madonna's design indicates she's very much the showperson, with the 2-14 Channel of the Alchemist turning raw energy into a dazzling spectacle. Having gate 33, the Gate of Retreat, turned on in her Throat suggests she is at her most creative when she steps aside from the world. Times of calm, away from the madness, are essential to refresh her nature.

We can see that her Crown, Mind, and Throat are interconnected, implying she can always speak her mind (and quite obviously does!). When she combines her Crown, Mind, and Throat with her Self and Sacral, she will sense a calming release of energy within her that gives her the drive and resolution to accomplish anything.

A defined Crown and Mind, activated to the Throat, means she is capable of answering all manner of questions intellectually. Behind that distinctive singing voice there is a great mind at work. She happens to be enormously bright and, because of a defined Self, knows exactly where she is heading in life, sure and resolute.

She has the Channel of Curiosity (11-56) which gives her the drive as storyteller, world traveler, and religious seeker, someone eager to squeeze the juice out of life in her search for meaning. Part of her storytelling through music will be an inquiry to see if her beliefs match those of her audience. If they don't, she will adjust them, sometimes embracing new beliefs altogether. It is an endless and often restless search for peace of mind.

The Channel of the Logical Mind, the 63-4 from Crown to Mind, means she probably sets high standards for herself and others, applying critical perceptions that, sometimes, are in danger of being taken the wrong way. She thinks logically and expects things to be a certain way, but this can be misconstrued as being overly picky and critical.

One media image of Madonna is that she might be motivated by money, but in actuality, according to her design, she is a true artiste striving to give birth to empowering forms of novel expression, and it is that pursuit of originality that just happens to have accrued great fortune and allowed her to play the part of a "material girl."

She does have two gates turned on within her undefined Heart. Gate 21 indicates she is inclined to seek control and must exercise caution in choosing administrators who always consider her best interests. Gate 26 implies she cannot allow herself to have people constantly disagreeing with her as she builds momentum to communicate her latest creation.

Madonna probably considers herself emotional, when in fact she's probably more sucked into the emotions of others, as evidenced by her undefined Emotions center. Her natural state, when alone, is cool, calm, and collected. But she does have gate 49 on in this center, which speaks of "emotional revolution," recognizing when something or someone has gone beyond its sell-by date. So she'll think nothing of turning her own life inside out when she feels the need to right an injustice.

An undefined Root indicates that Madonna is susceptible to stressful situations and will have found it essential to seek solace in meditation, exercise, dance, and quiet places. When she finds calm in the midst of furor, she knows the meditation is working!

Finally, in the Sacral, she has gate 59. You'll see this is activated twice in her life chart, with both a sixth line and a second line. Dual activations can often happen in a chart. Here, the second-line influence means she is naturally quite shy, regardless of the image she portrays, and the additional sixth-line influence means she is circumspect and discerning when it comes to choosing partners to be intimate with. Only those who meet her high standards will win her attention. Consequently, Madonna can appear to the world to be a sexually driven person, but in her private world she is quite reserved and very choosy!

An in-depth reading would take into account many factors of Madonna's Human Design, but a snapshot view illustrates that she is the consummate performer who brings a dynamic, revolutionary, and individual creativity into everything she does. At the same time, she is on a lifelong quest to find meaning in her life through her own sense of self-worth. The more easily she allows herself to use her gut response to guide her, the more happiness and contentment she will find in life.

BARACK OBAMA

Type: Projector
Authority: Emotions
Profile: 6/2

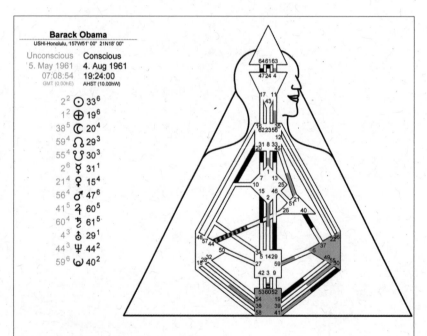

Your Individual Design Keynotes

TYPE: Projector (Chapter 3)

AUTHORITY: Emotional, Feeling Clarity, Patience (Chapter 4)

DEFINED CHANNELS: (Chapter 5)

      1. 30 / 41 Recognition. Focusing Imagination

PROFILE: 6 / 2 (Chapter 7)

On November 4, 2008, the son of a Kenyan father and a mother from Kansas made history when he was elected as America's forty-fourth president and its first African American president. Barack Obama symbolizes hope for a bruised and battered country and world. A sense of revolution was in the air when he addressed the nation from Chicago — and his Human Design suggests it's not merely rhetoric when he speaks of great change.

Whenever you come across a Projector chart like this one, with a lot of white and only two defined centers, do not think for one moment that you are dealing with an individual who lacks wisdom or intelligence. Indeed, it makes President Obama naturally empathetic, because his seven white centers bring a flexibility that changes with the different environments he finds himself in, adapting to the designs around him and allowing him to listen, share expressions, and have the flexibility to interact with a vast range of different people. On election night, when he said his victory was "not about me, but about you," it was clear that he was someone very much in tune with his true nature.

His undefined Self reflects the environment around him, so he can be all things to all people. His undefined Heart aligns with the wishes of the people he serves. His undefined Throat expresses things for the benefit of his audience, being able to better relate to matters and expressions that mean more to their lives than his own. In this respect, he makes an ideal leader — and his Projector needs for recognition and invitation will have swollen with fulfillment that night because an entire country elected him, recognizing his capabilities and inviting *him* to lead *them*. In such circumstances, a Projector simply thrives.

The two centers he has defined are the Emotions, which indicates he is a feeling man, and the Root, which gives him the thrust to act. It is somehow apt that the *only* channel activation in his life chart is the 30-41 Channel of Recognition, indicating he is a pioneering visionary with a passion for building a better future. This means he has tremendous focus and dedication that will be undaunted by any obstacle, crisis, or interference he may face. Admittedly, this channel also means he constantly balances between viewing his glass as half full and seeing it as half empty, and he can privately lurch between joy and despair. With such a design, he needs a steadying hand behind him, and I think he has this in the form of the First Lady, Michelle Obama.

In his undefined Throat, he has both gates 33 and 56, the two story-telling gates, and this explains why he is such a great orator, able to keep audiences spellbound with his experiences and visions. I watched him speak on countless occasions as he strode toward the presidency, and it was evident that here was a man who could spin a good yarn with consummate ease for the entertainment and excitement of others. I've also noted that he has gate 1 in the undefined Self, providing him with creative flair and the ability to be free to go beyond the tried and the true to bring about advancement.

Gate 59 in the undefined Sacral has the fourth-line element, implying he views all interactions on a brotherhood and sisterhood basis; he views his electorate as intimate family. Gate 29 in the same center means he must be wary of saying "yes" to everything and must weigh the needs of any given moment before he asserts "Yes, we can." But gate 44 in an undefined Spleen provides the balance, granting the president a "nose" for political and economical patterns, be they ones out-of-date or emerging. This gate grants him the ability to remain one step ahead, based on an innate sense of trends and patterns. Gate 19 within the Root also means that here is a man who yearns to end all division and bring about unification and wholeness.

His 6/2 profile gives him great aptitude as an authority and visionary with natural quality. It means he is someone wise beyond his years and probably feels this presidency is his destiny. He will require space and time on his own, so I would advise his advisers to create a sanctuary within the White House where he can withdraw and be alone.

What he will find in the White House, because of the flexible nature of his design, is that he may feel easily swayed by the influences of others around him, so it will matter that his core advisers understand his nature, share his visions, and honor his Human Design authority, allowing him to wait and not react to anything until he *feels* clear to do so. If he attracts the best people who understand him intrinsically, his triumph as president is assured.

An in-depth reading would take into account many more factors in the president's Human Design, but everything I see corroborates the vision he painted for America: here is a man with vision who has tremendous dedication and focus and wants to end all divisions in the United States and abroad and be a people's president. I look at the man, I look at the presidency, and I ask myself if the hope is well placed and he can rise to the challenge in front of him. And the answer that springs from his Human Design is "Yes. He can."

SANDRA BULLOCK

Type: Reflector
Authority: Outer
Profile: 2/4

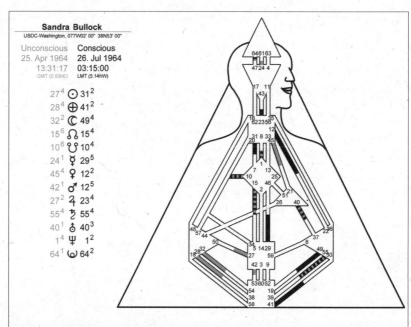

Sandra Bullock
USDC-Washington, 077W02' 00" 38N53' 00"

Unconscious	Conscious
25. Apr 1964	26. Jul 1964
13:31:17	03:15:00
GMT (0.00hE)	LMT (5.14hW)

27^4	☉	31^2
28^4	⊕	41^2
32^2	☾	49^4
15^6	☊	15^4
10^6	☋	10^4
24^1	☿	29^5
45^4	♀	12^2
42^1	♂	12^5
27^2	♃	23^4
55^4	♄	55^4
40^1	♅	40^3
1^4	♆	1^2
64^1	♇	64^2

Your Individual Design Keynotes

TYPE: Reflector (Chapter 3)

AUTHORITY: 29 day Review, Patience becomes wisdom (Chapter 4)

DEFINED CHANNELS: (Chapter 5)

No Definition

PROFILE: 2 / 4 (Chapter 7)

Movie star Sandra Bullock has been a ubiquitous presence on the big screen for more than a decade now, and she remains a hugely popular actress in Hollywood. She also happens to be one of those rare beings whose Human Design is that of a Reflector, with no defined centers. She therefore provides a fascinating example of someone with no immediately consistent way of relating to the world, someone who lives by trust.

I'm sure Sandra, like most Reflectors, has sensed at many points in her life that she is somehow different and has wondered how she will fit into the scheme of things. She will no doubt have felt an instinctive distancing from all conformity, tradition, and "the way things are done," seeking instead her own unique approach to people and situations. There is a glorious consistency to the inconsistent ways that Reflectors adopt when going through life, and this life chart illustrates that uniqueness.

I would suggest Sandra has the perfect job for this design, because Reflectors are always reflecting the natures and environments of people around them, using the lack of definition within their life chart to stand back and impart the wisdom that such a detached perspective allows. Consequently, they often find themselves playing many roles in life's dramas without necessarily getting involved or taking center stage. The fact that Sandra has found and established her gift as an actress is a tribute to her courage and vision, as well as a high degree of watchfulness and trust, but it may also have been influenced by her parents. Her mother and father were both involved in the musical performance world: her mother as an opera singer; her father as a voice coach. Sandra spent many years traveling between her mother's recitals in Europe and later the United States, and so, as a Reflector, she may have found it easy to absorb that lifestyle and adopt a similar one herself.

If you look at her life chart, you will note that she has six gates marked pink and black, indicating six areas of her life where there is a conscious/unconscious overlay. This means that she is very attuned to her own nature. All this, combined with the all-white nature of her chart, implies that she is someone who has the impetus to grow in wisdom very quickly. She is naturally empathetic as a result of this and no doubt finds that she's able to pick up everything about people: their habits, mannerisms, attitudes, and moods. This gift means that she is able to play out, reflect, and perfect any role that a playwright or director asks of her. This is because Reflectors are so open to the atmosphere around them and so sensitive to the energy of others. Sandra will have natural empathy for the roles she takes on but will also ride the energy of the actor she's playing against, utilizing it to bring out the best in both performances.

This sensitive tuning in to the energies of others is why many Reflectors tend to seek solitude, or at least to be removed from the masses. I'm sure the only thing Sandra longs to do after an intense spell on set or on location is retreat to a place where she can be by herself, away from the "noise" of others. Indeed, much of her adult life seems to have been spent buying, building, and dramatically remodeling houses and, more recently, a restaurant, and I'm sure this is all about meeting a personal need for solace and creating an agreeable environment.

Without even one center defined, Sandra is someone who will be susceptible to borrowing the identities of others unless she learns to turn these conditioning influences into impassive wisdom. Her sense of self need not be confused with the defined Self in others. Her undefined Mind need not get drawn into the racing thoughts of those with this center defined, and so on and so forth. She just needs to stand back, observe, pass on the wisdom of her reflected observations, and remind herself of her sensitivity to others' energies.

As a Reflector, she can literally be all things to all people. That's because people see themselves reflected back to them in her presence. She can also be a classic rescuer. Unwanted hangers-on and needy individuals may have attached themselves to her on occasion, and this reliance on, or demand for, her guidance can often feel overwhelming to her.

In a Reflector's chart there are no defined centers or active channels, so their "inside story" is always contained in the gates. Sandra has six gates that are both conscious and unconscious, and we will look at these here. In the Crown she has gate 64, the Gate of Diverse Possibilities. This indicates she is open to every conceivable source of inspiration in a way that can be dramatically moving for others. Gate 1 is turned on in the Self and is evidence of a highly creative flair, so she'll be forever seeking roles that push the envelope and break new ground. Also in that center, she has gate 10, the Gate of Behavior, which grants her individual expression that is unconcerned with what anyone else thinks. She is her own person and her behavior as a famous actress aims to positively influence others. Gate 15, Humanity, means she is a true humanitarian, and equality and fairness are the cornerstones of her attitude toward others. She is someone who is naturally committed to assisting or improving the lives of others. Having both gates 10 and 15 turned on in the Self represents a highly personal journey (the 10) evolving into a journey that embraces everyone (the 15).

In the Heart center, gate 40, Deliverance, means she has the will to work in the interests of everyone, delivering the goods each time, but will then need time and space to refresh herself and unburden her heart. In the Emotions, she has gate 55, Abundance, revealing a magnanimous spirit that shines through everything she does. I suspect that she can be whooping with silly delight one minute and deeply glum the next, and yet, despite all that, her spirit will radiate.

Gate 29, Commitment, gives her the tendency to commit to everything and everyone wholesale, only finding out later how overstretched she becomes when spinning so many plates in the air. Gate 27, Nourishing, means she probably ponders whether she has enough resources in life and yet doesn't hold back from being extremely generous. In some ways this may well have compelled her to achieve financial well-being so that her natural inclination to give back, in sometimes unexpected ways, can flourish.

Sandra has an Outer Authority that is honored by reviewing matters over a period of twenty-nine days, in synch with the lunar cycle. By giving herself the space of those twenty-nine days, she has the opportunity to sound out the opinions of others, do research, and reflect deeply on the matters at hand. I would guess that if she has honored her true nature, most big decisions have been made when she's at a distance from the source of the dilemma or question at hand. Reflectors need time, space, and isolation to distill and distinguish the influences of others from what authentically stirs and resonates with them.

Sandra has a 2/4 profile, indicating that she is naturally warm and sincere and ideally wishes to embrace the world and do good, yet she will be sensitive to criticism and easily bruised when misunderstood. It doesn't surprise me that she has twice donated a million dollars to the

American Red Cross, first to assist the victims of 9/11 and then to help the victims of the Asian tsunami. That's all in accord with the bighearted fourth line within her profile and the empathy within her type. But the potentially reclusive second-line element also reinforces her need to hang the "Do Not Disturb" sign on the door and be alone.

Reflectors are known for their penetrating insights about life. Such takes on the world come via their own failures and triumphs, which are digested and then reflected back to the world as wisdom. Sandra's own take on the essence of success is "Always choose people that challenge you and are smarter than you. Always be the student. Once you find yourself being the teacher, you've lost it."

An in-depth reading would take into account many more factors, but the snapshot conclusion is that Sandra Bullock is absolutely living her design as an empathetic actress who knows where she is headed in life and is determined to set the right example along the way. She has a generosity of spirit and true humanitarian outlook that assists the less fortunate and seeks to empower others.

Acknowledgments

This book has been the culmination of sixteen years' work and play with and mastery of the Human Design system, the most essential guidance tool for the twenty-first century and beyond. For every one of you who has trusted me over the years to read for you, or allowed me to offer my teachings, I thank you. I hope you have been able to see yourself in this book and find something to chuckle about.

I always wished to share this fascinating system with a wider audience, confident that its power and accuracy would speak for itself, and was blessed to be gifted that opportunity after spending more than a decade visualizing that very moment. It introduced me to the world of publishing and made me realize the Herculean effort that goes into a book's creation and the multitude of people who help make it happen.

None of this would have come to be without the vision, enthusiasm, dedication, and writing abilities of a man named Steve Dennis. He was just another male cynic cajoled into having a Human Design reading by his girlfriend in LA — and that was the start of this amazing journey. Aside from assisting the writing process, he forged introductions with the rest of the team who made this happen, whom I would like to thank: literary agent Jonathan Lloyd, at Curtis Brown, London, for his support and belief in this project; his assistant, Camilla Goslett; publisher Belinda Budge, at HarperCollins UK, for her trust, vision, and empowerment; and editor Katy Carrington, whose invaluable and meticulous input steered me through the woods. Without you, Katy, I would have been lost!

The moment I walked through the doors of HarperCollins in London and was embraced by Belinda and her team, there was no doubt that this project had found its correct home and the best team. In that regard,

I'd also like to thank Anna Valentine for her positive input and for taking on this project with so much enthusiasm, Elizabeth Hutchins for her penetrating clarity, and the rest of the cast whose behind-the-scenes efforts made this book possible in the production, IT, marketing, publicity, and rights departments.

My heartfelt thanks go to New World Library for their trust in taking on this book for release in the United States and particularly to Jason Gardner for guiding the project with great ability and humor.

Kim Corbin has a natural flair and spiritedness for bringing this book to the attention of a wide audience. And thanks go to Munro Magruder, whose wise overview helps direct the book where it needs to go. A special mention goes to Karen Stough, whose invaluable proofreading brought to light many aspects of the book that needed reshaping for the American audience. And also thank you to Tona Pearce Myers, who diligently oversaw the production and typesetting.

For a new author, it is a delight to work with such amazing teams in London and the San Francisco Bay Area! Thank you, each and all!

I thank and acknowledge Ra Uru Hu for being the one, back in 1987, who had the fortitude to receive and transmit Human Design to the world. It is no easy task being the messenger for such a brand-new concept. I also offer my heartfelt thanks to Juergen Saupe, who immediately recognized the beauty of Human Design and tirelessly promoted it, making certain that it was released to the world, and to Niketana for providing the initial support to get the Human Design project started. My sincere thanks go to Eleanor Haspell-Portner, PhD, for her extensive work in determining the statistical percentages of occurrence in the human population of the five types of Human Design.

My friend Erik Memmert is the highly gifted programmer who wrote the magnificent downloadable software, enabling a clarity that no words could provide. I thank him and commend his many styles of Human Design programs, which are available to anyone wishing to study this system even more and take their insights to the next level. Also, the constant presence, support, and sustenance provided by Lindy Harshberger commands special mention. Lindy, you are a star! Not forgetting the bright presence of Lynn Beaudoin; my stepdaughter Kristin Owens, whose precise insights provided invaluable input at a pivotal time; and the little man himself: Harrison MacTavish.

There is no question that I have been assisted by many people in my life, and my greatest thanks are reserved for two unique individuals: my father, Roderick Parkyn, who encouraged me to look further and deeper into life, and who first introduced me to the country and great spirit of America; and my mother, Patricia Parkyn, who has always tested, trusted, and supported my choices. Understanding Human Design has allowed me to fully appreciate some of the trials she has faced in her lifetime, and I honor her for the courage and strength she has shown and the unconditional love she has given me.

I must also convey heartfelt thanks to Gemma Cunningham, my loving travel companion and great friend through many a strange trip; Zeno Dickson, who initially introduced me to Human Design; and Rupa Westbrook, who walked beside me and reminded me to laugh at those times when it seemed that life was no longer funny. Thank you for holding such precious places in my life.

My special thank-you is reserved for the last: to the inspiration that is my wife, Carola Eastwood, who has dedicated her life to helping the world awaken to its true potential and who has always encouraged me in work and play. She has trusted herself to be my constant companion, so thank you, Carola! Your steady love and endless support are appreciated more than words can possibly convey. I'm also grateful for the countless hours you contributed throughout this challenging writing process with your creative input, and your help editing this work, which I know has been a long-held and shared vision. It's evidence, if evidence were needed, that a 2/4 profile finds perfect harmony with a 6/2 profile!

Finally, thank you for reading this book. I hope you found the journey fun.

Be in love.

Index

About the Author

Chetan Parkyn is a master of Human Design and has made it his mission to bring this extraordinary system to everyone. He originally qualified as a mechanical engineer in the United Kingdom and traveled worldwide troubleshooting diverse engineering projects. In 1993, he was introduced to the system of Human Design and began developing and teaching it in the United States. In 2001, he introduced classes and workshops in the United Kingdom, and he has since taught Human Design all over the world. He currently lives in San Diego, California, with his wife, Carola. He continues to give hugely popular one-on-one and partnership readings. He also does counseling, seminars, and classes worldwide.

© Sarah Clareheart

Visit him at www.humandesignforusall.com.

NEW WORLD LIBRARY is dedicated to publishing books and other media that inspire and challenge us to improve the quality of our lives and the world.

We are a socially and environmentally aware company, and we strive to embody the ideals presented in our publications. We recognize that we have an ethical responsibility to our customers, our staff members, and our planet.

We serve our customers by creating the finest publications possible on personal growth, creativity, spirituality, wellness, and other areas of emerging importance. We serve New World Library employees with generous benefits, significant profit sharing, and constant encouragement to pursue their most expansive dreams.

As a member of the Green Press Initiative, we print an increasing number of books with soy-based ink on 100 percent postconsumer-waste recycled paper. Also, we power our offices with solar energy and contribute to nonprofit organizations working to make the world a better place for us all.

Our products are available
in bookstores everywhere.
For our catalog, please contact:

New World Library
14 Pamaron Way
Novato, California 94949

Phone: 415-884-2100 or 800-972-6657
Catalog requests: Ext. 50
Orders: Ext. 52
Fax: 415-884-2199
Email: escort@newworldlibrary.com

To subscribe to our electronic newsletter, visit
www.newworldlibrary.com